Iris Krasnow is the author of the *The Secret Lives of Wives*, the *New York Times* bestseller *Surrendering to Marriage, Surrendering to Motherhood, Surrendering to Yourself,* and *I Am My Mother's Daughter.* She has appeared twice on *Oprah, Today, Good Morning America,* CBS's *The Early Show,* FOX News, NPR's *All Things Considered,* and several times on CNN. Interviews with Iris and reviews of her work have been featured in *The New Yorker; O, The Oprah Magazine; Time; US News & World Report; Redbook; Parade; The Washington Post; The Wall Street Journal;* and dozens of other local newspapers, radio shows, and morning TV programs from Baltimore to New Zealand. She is also a professor and professional speaker. More information on her speaking engagements can be found on www.iriskrasnow.com. She lives in the DC area with her husband of twenty-five years. They have four grown sons.

ALSO BY IRIS KRASNOW

Surrendering to Motherhood

Surrendering to Marriage

Surrendering to Yourself

I Am My Mother's Daughter

The Secret Lives of Wives

SEX AFTER...

WOMEN SHARE HOW INTIMACY CHANGES AS LIFE CHANGES

IRIS KRASNOW

GOTHAM BOOKS

GOTHAM BOOKS
Published by the Penguin Group
Penguin Group (USA) LLC
375 Hudson Street
New York, New York 10014

USA | Canada | UK | Ireland | Australia | New Zealand | India | South Africa | China

penguin.com
A Penguin Random House Company

Previously published as a Gotham Books hardcover

First trade paperback printing, February 2015

Gotham Books and the skyscraper logo are trademarks of Penguin Group (USA) LLC

The Library of Congress has catalogued the hardcover edition of this book as follows:

Krasnow, Iris.
Sex after . . . : women share how intimacy changes as life changes / Iris Krasnow.
pages cm
ISBN 978-1-59240-827-6 (hardcover)   978-1-59240-918-1 (paperback)
1. Women—Sexual behavior.   I. Title.
HQ21.K725 20104
306.7082—dc23
2013037177

Printed in the United States of America

1   3   5   7   9   10   8   6   4   2

Some names and identifying characteristics have been changed to
protect the privacy of the individuals involved.

Set in Bembo Std.
Designed by Spring Hoteling

*To the bodacious Golden Girls
who show all us women that attitude is everything*

CONTENTS

PART FOUR
ADVENTURES IN OUTERCOURSE

PROLOGUE

$\sim$

$\mathcal{J}$am walking through the maples, birches, buckeyes, and oaks on the campus of Kendal at Oberlin, a retirement living community forty minutes from downtown Cleveland. These verdant grounds are home to 320 residents ranging from ages sixty-four to one-hundred-two-year-old Esther, who credits wine and Coca-Cola as fuel that helps keep her going.

My tour guide is Maggie Stark, the pretty and perky admissions and marketing director of Kendal who reminds me of Julie, the cruise director on the TV show *Love Boat*. As Maggie ushers me through the facility, excitedly pointing out the ponds and cottages, the tennis courts and walking trails, I am tossed back in time to when I was being shown a summer camp to determine if the place was suitable for my kids.

Forget the children—Camp Kendal is where I would like to sign up to spend my final years. The place crackles with brain power (Kendal residents audit courses at neighboring Oberlin College for free), physical prowess (there are lots of hearty hikers, and a Kendal octogenarian was on the volleyball team that won the silver medal in the 2013 National Senior Games), social clubs, and blooming romances that have led to marriages.

In one large hall, a cluster of white-haired men and women

are hanging iridescent tropical fish decorations to prep for this evening's Spring Fling: A Night at the Beach. The creative, slightly flirty energy between them is reminiscent of a high school prom committee. Three women who appear to be in their mid-seventies are practicing a tap-dancing routine they will perform at the festivities. Their arms are swaying and they are clicking away to the Beach Boys singing, "Dom dom dom dom dom, dom be dooby, dom dom dom dom dom," the chorus of the song "Come Go with Me."

We stroll by the indoor lap pool where a female swimmer in a bathing cap made of layers of rubber petals is humming to herself and doing the backstroke. Outside, a tall and tanned man named Bill in a Western shirt with pearl snaps is digging and planting spring flowers. Maggie tells me that Bill has taken on the task of tending the courtyard garden of peonies, tulips, grape hyacinths, and irises.

He is eighty-eight, has biceps and a twinkle in his eyes.

The Kendal crowd is in the genre of hip older folks you will encounter in this book who are busting any residual stereotypes that advanced age means creaky, crotchety, lonely, and dried up. I am fifty-eight and awed by their vibrancy—and sex appeal—and hope to grow up to be equally feisty, and *alive*. They have taught me in countless ways how to push through illness and loss, and surmount relationship hurdles. I am eager to spill the fruits of my research, as my head is crammed, spinning, with stories on how to sustain intimacy no matter what comes our way.

During the past two years spent compiling *Sex After . . .* I have often felt like the commander of Operation Sex Central. Each day, I have been (happily) assaulted with a titillating stream of information from friends and fellow journalists, on new studies, new drugs, new toys, and new discoveries in the field of human sexuality and aging. It seems that everyone in my close friend and professional circles had a stake in this project, because as we all know, most people are deeply interested in sex, if not obsessed.

These leads and my digging helped me excavate everything I ever wanted to know about the interplay of sex and intimacy—as well as stuff I never wanted to know but was surprised, often staggered, to find out. (My most astounding find: a doctor at Wake Forest Institute for Regenerative Medicine attempting to grow human penises for reattachment, from the cells of soldiers with genital wounds. He has already successfully regenerated rabbit penises that, when reattached, functioned and produced babies.)

My interviews with 150 women of all ages caused me lots of sleepless nights as I was overstimulated by visions of great sex, bad sex, and how relationships shift throughout the female life cycle.

The combination of curiosity and insomnia have driven the composition of this book, which explains in unabashed detail the answers to questions such as these:

- How dangerous is my twenty-year-old's hooking-up culture?
- Why do I love my new baby and loathe my new husband?
- We have sex at most once a month: How often is normal for a married couple to do it?
- Will I ever want to sleep with anyone again after my painful divorce?
- What can I do about painful menopausal sex?
- How will I resume our sex life after breast or prostate cancer, or the amputation of a limb?
- What can I expect from sex when I am in my seventies and eighties?
- What the hell is a penis pump anyway?

If you picked up *Sex After . . .*, you are intrigued as I am by sexual behavior, our most pleasurable and most perplexing primal need. Given the book's subtitle, *Women Share How Intimacy Changes as Life Changes,* you are also likely interested in understanding how we can fan that flame for the rest of our lives. Along with my sassy seniors, there are plenty of tips herein from younger females who are revelatory and proud of their sexcapades in an era when it is no longer solely a man's role to initiate a pickup.

Perhaps the most memorable takeaways come from the mouths of audacious, bodacious babes three times their age, especially the wives who lost husbands of fifty-plus years—the only men they ever slept with—and are now as blathery as teenagers about their new "boyfriends."

My grandmother died at eighty-eight, outliving my grandfather by more than four decades. She did not date, and I never saw her clothed in anything but prim silk dresses, usually paired with white gloves. Many of the widows who sat down with me were wearing neon sweats and are on Match.com.

Hope sprung in all of us youngsters who have yet to turn sixty, watching Meryl Streep and Tommy Lee Jones in their delicious 2012 movie *Hope Springs.* After thirty years of a marriage that has turned tepid and sexless, they sign up for a couples retreat with a shrink, played realistically by Steve Carell. He gives them a set of sexercises, which gets them back into the bedroom, where they become sweaty and elated and more in love than ever.

That Meryl Streep still reigns as one of Hollywood's biggest draws is emblematic of this new age when women can flex, and own, their sexuality long past svelte midlife. Many of the people I spoke to in their twenties and thirties, and even some in their forties, were still floundering about love and intimacy. The older dames know precisely who they are, and what they want from their partners. And they are proof that prolonged intimacy has more to do with the mind than the body and is way more fulfilling than fleeting sexual highs. My most meaningful reward as a writer of relationship books is that I can pass on their sage reflections, wisdom that can sharpen and redirect our own journeys.

There is so much mystery surrounding sex, and that inexplicable magic is central to its sweet allure. I have left the ephemeral quality of sexuality intact but have added hard facts and statistics and true stories of sickness, struggles, and victories. My wish for all of my readers is that this book dissipates any scary mythology about what a woman could encounter as time goes by. And may that truth release you into becoming your authentic and fullest sexual self, after the honeymoon, after cancer, after boredom, after divorce, after wrinkles—until death do you part.

Although there are lots of senior citizens carrying on in *Sex After . . .*, I promise those of you who have yet to turn thirty that this is *not* an old lady's book. Rather, it is a valuable guide to how to pick the right partners and break off unhealthy ties. My research assistant, Nicole Glass, twenty-four, says she feels fully armed to face "any relationship" after days and months and years of helping me extract every morsel of news on how age and life changes affect intimacy.

"This project has prepared me for the weird and the wild stages of human relationships that can quickly sneak up on those of us in our twenties who tend not to focus on the future," says Nicole. "It was great to find out the news that seniors are often more passionate, and having more fun, than newlyweds!"

Some interview subjects have requested that their names and identifying details be changed. Those women are referred to by a first name only, a pseudonym. When first and last names are used, those are real names of persons who agreed to be identified on the record. If there is a story in this book that resembles your story, but I did not speak to you, it is not you. The only people whose experiences are printed in first-person narrative portions are people I interviewed.

SEX AFTER...

PART ONE

~

THEN AND NOW

CHAPTER 1
WHY SEX MATTERS

If we're truly open to our sexuality in the cosmic
sense, we're also open to our creativity, religious
awareness and sense of self-liberation.

—ERICA JONG

I am in San Diego scouring the shelves of a beachside book-
store for *Lady Chatterley's Lover*, the iconic work of erotica
I want to reread for historical perspective on this project. As I
flick through the pages of this slender loin-twanger (written in
1928!)—which I first devoured at eighteen and reviewed in my
pink teenage diary as "REALLY sexy"—a silver-haired sales-
woman tells me I should also buy *Fifty Shades of Grey*.

"E. L. James is *not* great literature like D. H. Lawrence, but
some of it is very arousing," she says, pulling the first book in the
series off the bestseller table and handing it to me.

I tell her I am writing a book on sexuality and aging and that
I probably need to read all three.

"I am seventy-five, and it was my *older* sister who recommended them," she adds. "My sister said some of the scenes gave her more orgasms than she'd had since her thirties. You do know that old people do it, too."

Oh, I know it very well. One of my most memorable interviews was with Delaware real estate agent Libby Zurkow, eighty-eight, who had recently lost her husband of fifty-eight years. Libby still drives herself around town in a Cadillac, and wears high heels and short skirts.

"To the end of his life at ninety-one, George and I never lost the magic of our physical attraction for each other," she told me. "This business that every woman over the age of seventy or eighty doesn't lubricate is nonsense. I guess people today would call us sex addicts, because we made love so often and thought about it every day."

Since the publication of my 2011 book, *The Secret Lives of Wives: Women Share What It Really Takes to Stay Married,* I have focused my research on understanding how sex and intimacy unfold in the female life cycle. Like most people on the planet, I am turned on and mesmerized by the physical pleasure we get from our sexuality. But my deeper goal with this book is to show the critical association between sexual fulfillment and the healthy functioning of intimate relationships.

I am often the keynote speaker to large audiences of women, and during the question-and-answer sessions, two subjects dominate the conversation: sex and change. Whether they are worried about marriage or divorce or illness and death, they all want to know: "How do I handle the shifts in my marriage or love partnership that these events have caused?"

This book is my lengthy answer, penned in hope of releasing readers into accepting, and celebrating, their unique sexuality throughout all of life's passages. We all want to have great sex because we think everyone else is having great sex, a myth perpetuated by a sexually obsessed media that spotlights thin and perfect women who have no trouble bedding down hunky and perfect bedfellows. In this book you will discover the real deal—there is no perfect sex because there are no perfect people. And it is ironically the frailty of imperfection and vulnerability in our relationships that solidify them, and make them endure.

I take you from the perils of hooking up in your twenties to the dating landscape widows are now facing in senior communities, where hooking up is also happening and STDs are on the rise.

The best way to learn how to navigate our own intimate relationships is to hear from others who have pushed through the obstacles we can expect along the way. There is plenty of prescriptive wisdom in these pages from dozens of women of all ages—as well as sex researchers such as Dr. Ruth and Dr. Kinsey—on how intimacy evolves after college, the honeymoon, pregnancy, midlife malaise, adultery, menopause, cancer, AIDS, Viagra, and widowhood.

These women are black, white, liberal, conservative, rich, and poor. They range from a superior court judge who speaks out on recovering from adultery to long-married wives who left their husbands to be with women. In this cross-societal bitch-and-learn session that airs the most private niches of girl talk, you will also meet waitresses and housewives—and a few wise men.

However varied they are in life experiences, each of these people has learned—often the hard way—that the ability to achieve intimacy, a state that requires far more than mind-blowing sex, is vital to the survival of relationships. Many of their snags in intimacy are far more urgent than the typical complaints that accompany long-term commitment, such as: "He snores. He is too tired for sex. I am tired of him. I met another guy."

You will meet a twenty-three-year-old wife whose husband came back from Afghanistan without a leg and a dynamic septuagenarian who has had AIDS for fifteen years.

You will also hear from wives in transition after mastectomies, after their husbands' erectile dysfunction—and from women who have lost the desire to have sex with the same old partners, including one who is repelled because her spouse has become obsese. While rocking grandmothers lend some spicy tales to this book, young women also get a good chunk of the spotlight, speaking out on how random sex and hooking up is affecting their ability to truly love. And pregnant women will learn from new moms on how to get their mojo back.

With women in their late eighties to early nineties constituting the fastest-growing segment of the aging population, a college-age female who stays healthy can look forward to a seventy-plus-year sex life. These young women are also coming of age in an era when even the kinkiest areas of sexuality are no longer subjects that make people stammer, but are shared openly.

"Sexting is as normal as talking, like no big deal," a college junior is telling me as she shows me a photo of a man in a white T-shirt and no bottoms she met at a bar the past weekend. "My mom calls us the 'Whatever Generation.'"

"I've had the same f—buddy for two years," her friend chimes in. "We just have great sex together, and we call each other when we want it. So it's like once a week or twice a month, and both of us are seeing other people. This guy sometimes refers to our dates as lovemaking. I kinda laugh and remind him that this is not love. It's just sex."

People always ask me how I convince women to speak candidly about their intimate relationships. It is much easier than it used to be. In the late 1990s, while researching my first marriage book, *Surrendering to Marriage,* it was like prying open a stubborn oyster to get couples to share what was really going on behind closed doors, even when they were offered anonymity. Eventually, I got the goods, but it took much cajoling and wine. These days? The wine is optional.

Every woman I've talked to agrees: There's no such thing as *just sex*. Sexual success requires emotional energy and communication, and those qualities change as life changes. The good news, as you are about to discover in these pages, is that this means sex often gets better.

"That's one of the most fantastic things about sex," says Debby Herbenick, a research scientist at The Kinsey Institute for Research in Sex, Gender, and Reproduction and a sex advice columnist who writes MySexProfessor.com.

"As couples age and have history together that intimacy really enriches sex, particularly for men. When men are younger, sex is so genital focused, and often not as satisfying for the women. But as the natural change in erectile function occurs, the couple can have a much richer experience about sex than when they were younger. Because the wives can then prompt the men to reconsider what sex is, what it means, the importance of expressing their feelings. And when men are confronted with that depth of meaning about sex, they rise to the occasion.

"When we ask people about the importance of sex, many talk about the physical aspects, the enjoyment of orgasms and kissing," Herbenick continues. "But what comes up most of all is how sex brings on intimacy and connection and love, and feeling like they are part of something bigger with somebody else."

As many great sex stories as I have gathered from the Whatever Generation, there are lots more—and surprisingly ones that are just as hot!—from women with arthritis and hysterectomies, extolling the joys of elder sex with the zeal of horny teenagers. One of the words I have added to my vocabulary because of these adventurous Golden Girls is *outercourse*, which is sex that encompasses everything but intercourse. These are sexy seniors who are merrily experimenting with vibrators and new positions as they tackle the last lap of life with increased health and vigor, and fruit-flavored lubricants.

One of my prize discoveries was the little-known film *Play the Game*, starring Andy Griffith, whose character, Grandpa Joe, moves to a senior community after the death of his wife of nearly sixty years. Joe meets a horny widow named Edna (played by Liz Sheridan), who discreetly crumbles a blue Viagra pill into his cocktail. The two end up with Andy of Mayberry, at the age of eighty-four, doing the first bedroom scene in his acting career. Grandpa Joe is thrilled to get a rise again and Edna gets so excited during foreplay, she has a heart attack. My last chapter features an interview with Marc Fienberg, producer of *Play the Game*, a movie based on his grandfather, who lapsed into an immobilizing depression after the loss of his wife. He was then transformed into a spirited hottie after becoming involved with a welcoming widow.

Of course, a preoccupation with sex across the ages is hardly an invention of millennium medicine. In the Book of Genesis, Sarah supposedly was fooling around with Abraham at the age of ninety when she gave birth to a son, Isaac, following seven barren decades. This after enticing him away from their fertile slave, Hagar, with whom Sarah allowed Abraham to bed in order to conceive a firstborn. Indeed, some of the twisted antics of characters throughout the Bible could easily be plots of modern dramas: the passion, jealousy, lust, and adulterous sins, and lots of invitations to "lay with me" for procreation and for entertainment.

The timeless reality of human sexuality as a "garden of good and evil" started when Eve tempted Adam with the apple that God forbade them to eat, with this warning: "In the day that you eat from it you shall surely die." Instead they fell for the promise of a serpent wrapped around the forbidden tree, who basically tells them to get it on, teasing them with this: "Ye shall not surely die; for God doth know that in the day ye eat thereof, then your eyes shall be opened and ye shall be as gods, knowing good and evil."

Their chomp on the apple, disregard of the Lord, and surrender to the writhing and phallic serpent offers a first glimpse of the mystical, uncontrollable power of the human sex drive, a force, then and now, that can cause the greatest joy and deepest pain we feel in our lifetimes.

Gone is the shame over nudity of Adam and Eve and the urge to cover their privates with fig-leaf shrouds in our brazen introduction, in the Book of Judges, to BDSM, or Bondage, Dominance, Sado-Masochism. This scenario occurs centuries before the gray silk tie Christian Grey uses to tether Anastasia to his bed in *Fifty Shades of Grey*: In the Book of Judges, Delilah, professing to be "helpless," ties up the lead-bodied Samson to enhance their erotic encounters, so, as he puts it, he can "become as weak as an ordinary man."

Another biblical bodice ripper is portrayed in the Book of Samuel, when King David catches a glimpse of the gorgeous Bathsheba, another man's wife, naked on the terrace below his swooping hilltop digs. Intoxicated by her beauty, he invites her into his royal chambers. Things get really messy for the couple, as it generally does with adultery—they begin an affair, Bathsheba gets pregnant, and to keep her husband, Uriah, from finding out, David sends him into a dangerous battle with the intention that he get killed, which he does. Sinning with another man's wife, then getting that guy obliterated, doesn't sit well with God, who remains true to this warning to David: "The sword shall never depart from your house."

While David tries to sanctify the tryst by marrying Bathsheba, this king glorified for such feats as striking down the giant Philistine warrior Goliath and writing the Book of Psalms is struck with a series of divine punishments. His baby with

Bathsheba is sickly and dies soon after his birth. Another son, Absalom, born to another wife, Maacah (the Bible states that David had at least seven wives), rebels against his father, mobilizes an army to take over his kingdom, then dies in the Battle of Ephraim Wood. David falls into an agonizing spiral of grief and remorse, wailing like any parent who loses a child: "My son Absalom! O my son, my son Absalom! If only I had died instead of you!"

I ask Rabbi Ari Goldstein, a biblical historian based at Temple Beth Shalom in Arnold, Maryland: "What is it with all this sex in the Bible?" He chuckles and compares some of the antics splashed across the sacred tomes to Jerry Springer episodes:

Rabbi Ari Goldstein

While no person would ever think that sexuality, itself, is a recent concept, many might consider the various expressions of sexuality to be of a more modern vintage. This, however, could not be further from the truth. Chapter after chapter of the Bible leaves the reader wondering if the subjects of these stories are not lifted directly from a season of The Jerry Springer Show.

"I got my father drunk and had sex with him" is the story of Lot and his daughters in the Book of Genesis. "My boss's wife tried to seduce me" is a pivotal moment in Joseph's life. "I think my daughter is in a sex cult" can be found in the story of Jephtah. "My exhibitionist husband dances naked in front of an entire town and then ignores me" is Michal's primary complaint about King David. These are but a few of the many scores of stories in our holiest text that plainly speaks about sex and its multiple expressions.

And then of course there is Shir HaShirim, the Song of Songs. This portion is 117 verses of biblical erotica. The entire scroll details two lovers dwelling on each other's physical beauty and sexual interactions. Amazingly, it is the woman's voice that we hear both first and last, contradicting any preconceived notion we might have that ancient women were sexually passive. Strikingly absent from this entire book of the Bible is any reference to God.

Yet, despite God's absence, our earliest sages considered Song of Songs to be holier than any other book of the Bible, as indicated in Mishnah Yadayim 3:5: "For all of eternity in its entirety is not as worthy as the day on which Song of Songs was given to Israel, for all the Writings are holy, but Song of Songs is the Holy of Holies."

Indeed, the Bible chronicles with an understanding, even approving, tone the multitude of sexual behaviors and mannerisms in humans. Yet it is thoroughly misunderstood and misrepresented as disapproving these most basic needs.

Hearing from Rabbi Goldstein and flicking through the pages of the Old Testament, I am reminded that sex was man and woman's original thought, and remains our primal need, in body, psyche, and for procreation.

I am flashing back on the legacy of the philandering King David and it is not all about the dark repercussions of flouting the commandment "Thou shalt not covet thy neighbor's wife." His relationship with Bathsheba, which started as purely sexual but turned into a loving and abiding bond that produced a second and healthy son, is poignantly interpreted by author Naomi Harris Rosenblatt for a modern audience in her book *After the Apple: Women in the Bible,* published in 2005 by Miramax.

"David and Bathsheba move beyond simple lust, as every couple must if their partnership is to endure," writes Rosenblatt. "They share their grief with an emotional intensity that David has not found with any of his other wives. Paradoxically, the death of their son ushers in a lifelong partnership that will mature and deepen through the years."

What I have found in my conversations with women in longstanding relationships is that they do consider emotional intensity, a pilot light of love flickering within and not roaring bonfire sex (that can never last for thirty-plus years), as the primary secret to their endurance. The pairing generally starts with infatuation and sexual attraction, but the bond gains traction through commitment, friendship, and shared history. Of course, engaging in some degree of continued sex play along the way helps greatly in solidifying a lengthy union. That is, if partners *want* sex and *need* it.

I'll give you a snippet of one story, to follow in full, of a marriage between partners who prefer the softening of their intimacy to the rock-hard variety. Lynn is a sixty-year-old woman married to a man of sixty-four, with whom she used to "screw twice daily" in the early years of their marriage. Postmenopausal, she has zero libido and he has low testosterone and erectile dysfunction. Lynn does not want medical intervention, and her husband does not want supplementary testosterone, because they are content with this phase of what she calls "deeper loving over deeper sex."

"We haven't had sex for more than two years," says Lynn, a schoolteacher with short white hair and penetrating blue eyes.

"I had my children by C-section, and over the years, penetration has become very painful for me. My vagina has closed up in a way that women who birthed naturally may not be experiencing. And it is difficult for my husband to get hard. Neither of us even tries to initiate intercourse anymore. We are very good communicators, and we talk about the fact that we're not doing it anymore. We both agree that neither of us miss it that much.

"So what we do have is more cuddling and kissing, and a friendship that feels very deep and sexual without the sex," adds Lynn. "You may find this hard to believe, but in the absence of intercourse, we have entered a period of our marriage that feels closer and more intimate than we have ever experienced in our twenty-four years together."

Lynn and others in this book have a clear message: There is no gold-standard sexual relationship to which women must aspire. Their stories are proof that you should never compare yourself, or feel inadequate to, a girlfriend or sister or cousin who swears she has the best, sexiest, tightest partnership of anyone she knows. Because I can assure you of this: After speaking to hundreds of women over the course of a thirty-five-year career spent researching relationships, I am confident there is no such thing as *normal*. As you are about to find out, or may already know from personal experience, some women would rather sleep, or garden, than make love with their mates, and others cannot live without sex. Yet we all need some degree of intimacy to fortify our relationships, and it helps if both partners are open to fluidity in expectations and performance throughout the aging process.

Sexual chemistry has always mattered, as the cause of heartbreak when it wanes and as the crackle that fuels happily-ever-after. In the truth-stranger-than-fiction category, we witnessed one of the most incredible and mercurial displays of insatiable attraction in the breakups and makeups of Elizabeth Taylor and Richard Burton. Of this fiery and toxic and undying union, Burton wrote in his journals that it was filled with "famine, destruction and plague . . . she was, in short, too bloody much."

Yet they could never completely sever their bond, marrying and divorcing twice, making up and breaking up in-between, intoxicated by what Taylor called an "incredible chemistry together" in an exclusive interview that appeared in the June 2010 edition of *The London Daily Mail*, in which she also allowed editors to print excerpts from Burton's love letters.

"We couldn't get enough of each other," recalled Taylor in the interview, revealing how they would "make love, and play Scrabble, and spell out naughty words for each other, and the game would never be finished. When you get aroused playing Scrabble, that's love, baby."

They fell into lust on the set of the 1963 movie *Cleopatra*, shot partially in London and mostly in Rome, the city from which fittingly the word *romance* derives. Desire was apparently like a drug to Burton from the moment he saw Elizabeth as Cleopatra naked in a bath. His response to the voluptuous actress then and as their relationship unfolded was both tortured and worshipful. As he observed:

"Her breasts were apocalyptic, they would topple empires before they withered. . . . Her body was a miracle of construction. . . . She was unquestionably gorgeous. She was lavish. She was a dark, unyielding largesse. . . ."

Hollywood legend has it that their first screen kiss together lasted longer and longer with each take, causing director Joe Mankiewicz to demand: "Would you two mind if I say cut?" And the kiss still did not stop. Her body, her violet eyes Burton said had "an odd glint," a woman he considered "more beautiful than the dreams of pornography" stirred Burton to lyrical highs, as he wrote in a love letter:

"I lust after your smell . . . and your round belly and the exquisite softness of the inside of your thighs and your baby-bottom and your giving lips and the half-hostile look in your eyes when you're deep in rut with your little Welsh stallion."

The Welsh-born Richard Burton was no stallion when he died boozy and broken at age fifty-eight. Yet he was always an irresistible man to whom Taylor remained twined throughout both of their multiple marriages, as she described, "like chicken feathers to tar."

The modern cast of women herein demonstrates that while many civilizations have passed since the randy biblical tales, there are primal and timeless emotions that accompany getting naked of body with a partner who can either build you up or strip your soul. In the case of Burton and Taylor, the flare of their relentless desire did both.

What is pointedly new about relationships American-style is the amped-up public chatter about private sexual experiences, as real life follows *and* inspires the unprecedented sexualization on TV and in Hollywood. One of my fifty-four-year-old friends started playing Ping-Pong topless with her husband (her kids are in college) after watching Lena Dunham's Hannah character, in only a thong, slamming the ball across the table in *Girls*. A seventy-seven-year-old widow told me she was inspired to try fellatio for the first time with a new man friend after watching a YouTube video titled *Learn How to Give a Blow Job Like a Pro*.

She practiced on a banana, which is what Dr. Ruth Westheimer advises. Dr. Ruth is the original sex advisor, now eighty-five with her own YouTube channel on which you can learn about everything from masturbation to how to control your fantasies about celebrities. The incomparable Dr. Ruth dishes more during an interview featured in a later chapter.

Many in my own aging friends circle are as mesmerized by the HBO cult show *Girls* as are their daughters. We are also disturbed by some episodes of this comedy-drama that tracks a clique of twentysomethings living and hooking up in New York City. We are the unashamed Boomers who birthed free love and embraced Erica Jong's "zipless" take on sleeping around, yet nipples and bare butts did not show up on prime-time television when we were starting to become sexual beings. Sex was a force of real life, not the life force of media.

The rules about nudity and cussing on cable are more lax than on the major channels, yet we will likely see more flashing of breasts and crotch shots on most stations in the near future. The Federal Communications Commission currently prohibits nudity and obscene language on public, educational, and governmental television channels but is considering lifting its ban on frontal nudity on all broadcast media.

Even the steamiest *Sex and the City* episodes seem tame compared to some of the smut that routinely unfolds on *Girls*, whose players are emerging as the Misses Manners of the hooking-up culture. Their only barometer of propriety seems to be that anything is permissible short of rape, though some critics felt a particularly graphic episode from season two was a hair away from sexual assault.

This was when the character Adam commanded his new girlfriend, Natalia, to get on all fours and crawl to his bedroom. Reluctantly, she obliges, scratching her way across the floor to Adam, who then proceeds to have sex with her from behind, despite her protests. He then masturbates and the ejaculation is obvious, as she grumbles that the fluid will soil her dress.

Unlike Dunham's salacious tribe, there was no doggie sex or gay sex or any real sex portrayed on *Love, American Style*, the romantic comedy that was designed to capture what its producers billed as the "new morality" of the 1970s. It was flirty and funny and my favorite show, without showing body parts or wet spots. This program, which ran from 1969 through 1974 on ABC, teased audiences by alluding to the emerging promiscuity of the era without shoving it down our throats, starring actors you would never have pictured showing up in sexy situations.

In one episode, Jane Wyatt, who played Kitten's prim mom on *Father Knows Best*, mulls over buying birth control pills for her daughter. In another segment, squeaky-clean Ozzie Nelson plays a husband considering infidelity.

The most scandalous episode I recall was when a young woman takes her fiancé to visit her parents, who live in a nudist colony. Yet all you see of their bodies are their shoulders—way different from seeing Hannah sitting naked in the bathtub with her friend Jessa. I do like that Dunham is not skinny and she flaunts an imperfect and ample body without a trace of self-consciousness.

Dunham's fearless forays into television programming with a show that has risen to the number one spot on HBO has wowed the most prestigious of Hollywood players. At the 70th Golden Globe Awards, staged in 2013, *Girls* won Best Comedy Television Series, and Dunham won Best Performance by an Actress in a Comedy Television Series.

In Cabernet-laced conversations with my graying girlfriends about the new normal in sexuality, I am struck that we were not as hip as we believed in our youth. Our Sexual Revolution, which endorsed premarital sexploits and birth control, was considered countercultural, a sideline show perpetuated by hippies and sniffed down upon as dirty by most of our elders as well as by many straight people our own age. (*Straight* when I was young meant "conservative," not "heterosexual.")

These times and these men and women of now are creating a genuine gender-bending, "whatever" sex revolution in which anything goes, not on the fringes of society but in a bombastic center-stage performance.

When I was growing up, my dad's *Playboy* magazines were stuffed into a bottom drawer in his office and covered with business papers—which of course his kids put neatly back in place after ogling the magazines. The pinups were airbrushed and stiffly posed in studios, sexy but unreal. Decades later I am looking at a February 2013 supplement to *Purple Fashion* magazine, which features a collection of shots by the talented young photographer Ryan McGinley, of real people, young and in all sizes, romping nude in nature, engaged in sports and doing ordinary tasks.

Page after page of a variety of vaginas, breasts, and penises in a popular indie publication is both alluring and surprising. When I share the images with a young man of twenty-three, his expression does not alter as he takes in a nude woman frying up breakfast, nude couples doing handstands with their legs wide apart, a nude male bungee jumper in a harness that circles his erection.

"It's just people naked," he finally says, and shrugs.

His nonchalance about sex mirrors a prevailing attitude among his age group, a comfort level and sexual confidence that McGinley's photographs reveal. The men and women on the pages of the *Purple* supplement titled "I Was Naked Here" look like nymphs in the forest, as untamed and unconscious of their bare skins as animals. They are saying with their stances and poses: "I was naked here. Get over it."

I cannot envision our closest couple friends accepting an invitation to our home for a "Naked Sunday Brunch." Yet I do know from the dozens of midlife and older women I spoke to for this book that they do often envy the sexual confidence their kids seem to have, a generation that is coming of age with an unashamed acceptance of their own bursting libidos.

The power of sexual confidence, and lack thereof, is the theme of the raunchy and smart Canadian film *My Awkward Sexual Adventure*, which came to the States in January 2013. An opening scene has Rachel (played by Sarah Manninen) and Jordan (played by Jonas Chernick) naked in bed. The couple are in their early thirties and have dated for two years. Jordan is vigorously pumping Rachel in a missionary position, and when he looks down in rapture, she is asleep.

He wakes her up, and she tells him he is a lousy lover, that he lacks prowess and a sense of adventure, has bad breath, and that his "sexual insecurity" is a turnoff. "I can't spend the rest of my life just having sex with you" is her final breakup line.

Jordan ends up turning to a stripper named Julia (played by Emily Hampshire) whom he takes on as his "sex Yoda" so he can woo Rachel back. Jordan and Julia cross-dress and experiment with chains and other sex toys, and she teaches him the art of cunnilingus by having him practice on a cantaloupe cut in half. He then transfers his new skills to Julia in a manner that demonstrates he has been a star pupil. When Jordan shows off his new-found sexual confidence with Rachel, she of course wants him back, having had her first orgasm of their relationship.

Alas, Jordan chooses to stick with his sex Yoda stripper, who shifts professions to restaurateur, and their explosive sex simmers into love. This is the best of Hollywood endings, and in my view the best way to have sex—when love comes with it and turns into a genuine relationship. Feeling sexual attraction and sexually attractive, interwoven with loving sex, is a surging charge like nothing else.

Sex even helps us live longer.

There have been numerous scientific studies on the effects of oxytocin, called the bonding hormone, on a human's impulse to relax, which lowers stress. Oxytocin is released with a gesture as simple as fingers brushed across someone's cheek. Even daily hugging has been proven to lower blood pressure, which leads to the reduction of heart disease. Take that further into regular fondling and lovemaking, and the oxytocin is steadily flowing, cutting the risk for other stress-related diseases such as stroke and clinical depression.

For the most part, this book is focused on heterosexual partnering because the themes of my books, while they are not memoirs, stem from my own convoluted journeys. I am the wife of one husband for twenty-five years and the mother of four sons in their twenties. Yet this book does include a long chapter on coming out after marriage, highlighting stories from ex-wives that trace the emotional and physical shifts that accompany leaving conventional heterosexual marriages for same-sex unions.

With testimonies from females spanning recent college graduates to those nearing ninety, my goal is that you find answers to anything about sex that piques your curiosity, and that you create richer and more exploratory dimensions in your own relationships. For whom we love and how we love are ultimately the definition of our humanity. And that means everything.

I follow a long line of authors, researchers, and therapists who chronicle the importance of intimacy as the most vital artery of life. Luckily, I also inhabit an era when there is an enormous amount of information available. At every stage of our growth cycle, whether we want it or not, we are drenched, drowning, in sexual images.

Correspondingly, people are discussing their sexual proclivities with unblinking candor, even with strangers. I felt this cultural shift personally when I was finishing book one of the Fifty Shades of Grey trilogy, on an airplane from San Diego to Baltimore. The female flight attendant, who appeared to be around sixty and was wearing a wedding ring, asked me, "Have you gotten to page 196 yet?" I skipped forward to find Anastasia extolling how Christian "slaps me hard. Before I can react, he plunges inside of me. I cry out—from the slap and the sudden assault, and I come instantly, again and again, falling apart beneath him as he continues to slam deliciously into me."

When the flight attendant returns, I order two vodkas.

This incident reminds me of how I had no hesitation about flaunting the cover of *Fifty Shades of Grey* in plain view, a book that everyone knows is filthy. In 1982, I cloaked my copy of *The Sensuous Woman* in a cover made from a brown paper bag so my seatmates on a plane from Dallas to Chicago did not think I was a pervert. When I reread *The Sensuous Woman* today, even the "whipped cream wriggle" that involves licking the confection off body parts seems innocent. There is, however, a phrase in this vintage bestseller by "J" that encouraged good girls to be naughty and is a timeless truth; it is the crux of this book.

"The best benefit of all in lovemaking is that you are not alone," J writes in *The Sensuous Woman*. "You have a companion who, if you choose well, . . . helps you build a bridge of intimacy that reaches into the heart, mind and soul of each of you."

It is the range of ways a relationship benefits from sex as "a bridge of intimacy" that is my intended takeaway, told through the voices of real women dealing with real issues. May their raw and heartfelt stories make you feel better about your own carnal highs and failures, experiences that have thus far been buried, painful, or incomprehensible. *Sex After . . .* will serve as a GPS on how to forge onward, no matter what pothole or swerves in the road lie ahead.

CHAPTER 2
THE NEW FREE LOVE

The twenties are about experimenting to figure out
what you want. Your thirties are about going out
and getting it.

—JESSICA BARI

In the undergraduate journalism and adult women's studies
courses I teach, there are often discussions about relationship and marriage trends. Not surprisingly, the opinions sharply
differ between the youth and grown-ups in the era of their moms
and grandmas. Yet this shared sentiment is becoming more pervasive in young and old alike: There is a lot of confusion about
the repercussions of hooking up.

In this chapter, I open up a real conversation featuring real
characters in a youth culture in which marriage is on the decline
and random sex is on the rise. I am writing from a mother's point
of view, so if you, too, have offspring in their twenties, these
pages will be like a forbidden peek into your own child's texting

stream. I admit to being very concerned that the new free love means a torrent of promiscuity that is destroying romance, courtship, and the ability to commit. Alas, my own parents thought the same thing of our 1970s free love, and yet I ended up married and embedded in a traditional family structure. This chapter allows people our childrens' ages to air their own defenses, definitions, and angst about their new brand of free love.

I have set out to discover what your children are not telling you.

In my own home with four sinewy sons in their twenties, I adhere to one of the golden rules of Dr. Ruth: Don't grill your kids about their sex lives. If they were girls, they would likely share more openly, as my friends with daughters attest. So instead, I grilled dozens of other young adults on their views about the death of dating and the ascent of F-buddies and friends with benefits. These observations from the frontlines show a prevalence of casual sex in the eighteen-to-thirty age range, often initiated by terse text messages. I also picked up among those same young adults a sense of being baffled by their own behavior, since love has very little to do with it.

A hookup can mean making out with a stranger, oral sex, intercourse, or a combination of these selections. While the menu may vary, the shared component is that these encounters are *supposedly* conducted without emotional bonding or expectations that a romance will ensue. Getting someone in bed, a goal that used to take weeks, even months, of anticipation and courtship, now can take less than two hours—even less than thirty minutes. It starts with a text message, "Let's meet for a drink," that suggests the pretense of a social outing but the actual intention is a hookup.

"Things can happen very quickly," says Karla, twenty-five, an attorney in Manhattan, in a green wrap dress from Venus.

com, the company that claims to be "the sexiest clothing on-line." She stamps out one Salem, then lights another.

"I can send a text right now and in less than an hour be in bed with somebody I met once briefly, and may never see again. Men like when girls talk naughty to them in a text. I don't do the kinky, steamy, dirty chat messages. It's more of a sexy-textie like 'What would you do to me now if you could?'

"It's playful, it's coy, guys love it," continues Karla in a growly whisper. "People call us the hooking-up generation; really we're the text-up generation. A text message starts a meet-up, and it's the tool that keeps things going. You know it's over when a text message or a sext message gets no response."

Along with Karla, Jessica, Stephanie, and Hank report on hooking up in the States; Rachel and Olivia weigh in from London, where during a recent visit I found a rollicking club scene. Another reason to add young British women was because they were reared in a historically edgy country that was a front-runner in pushing the boundaries in sexy fashion, sexy music, and sexy TV.

The United Kingdom was beaming explicit sex into living rooms as early as 2000 with the debut of *Coupling*, a racier rendition of *Friends*, though similar in its group-genre interactions and romantic mishaps. Unlike in *Friends*, the stars of *Coupling* do not sit around as much, processing their sexual encounters in living room encounter sessions. Couples on *Coupling* show more than tell. The show was named Best TV Comedy at the 2003 British Comedy Awards, but when the American rendition made its debut that year on NBC, it was canceled shortly thereafter—*too* much sex!

While my roster of youthful sexperts offers some contrasting takes on how quickie romps affect their extended emotional health, there is unanimous agreement that casual sex is rampant and "expected." And there is pride among some of my sources that no-strings-attached sex has become acceptable to be initiated by either gender, giving women equal power.

"I used to feel guilty about making out with a stranger at a bar, then bringing him home that night," says Stephanie, twenty-six, who works at an upscale Italian restaurant and is decked out in her uniform, a starched white blouse and chinos. "But at the same time, it is empowering, not demeaning, because it is a choice that I am making and I am making it to feel a certain way—strong and attractive. The game is no longer one-sided. I picked up one man at a bar a year ago, and we continue to hook up once or twice a month. He was caught off guard when I made the first move, but he has never turned me down.

"I am aware that our interests are never going to align, and that our relationship is not headed for a soul-mate sort of thing," adds Stephanie. "I am using him for sex, period, and we are settled in our routine. My F-buddy is a special friend who is available when I need him to be. I have never left my fragile heart on his pillow. Instead, I leave a few drops of sweat and feel empowered knowing that I satisfied both of us, on my terms. We both use protection, so I consider this the safest sex there can be: I don't love him, so he can't hurt me."

There are no exact statistics on the spread of sexually transmitted infections (STIs) because many people are unaware they are carrying the diseases, which often show no early symptoms. Reports compiled by the American Sexual Health Association estimate that up to half of sexually active persons will contract an STI by the age of twenty-five, and that as many as one in five Americans has the incurable herpes virus. An average of 14 percent of American female college students get infected with genital human papillomavirus (HPV) each year. And according to a report by the Centers for Disease Control and Prevention, between 28 and 46 percent of women under the age of twenty-five are infected with HPV, and some 14 million people become newly infected each year.

Michael Douglas blamed the HPV he contracted during oral sex as the agent that trickled down the pipe to catalyze his cancer, which doctors agree is possible. This virus comes in some forty different strains and is also linked to cervical, vaginal, penile, and mouth cancers. The HPV vaccines Gardasil and Cervarix, which together protect against cervical cancer and genital warts as well as cancers of the anus, vulva, and vagina, gained FDA approval in 2006 and 2009, respectively, and have been recommended to be given to all adolescent girls before they become sexually active. The good news about a dangerous infection is that the majority of HPV cases can disappear on their own within two years. But it is the 10 percent of persistent strains that are responsible for the 33,300 HPV-associated cancers occurring each year.

Young people discuss HPV and herpes as a "hassle but not a curse," says the young attorney Karla, adding: "We talk about having HPV as casually as having a cold. Out of my ten closest girlfriends, four of them have an STD."

Author Paula Kamen was early in documenting the emerging breed of young females on the prowl whom she calls super-rats in her groundbreaking book *Her Way: Young Women Remake the Sexual Revolution*, published in 2000 by New York University Press. Kamen explains in the first chapter her choice to compare young women to resilient rodents.

"Although this label may seem insulting at first, I use it with all due respect to refer to an often confounding, sexually savvy breed of young women, who have evolved to become more un-stoppable and more prevalent with every generation."

Kamen writes, "Imbued with a large streak of traditionally male (aggressive, self-gratifying) attitudes and behavior, these women illustrate some of the most dramatic sexual changes of the past three decades. These superrats may look different, want a variety of things, come from different backgrounds, have libidos of varying capacities and demands, and confront different obstacles, but they are united by one common trait: the expectation of and insistence on conducting their sex lives on their own terms and with a new degree of openness."

While some women I interviewed did express gratification that females can now openly be the seducers, other superrats complained that when it comes to sex, the two genders will never match up as equals. This latter group described hurtful hookups that left them sexually satiated but hungry for intimacy. They tell stories like Jessica's below of how women can bruise more easily than men because of an imbalance in intent and expectations.

Jessica Bari is the proprietor of Power Coaching Today in Miami, a life coach practice that consists mainly of single women between the ages of twenty-five and forty. Jessica speaks from the heart of a woman who spans both the worlds of her clients and that of her own: as a single, twenty-seven-year-old female living in what is often classified as America's sexiest city.

Very blond, in a skimpy black skirt and black high heels, Jessica comes off more as a *Sex and the City* sophisticate than an insecure girl from *Girls*, with her husky laugh and seen-it-all attitude. As she coaches others through their hookups and break-ups, Jessica is navigating the new normal in her own romances as well, a landscape in which, she says: "Dating is definitely a dying art."

JESSICA BARI

What I see in my practice and among my peers is that a single, fairly attractive guy has slept with anywhere from twenty to forty girls by the time he is twenty-nine. A girl could have easily slept with fifteen guys by the time she is twenty-nine. In the absence of one-on-one dating, people just hang out as a group and in somewhat incestuous ways hook up with each other—friends sleeping with friends swapping with friends of friends, and so it goes.

Sex comes easy and often. Courting is very outdated for our generation. In Miami and other big cities, the hookup culture may start as early as high school and continue through the thirties. What I am seeing, both among my peer group and my clients, is that guys in their twenties for the most part will sleep with anyone who is willing to sleep with them. Usually it's all about sex for the guys. And more and more of the women are allowing it. They are not mandating anything substantial from these guys, although many of these women are hoping for more.

Most women I see have to at least feel the possibility of love if they are continuing to hook up with a guy. While a lot of women are looking for love, women also like sex just as much as men, so many females are no longer holding back and making the men wait. The result is a lot of meaningless sex.

There are categories among women in their responses to casual sex: Some women don't say so but they silently are hoping that if they play their cards right, eventually the hookups will turn into more. Others get tired of being a booty call and demand to know "Where do we stand?" Then she either gets told some bullshit to string her along or the guy is honest and says he is not looking for a real relationship, that he is happy with the way things stand. Then there are women who aren't looking for anything other than a good time, but those tend to be in the minority.

Here is a story of one of my clients, and it's actually pretty typical of what goes on with young single women. She is twenty-six and has a steady sexual relationship with this guy one night each weekend, but doesn't hear from him all week. Friday around 8:00 P.M. he texts her, "Hey, my friends and I are going to this bar if you wanna come by?" Sometimes she doesn't hear from him until the back end at 1:00 A.M., asking, "Hey, are you awake? Want to meet up?"

Here is what she says about her situation: "If I meet at the bar or come over late, we hook up. If I am unable to or don't answer, he just texts someone else."

I see a lot of women confusing sex with love. Their usual MO is to get physical first and deal with the emotions later. As a result, they suddenly find themselves with ridiculous expectations about a guy they would normally be indifferent about, simply because they have been having mind-blowing sex. It feels like love should be the next step, but that's not how the guy generally sees it.

Observing my circle of single girlfriends my age, I'd say two things: Most of them are having sex with someone. And most of them are hoping the relationship deepens into something else. It is not easy for women to keep their hearts from getting bruised. Women for the most part are just not capable of having nonemotional sex. If you sleep with someone, you usually can't help but become attached in some way. Sadly, a lot of those women are falling in love and think they are going to win them over with sex. And if the relationship doesn't turn into something else, too many of them still stick around and just take what they can get.

When I go out to Miami clubs and bars with my girlfriends, we are meeting men all the time. I am not ready to settle down right now after ending a committed relationship that lasted for more than three years. So I, too, have had insignificant meet-ups that are going nowhere. I am very careful, though, because of the work that I do, to make sure not to enter into a superficial physical relationship with someone with whom I think I could become serious. That is a mistake.

It is important to hold out for a multitude of reasons. For starters, if you like the guy, you want him to respect you. Also, it is human nature to want what you can't have. Sex has almost become like a sport to them. Sex is the goal line for men. If you don't have a good defense, then you're really no fun to play with. A man will sleep with just about any girl. But he will fall in love with the woman who makes him feel like he's playing in the NFL. Making a man wait behooves you, not simply because it makes them want you more but because it spares you from falling in lust that you mistake for love with a man who probably, when tested with time, would be totally wrong for you on all the other important levels beyond sexual highs.

There certainly are instances where great hooking-up sex can turn into love if the timing is right. But most relationships in your twenties are based on lust, not the marriage hunt. The twenties are about experimenting to figure out what you want. Your thirties are about going out and getting it.

And while ours is also the generation nearly half of whose parents got a divorce, including mine, many of us still deep down want to find permanent love and to have a healthy family life. So there is a lot of confusion: How can you tell if it is just sex? What is love anyway?

Sleep with enough assholes, and your hopes of finding real love are sure to diminish.

Jessica's take on her generation is delivered with tough-talking wisdom reflecting experience from both perspectives, as a life coach and as an attractive, sexually active single. She knows enough to not be like some of her clients who are prone to "sticking around and just taking what they can get." As a college professor for more than two decades, I am seeing more and more Jessica types, emboldened females in their twenties who are speaking up about owning their power. They are ditching partners who are bad for them and they are smart enough to take a breather between harsh breakups. They don't *need* to be in romantic relationships.

But this is an age group that does need sex.

Tracking the physical and emotional dents that loveless sex is making on youth has become an obsessive field of study for psychologists, academics, and scientists. Dr. Justin Garcia, a research scientist at the Kinsey Institute for Research in Sex, Gender, and Reproduction, coauthored a comprehensive assessment of the subject published in a 2012 volume of the *Review of General Psychology* titled "Sexual Hookup Culture: A Review." Based on the report, which combines multidisciplinary research, hooking-up behavior does seem to be tougher on women than men, yet overall, most young people surveyed feel positive about their sex lives.

My interviews are reflective of that finding. Even the cynics about loveless sex were largely satisfied that they were gaining valuable relationship experience, despite the fact that many of those liaisons caused some pain and confusion.

Garcia spoke to me about the proliferation of uncommitted sex among a population he refers to as "emerging adults." He stands on the shoulders of past Kinsey researchers who have been studying human sexual behavior since Dr. Alfred Kinsey and his colleagues published the two-volume Kinsey Reports in book form in 1948 and 1953. The earliest Kinsey studies, based on interviews with some 14,000 adult males and females, were considered shocking at the time.

Not only did the Kinsey researchers use frank language, but they shattered long-held beliefs that it was primarily the men who craved sexual experimentation. More than a quarter of the married women interviewed during a time frame known for its 1950s Happy (Repressed) Housewife image admitted to at least one act of adultery, and half of them did other fun things in bed aside from just intercourse.

At the age of twenty-eight, the single Garcia, who is also an assistant professor of gender studies at Indiana University, where the Kinsey Institute is based, is part of the demographic he finds "fascinating and mystifying" to study. Here is his scientific overview of a generation that in his words have "turned electronic flirting into the new foreplay."

Dʀ. Jᴜsᴛɪɴ Gᴀʀᴄɪᴀ

Among heterosexual emerging adults of both sexes, hookups have become culturally normative. Our most recent data suggest that 60 to 85 percent of North American college students have had some sort of hookup experience.

There is a tendency for developmentalists now to refer to the period between eighteen to twenty-five years as emerging adulthood. This is really a phase of extended adolescence in which individuals are not fully launched and independent. Among this demographic, hookup behavior is becoming a dominant script, as dating culture has become virtually dead on college campuses.

I'm an evolutionary biologist by training, so this area of study is particularly fascinating to me: Humans have evolved over millions of years as a highly social species, getting to know one another and eventually coming to love others over a period of time. We have removed so much of that courtship with rapid electronic communication. We are really in uncharted evolutionary territory. You don't see, hear, smell, feel, and taste in a text message, so we are now at a point where we are changing the way we communicate as a social species and, as a result, how we find love.

In our recent review, we found that women do experience more frequent negative emotional side effects from hooking up than men. But, at the same time, when the average college student was asked if he or she was generally happy following his or her most recent hookup, the majority of them say "yes."

So, while there are very real physical and psychological risks associated with uncommitted sexual behavior, I worry about the overuse of a disaster model among parents concerning emerging adults. The data simply does not support this model that so many older people ascribe to: the notion that having uncommitted sex, outside of a traditional marital union, may lead to the destruction of the individuals' moral compass and soul.

American society is often worried, perhaps too much, about young people having too much sex. In so doing, we neglect to accept the fact that sexual activity is a normal part of emotional and sexual development. Part of emerging adulthood is testing boundaries and defining the edges of who you are as a person. We also know there are some negative consequences, such as feelings of regret, feelings of shame, feelings of being used.

The fact that many scientists have demonstrated that women have more negative feelings following hookups is partially due to the gender double standards of our society. Some feminist scholars refer to this as "slut shaming": the idea that if you are having sex outside of marriage as a woman, you must be a slut.

However, there are a variety of other factors that also impact how people feel following a hookup. Many emerging adults are aware of the risks of sexual activity, such as unintended pregnancy, sexual violence, and sexually transmitted infections. However, in one of our current studies conducted at Binghamton University in New York State, we found that 70 percent of college students reported condom use in their most recent hookup.

Researchers have noted that one of the interesting aspects about sexuality today is that so much is now discussed openly. I admit that I am sometimes shocked when, during a lecture to undergraduate students, they start talking about their own personal hookups that weekend. While there was a sexual awakening during the 1960s and '70s, this type of discourse is different: Students today aren't trying to incite a sexual revolution or to make a point about their sexuality. They view sex as a natural and open part of the cultural discourse, and there is almost an expectation that young people will regularly engage in some form of hookup behavior.

Yet, despite a prevalence of uncommitted sexual behavior, in our research we have found that a substantial majority of both sexes in the developmental stage of emerging adulthood would prefer a romantic relationship. In one of our 2008 studies, over half of both men and women stated they hook up because they wanted to initiate a romantic relationship with the other person. In some of our more recent data, it is a majority of men and women who identify romantic relationships as more rewarding and preferable to hookups.

While there may be some bravado in hookup culture, where sex doesn't matter or carry meaning beyond pleasures of the flesh, of course sex does matter and it often does lead to romance. Sexual behavior evokes real feelings, beyond just following a script. And for some college students, these experiences and expectations may result in confusion.

Research has shown that these feelings emerge with friends-with-benefits situations, for example. The partners are platonic friends; they start having sex and they start to develop more complex feelings for each other. It becomes complicated, not because of the sex but because the script explicitly says you are not supposed to be having romantic feelings. Yet, perhaps inevitably, many of these relationships contain romantic elements.

Friends with benefits is often functionally distinguished from hookups, because FWB situations represent a greater degree of friendship, trust, and emotional comfort. Hookup scenarios do not implicitly include a friendship component as a condition. FWBs pose another challenge as well: Individuals have to work at avoiding predictable natural responses, such as feeling jealous when your friend starts wanting to see someone else.

From my perspective, I think it is a generally good thing that some of these relationships are more out in the open. Love and sex are some of the most consistent human experiences, across cultures and across time. So perhaps this openness is getting us to recognize the centrality of sexual relationships in our lives, and their importance to the health of individuals and populations around the world. As a society, we genuinely need to be more comfortable addressing these topics.

While sexual activity can be extremely fun and emotionally rewarding, we have a responsibility across age groups to talk about what distinguishes good and healthy sex from behaviors that can be dangerous. There is too often an absence of real, productive, honest conversation about some of the more worrisome aspects of casual sex. A majority of hookups involve alcohol and drugs, and the experiences can be coercive; sexual assault can take place. We have to address these more serious topics with kids before they go to college if up to 85 percent of them are going to end up having these casual sex experiences at some point. We can't pretend that it doesn't happen.

The period in which emerging adults are engaging in hookup behavior is a historically unprecedented time gap, since puberty starts earlier while marriage and child rearing are now being delayed. While we are gaining knowledge about this growing field, our understanding of the ramifications remain mysterious—both the historical transformations that have resulted in the reordering of sexual behaviors and scripts, and the demise of traditional romantic courting. The rise of casual sex is really one of the defining issues of youth today.

What is particularly interesting to me as a scientist is that so many different disciplines are fascinated by the issue: scholars in fields of gender studies, sociology, psychology, anthropology, biology, social work, nursing, medicine. America's youth has captured all of our attention.

The sexual youthquake, whether we like it or not, has indeed captured everyone's attention. It has even shaken awake the most rigid of politicians, such as U.S. Representative Rob Portman, who turned around in support of same-sex marriage after his young son came out as gay. Portman joined legions of other conservative parents who are being forced to abandon sexual stereotypes about what constitutes "normal," as gender-bending, hooking up, and the new free love have become an overarching cultural script that is impossible to avoid.

The acceptance, albeit reluctant, among American moms and

dads that sexual experimentation is now an intrinsic part of mainstream youth is in pointed contrast to the outrage voiced by most adults to the horny hippies of decades ago. Those were the hippies who warned their peers, "Don't trust anybody over thirty."

The oversexed players in the current sex revolution are not singing "One, two, three—what are we fighting for?" like their ancestors did at Woodstock. Those were the activists fighting to end a war, for equal rights for women, for the right to have premarital sex without reproduction. Today their grandchildren of college age and beyond just want to have sex and are increasingly able to do so loudly and proudly, without stigma or cultural checks.

Hayley Samela, twenty-three, is a freelance journalist who splits her time between Washington, DC, and New York City. She wears black jeans with back zipper pockets and a billowy black-and-white polka-dot blouse, both from Zara. Of Korean heritage, Hayley is a stark beauty, enhanced by her unique style and self-assuredness.

HAYLEY SAMELA

My girlfriends and I all agree that dating someone who hasn't had sexual experiences would be strange. We want partners who know what they're doing. The girls I know would never marry someone without sleeping with him first. Even my most religious friend has sex with her boyfriend—although she cried afterward the first time. But now she doesn't feel bad about it, or think it was a wrong thing to do. She jokes that "God has more important things to worry about than me losing my virginity to a guy I love."

But I've never had a relationship where I was physical with someone I didn't care about or wasn't attracted to on some level. For me, the relationship is always about more than just sex. I do know, though, very quickly whether or not we will be compatible sexually: I measure a man in the first moments of meeting. Not just the size of certain body parts, but if they meet criteria to my liking—such as age, profession, appearance, and then personality. If they don't meet most of those things, why waste time pursuing them further?

I need to like him and respect him. He needs to make me feel good about myself. He also needs to make me laugh. But I don't have any friends who wouldn't want to sleep with someone before getting into a serious relationship. You need to know if there's chemistry beyond just good conversation and feeling like he has nice manners.

If you're having a hard time being intimate with someone now, it's just going to be that much more difficult once you're married to him and have all these other issues, like kids and money problems. You have to work at the relationship, but you shouldn't have to work at sex. The attraction is either there or it isn't there.

Sex can get better with time, if you are honest and open with what works and doesn't. I don't think our generation has many problems with being really open. We talk about sex all the time without censoring ourselves. We're not whispering, there's no secret code, even in public places when there are strangers at the other end of the table. Our mothers and grandmothers were so hush-hush about it. Yet we're never afraid to ask another girlfriend on a bus or over brunch, "How was it?"

I am thinking that the straight-shooting Hayley and the Salem-smoking Karla would have fit in well with the flappers of the 1920s, who stepped out from under the Victorian prudes known for covering their bodies from neck to toe. The flappers bobbed their hair and wore flimsy skirts and smoked cigarettes and had many men. But unlike the gloating inhabitants of the new sex-texting society, the flappers had to conduct their chatter on petting and drinking gin during Prohibition in clandestine whispers. God forbid their mothers, tightly cinched in corsets, would catch wind of their shenanigans.

Even a decade ago, our more sexually progressive European neighbors would have considered most Americans to be psychologically corseted about sex, stuck in our Puritan past. That put-down does not define us anymore. Finally, we are acknowledging, and yielding to, this fact of life: Sex is occurring among the majority of youth, long before they enter committed relationships—if they ever do so.

While some 90 percent of Americans will marry at some point in their lifetimes, there is no sense of urgency to do so before the age of thirty. If a young woman wants a baby, she certainly does not need a husband. She can bank her eggs, buy some sperm, and even hire out a donor womb. And cohabitation outside of matrimony does not even raise an eyebrow.

More than five million unmarried couples live together in the United States, nearly eight times as many as in 1970. And unlike previous generations of libidinous youth, these sons and daughters do not view their sexual behavior as a rebellion against their parents, nor as something they must hide. Most moms and dads assume that their kids will follow the statistical norm of having sexual intercourse by age seventeen, and often help them do so safely, accompanying them to doctors for contraceptives. Succumbing to the reality that sex happens early and often signals a more astute cultural intelligence than the days when long-haired hippies with hefty carnal appetites were deemed the enemy, and chastised.

We need to be moms out of denial and not preaching

chastity, but instead mandating that condoms belong in night-stands, purses, and backpacks. Because this story from Olivia is not all that rare.

While clubbing in London with a group of young local women, I was introduced to this sassy twenty-five-year-old who relayed, calmly, how when smashed on a Saturday night, she picked up a man on a bus. A half hour later, they were in his flat. (And she *did* use condoms.)

Five feet nine with bright red hair and matching lips, Olivia wears a white see-through sweater and skintight jeans tucked into ankle boots. Here are her reflections on The Man on the Bus and what it all means—and does not mean.

OLIVIA

The guy on the bus—that was something I hadn't done before. I've gone home with a guy from a club, but never from a bus about thirty minutes after meeting him.

It was quite wild—we just started talking at the bus stop while we were waiting. Then on the bus we got to talking more about where we lived; we didn't talk about jobs at this point or nothing very personal at all. We actually started kissing on the bus. Then we started walking toward our houses. We live near each other, and I went to his place instead of mine. I was quite drunk, but I knew what was happening. I know it doesn't sound very smart, but I was in the right state of mind for him and for this experience.

He is Polish, an artist, twenty-eight years old. But that first night, we didn't exchange a whole lot of information. I think I even remember him saying, "Don't you like that we don't know much about each other?" The sex was really, really, really good. I didn't know if I'd see him again, but I gave him my cell number.

I frankly didn't really expect him to text me. He did, though, two or three days after. I went back to his place, and we hooked up again.

The thing about this man, though, was that it wasn't only that the sex was very sensual and good. He was affectionate and fun, inviting me over to watch comedy videos and eat ice cream as well as hook up.

Other casual sex experiences I've had have not been enjoyable because the guy has been quite selfish and mechanical, not caring really about anything except pleasuring himself. This was different—and I liked that he paid attention to me. He was experienced, and above all, he was very good at expressing himself. He even told me he wasn't really into just f—ing for no reason. He said sex was about the desire to be intimate with someone he liked as well as to be physically expressive of an animal need.

We both understood it was a casual thing, and we kept hooking up on weekends. This lasted for about two months. Then one weekend, he went away for business to Madrid, and I didn't know if that meant the end and I wouldn't hear from him again. And I did start feeling a bit too anxious, like "When is he going to text me? Why haven't I heard from him?" In the end, I texted him and asked him to come 'round to my place, and he stayed over.

We talked for hours about stuff that we hadn't talked about before, about our fears and school experiences, about what we were like when we were growing up, about our jobs. It was an intimate few hours of talking, and I could feel that I was getting closer to him. After that night, I didn't want him to leave. I felt vulnerable and just generally more insecure than normal. So I knew it was time for the relationship to stop before I got too deep into it.

What changed was that I cared. When that feeling suddenly became too stressful, I called him and explained that I wasn't 100 percent happy to keep things casual. I was clear about how I felt, and gave him opportunity to say how he felt. He said he understood, but then he was a bit like, "Why would you leave this? Don't I make you feel good sexually?"

I was like "No, that's not it. I just want something more reliable." There was an opportunity for him to object, to say he wanted to keep seeing me, but he didn't. So we said our goodbyes.

I was proud of myself; I wanted more and wasn't scared to ask for that. When my emotions started coming into it, I had to protect myself. I never asked if he was sleeping with other people, and he never asked me either—it was just not necessary. We always used protection, and I'd been checked for STDs since we started seeing each other.

I want something now that I can count on, someone more reliable and less dangerous to be thinking about. I think I was aware that even though I had varied, sometimes quite meaningful conversations with The Man on the Bus, he hadn't asked me out for a real dinner or a movie. We were bedroom buddies. And that wasn't enough.

Still, I don't believe the random hookups have been bad for me. If anything, I think it's better to have experiences that are fun and casual while you can. I do want to commit to someone someday, and my experiences in my twenties have helped me know what I want. Now I can recognize when someone is good for me, or when the situation is not worth fighting for anymore.

I've only really had one relationship that lasted more than a year—it ended when I was nineteen. When I broke up with that first serious boyfriend who was my first everything, I realized how important it was as a woman to learn how to be alone and happy. I want to be okay by myself and with myself, first and foremost. Because then when I do fall in love again, I will know how to have a fulfilling, dedicated relationship with that person, without losing sight of who I am, and without relying on him to be my world. Because I will already have my own world.

My British buddies are atwitter about a new play at London's Soho Theatre, called *A Guide to Second Date Sex*, written by twenty-four-year-old playwright Rachel Hirons. Of course, the title intrigues me, and I was further enticed when I read Hirons's blog post in the February 18, 2013, *London Evening Standard*, in which she describes the origin of her project.

"I, like you, live in a world where adverts, daily spam e-mails, film, and TV all work together constantly reminding me I should be having sex, should be having better sex and however much I'm having, I'm not having enough sex. . . .

"Seemingly these ideals just don't translate well in real life."

Within the article, Rachel describes one of her own humiliating second-date sex dalliances with a man who turned out to be a virgin. Attempting to tutor her novice partner, she went at it in a near-standing position after her partner somehow ended up in a "yoga crab position." Candles lit, limbs twined, their awkward yogic moment was interrupted by his red-faced mommy, who was supposed to be out for the night, and who screamed, "What the hell are you doing to my son?"

And thus a play was born.

"To this day I am still not 100 percent certain what I am meant to be doing to the sons of these women," Hirons concluded. "And neither do most of the women I encounter. So I decided to ask the men. I was shocked to discover a list of insecurities and anxieties that almost went beyond that of women.

From the blatant, to the bizarre, I decided to collate these findings into *A Guide to Second Date Sex*."

The one-hour play, which has only two characters and takes place entirely on a set resembling a bedroom, opened in August 2012 to fawning reviews at the Edinburgh Fringe Festival. During its two-week run in London, it sold out every night, with extra shows added to cater to the demand.

I sought out Rachel to talk further about her own angst and discoveries about sex and relationships. A short and striking woman with a rapid-fire megamind, she has what she calls "fake blond hair," and a genuine take on the insecurity of a generation being force-fed unreal expectations.

RACHEL

What I really wanted to get across with my play is that it's time we start looking at the reality of sex rather than this glossed-over, sugarcoated rubbish we are constantly otherwise subjected to. It is ridiculous. We are conditioned through every media outlet imaginable that sex is something that we are good at or bad at, rather than the whole thing being relative. This results in us viewing sex like a sport, performance, or impersonation rather than something we experience.

Sex, in reality, is nerve-racking. Ultimately, we all want to come across as sexy, funny, charming, sensual, skilled, and confident in the bedroom. However, no matter how experienced we are, being intimate with someone new and revealing our bodies to them for the first time is always enough to cause heart palpitations.

Although the play is called *A Guide to Second Date Sex*, the only guide within the play is basically saying to the audience: "You know all of those sex tricks, insecurities, and embarrassed, panic-stricken thoughts you have? Well, you're not alone—we all go through exactly the same thing."

The depiction of hooking up on TV shows as glamorous and carefree is absolutely not true in real life. Most of what we are shown is attractive, triumphant, constant sex. Maybe this is somebody's reality, but certainly no one I've ever encountered. I'm sure if an alien came to earth and read our magazines or watched our movies, they would think we all lie around having constant sex, while looking like models.

You can't learn satisfying sex from a book or pornography or anything else. Good sex is practiced; it comes when two people know each other really well. Know each other's bodies intimately, and know what the other person likes and doesn't like. And good sex comes when you are comfortable enough with that person to communicate all of this freely.

When you reach the comfort point with someone, where you are not worried about smells, sounds, or impressing them with technique, there is no bad sex: It's just an experience.

The casual sex of our generation makes many of our elders believe we may not recognize true love when it finally does arrive. I don't think it's a case that we don't recognize it, but arguably perhaps we are just not as interested in finding it as we used to be. Romance in our age group has become less about finding that one person who you will always be with, and more about finding whomever is right for you at that point in your life. We don't seem to have the time or inclination to keep trying to make something work if it isn't doing so naturally. We are the instant-gratification generation. If your cell phone breaks, get a new one, for example, and I think we have come to view relationships in much the same way.

Of course, this approach to relationships is not without its own issues of stress, perhaps more among the women than the men. Women do eventually become more concerned about commitment for simple, evolutionary reasons such as childbearing and rearing. Not to mention that the actual act of sex is far more intrusive for a woman than for a man—you are literally letting someone inside you; you cannot escape the intimacy of that. Naturally, hooking up is bound to have an emotional effect on women. Due to the saturation of promiscuity and images of wild sex in the media, we women feel as though the idea of us actually being able to be enough for a man in order to keep him forever is an unlikely pipe dream. After all, there will always be someone younger, prettier, sexier, more exotic, and more charming than we are. We are constantly made to feel as though we need to improve, to be fixed, to be better, to be perfect.

I am completely obsessed by the psychology of human relationships and have always been a voyeur with couples, trying to understand the dynamic and chemistry. Given this intense curiosity, it probably won't surprise you to hear that my parents are not together. They divorced when I was only a couple of months old, so I have no memory of their marriage.

While my dad married another woman shortly after the divorce, had my half sister, and is still happily married, my mother has had a chain of rocky relationships with often bizarre suitors—men half her age, married men, gay men. She is a very funny woman with whom I am very close and she would probably say she has given me too much information over the years. She has no issues with saying things like "Okay, I'm getting with this man. . . . He is married" or "I met this guy; he's twenty"—and she would be forty-five. She talks candidly to me about her insecurities and attitudes. Witnessing the experiences of my mom has given me this drive to figure out the nuances and difficulties of relationships, and motivations behind romantic decisions.

In truth, I tend to be a long-term relationship person rather than one for one-night stands; they are far more interesting and revealing. I am currently with someone for going on a year now. Things are going well, but I don't think either of us is thinking about forever. What's more important is the pleasure I am getting from the relationship today.

But as promiscuous as our generation has become, it would be a bitter thing for me to say that sex isn't sacred. There is meaningful, even sacred sex out there. But it doesn't come from replicating instructions for lap dances or wild techniques seen on TV or in guides; that's rubbish. Good sex has always been dependent upon how you feel about yourself, and how you feel about your partners. My message is that we finally should be talking about real sex for real women, and that sex is insecure and imperfect for everybody. I'm sure that even women who look like Mila Kunis have panic-stricken and embarrassed moments with sex.

Listening to the voices of youth I am replaying conversations of long ago with my best college pals when we were the age of Rachel and Olivia. There was plenty of confusion about the preponderance of free love, and how the pleasurable thrashing of our bodies seldom matched what was thrashing through our unsettled minds. This sprang from experimenting with lovers we did not love, or didn't even like that much. Many of us early protégés of hard-line feminists still felt that ancient yank of the womb, and softness of heart, that comes with being born female.

I do detect a hardening bravado in some of the young women I meet, but there remains an inherent sentiment about relationships that mirror what we felt: We women often made the mistake of believing, hoping, that sexual chemistry would lead to a lengthy emotional match.

Along with breathy celebratory vignettes about sexuality, I heard as many tales of despair, from young women who fell for men who were inconsistent in their affections, even iffy at showing up. I tell the lovelorn that finding out yo-yo patterns early on in a relationship is a good thing. Because the most important quality they should look for in a lifelong partner is reliability.

Bad, sexy boys given to spontaneity may be amusing to sleep with but can become disasters when sharing a mortgage and childrearing. The man I married at the age of thirty-three was the first suitor who always did what he said he was going to do; he called on a Monday for a weekend date; he showed up on time; he did not bolt when I told him I was ready for commitment and kids.

Twenty-five years later, that husband is still here, unfailingly— watching hockey, drinking longneck Rolling Rock beer, in a tattered La-Z-Boy chair. I do not share his passions for hockey or sitting still. Yet at least I always know where to find him, which is a lot more than many wives can say about their spouses, and is definitely more than modern singles can say about their mates-of-the-moment.

I find myself offering unsolicited maternal advice to young women in random romances, warning them that sex on the fly with a revolving cast of strangers at some point takes its toll. Ironically, it was a young man with wild curls and an elegant spin with sentences who was one of the only active hooker-uppers I spoke to who said: "I'm done with this. It's making me crazy."

Hank is a twenty-five-year-old who works at an environmental think tank. After a wave of promiscuity, he recently entered a stage of "self-loathing" that has prodded a transition in how he conducts his romances. This tall and thin young man from

Wyoming has found himself in the "previously unthinkable state where I am actually dating!" Here is more from Hank on his turn-around and a new relationship that holds the promise of love.

HANK

I haven't been in a functional monogamous relationship since, like, Bush Two was in office. I dated someone I met in college for three years and we broke up when we were both twenty-one years old. It was off and on and not exactly healthy.

We were very much in love, though, and the narrative going through our minds was spending the rest of our lives together. It was definitely one of those head-over-heels relationships, and then we just started to grow up and grow apart. Since then, I'd say I've slept with something like twenty-five women, five or six of whom could probably be considered "girl-friends," but only in a very low-grade, air-quotation sense of the word.

I say that because while I was sleeping with one of these women and spending inordinate amounts of time with them—cooking meals, going to movies, meeting each other's friends—there was never a confirmed understanding of where each of us stood with the other. There was always a proverbial foot out the door. I looked at these experiences as cheap pleasure and cheap entertainment.

There was very little vulnerability on my part: I did not meet parents, and took almost no responsibility for the relationship. For the most part, this person would function as someone I could call on short notice to go to a movie, eat dinner, and f—k. I know this sounds very calculated and sociopathic—perhaps misogynistic—but there was always some conversation in the early running which went something like:

Me: I don't know what you're looking for with this, but I'm not really in an emotional place right now to be in a relationship.

Her: Okay, good. Because I'm not either. My job is crazy, and I might be moving, and I just don't know. But I want to spend time with you.

Me: Same here.

This effectively puts a shelf life on the relationship from the start and clears up any perception that intimacy is the goal. The relationship exists on this level for, say, a month or two before things fizzle. Because of the loose sense of commitment, there's almost never an emotional breakup. The obvious result of this is a lack of closure and a sort of open invitation to maybe walk through the door again. I've recently slept again with probably five of these women, for example.

It really is this sort of weird addiction cycle. The hookup culture is simple and effective direct pleasure to your nervous system. People are going to go back to that pleasure time and time again in an addictive way. Slowly and surely, you realize it's not nutritious, in the way that eating candy all the time might taste good but has no nutrition.

I've had a lot of sex with women I don't particularly like, sex that had almost zero implication for my desire to date the person. This of course ends up feeling contrived and vacuous and can go on only as long as the person sexually excites you, which is a very short time for me.

So perhaps a working definition of dating in the twenty-first century, at least for male twentysomethings is: an informal vetting system wherein both parties are removed from relationship implication by meeting up and participating in casual sex as a litmus test of vulnerability and connection. If she is fun and smart and sexually exciting, a one-on-one relationship does become a possibility down the road.

Recently, I met a woman through a friend and actually asked her out on a date, to dinner. The implications for the relationship were clear—it wasn't a hookup—the setting was fairly formal, and we had a great time. My intentions were clear and confident, instead of blasé. Blasé is the right approach when you're just trying to get laid. I'm starting to feel that I've done the avoid-vulnerability-via-sex-route enough. I am becoming more interested in one-on-one, to experience a person right up all my nerve endings instead of trying to let sex do the talking. That other route hasn't been working for me.

I have now gone on five dates with this woman. It's going great—this is going to make me sound incredibly shallow, but this is the first time in a long time that my first point of attraction to a woman is not purely physical. I genuinely admire her mind and her value system above how attractive she is, although she is attractive.

My mother has sort of talked to me about the value of courtship and not sleeping with a person early on, how drawn-out foreplay can be romantic. And I am thinking she is right; you develop some mystique. It also connects you more interpersonally, which is a prerequisite for me to have good sex. I've had a lot of sex in the past few years, but not that much good sex. As I said, I have slept with people I didn't like that much. It's a little bit easier for men to think with their penises than their heads, but in the end, you are going to have good sex only when your head does the thinking.

But the cliché that it's only men who think with their genitals is some Old World shit that I think most feminists would balk at. Women are plenty capable of thinking with their vaginas, and they often do so. Ask any of the women who use OkCupid, and my point will be confirmed in spades. Men do think with their genitals more often only because we've been allowed to. I don't think the problem is biological as much as it's sexual politics.

I still think sexual politics is lopsided. The way I've been living my life for the past three years is much more socially acceptable. Although people my age are becoming a lot better at gender equality, if I were a woman, there would be a tendency to label me a "slut." For men, our many sexual experiences are deemed notches on our belts.

My parents have been married for thirty-some years and are still big fans of each other. They respect and love each other deeply, recognize and compensate for each other's blind spots, and don't derive meaning wholly from the other. They married within weeks of meeting, both leaving other romances to be together.

I used to feel tremendous romantic pressure to replicate my parents' whirlwind meeting and run off to get married with a soul mate. Once that first love fell apart at twenty-one, my response was to count my parents' relationship as rare and special and accept that I'd probably never get that lasting relationship, and would be divorced at least once, per the statistics. I just kind of accepted that not everyone gets one of the really great relationships and that I'd be okay with falling short, as long as it gave me companionship and children.

I've come to a middle ground. I'd love nothing else than to one day be in a long-term monogamous relationship and to have kids. That would be awesome. But I don't want the all-consuming love I had before; that college relationship flamed out in a hard serious way like space debris coming back into orbit.

I'm almost willing to think that love should be a little more placid. It doesn't have to have these intense chemical reactions. It can be a really comfortable blending of agreeable forces. I'm happy to be getting to know this new woman's mind first, rather than her body. This is really a decision based on my deteriorating mental health.

I had gotten to this place over the last several months where I was self-loathing about participating in one-night stands and one-month stands. You can't help but kind of get involved emotionally and mentally with these people. I could not continue to live that way. It was slowly taking a psychological toll and driving me into a downward spiral.

Sure I got fun. I got pleasure. I got affirmation. But I wasn't getting stability or companionship or loyalty or love. This new woman is someone with whom this seems possible.

Sex is exalting, sex hurts, sex does a lot of things to the physiology and soul, as Hank and others in this chapter reveal in pained honesty. Many of them, such as British playwright Rachel Hirons, also realize the depth to which media images of sexual perfection and perfectly sexy bodies corrupt concepts of self-worth and induce false expectations. Sara Wilson was my longtime editor at *The Huffington Post* for my blogs in the Weddings and Divorce sections. She is now a manager in Strategic Partner Development/Lifestyle for Facebook.

Single and thirty-three, the super-savvy Wilson is a purveyor of the most critical—and edgy—behaviors and trends that are shaping youth culture and their intimate relationships. I asked the wise young journalist to help me make sense of the chorus and clash of voices I have heard on what hooking up really means, and for her view on how casual sex might impair or improve a young person's future shot at commitment.

SARA WILSON

It's not exactly a news flash that sex, or at least images of sex, are everywhere these days. In magazines, on billboards, in video games, on prime-time TV shows. I'm not even talking about porn. I'm talking about mass media. Popular culture. And it's overkill. At this point, can't we come up with a more creative way to communicate on a mass scale? That said, I think these images and their prevalence affect us more than we know.

When we talk about the effect of these images, and the messages they send to kids, the discussion often turns to "hooking up," which I think is probably one of the most misunderstood and overused terms ever. What does *hooking up* really mean? I wonder sometimes if it's just nostalgia for a long-ago time when young people abided by clear-cut rules for dating instead of the casual way they do it today. Too often the discussion verges on hysteria—like "Oh my gosh, they're growing up too fast!" We as a society have long been obsessed with young people's sexuality, especially young female sexuality, and in many ways, I think, this is just the latest incarnation of that.

I also think hooking up can be good. It can really help people—especially women—figure out their own sexuality and what they want in a partner. In generations past, people who wanted to have sex got married, and that was that. Many of those people probably shouldn't have gotten married. They ended up in miserable marriages. The pill allowed women the opportunity to experiment before marriage, evidently at younger and younger ages. So with some exceptions, I don't think that's necessarily a bad thing.

That said, I think the fact that sexual images and messages are everywhere affects kids in very real negative ways, too. I saw this very clearly in 2004, when I wrote an article for *The Globe and Mail*, a Canadian newspaper, titled "Good Girls Do." It was about middle schoolers and sex. After talking to a lot of kids at length, I wrote a story that included firsthand details about how middle schoolers were handling their own sexuality. Specifically, how the attitude toward sex of all kinds had shifted to one that was completely casual, so that oral sex was seen as "no big deal" (that was a direct quote).

The article caused a huge stir, and it ignited conversations on both coasts of Canada about teenage sexuality and what it all meant. But what kind of got lost in the noise surrounding the piece was the much more subtle point I had made about kids' shifting attitude toward sex in general.

To me, that was the bigger story. And I think there's a lot more to be explored there. For starters, why is this happening? I think we have to look at the messages kids are getting from the culture, which in many cases are more powerful than the ones they're getting from parents and teachers. And be honest about what those messages are doing to kids, and try to help them navigate through the morass of information.

The fact that sex is everywhere in the culture affects adults, too, in a big way. For one, the prevalence of this imagery would seem to suggest that everyone in the world is having a lot of sex all the time. Which just isn't true. You want to talk about epidemics? Let's talk about sexless marriages. The numbers vary, but the latest one I heard is an estimate that 15 percent of married couples have not had sex with their spouses in the last six months to a year. Six months to a year!

So when you go into a long-term relationship or marriage with the belief that everyone else is boinking each other at all times, it's a double whammy—it sets up unrealistic expectations that makes you feel inadequate when you don't meet them.

Many young people still cling to the fairy-tale fantasy that marriage will always be romantic and full of hot sex; and that is completely unreasonable. You can't possibly sustain it. You can sustain lots of other wonderful things within a marriage, like a deep friendship and starting a family and building history together. But the idea that you'll have fiery sexual passion until the day you die is crazy.

At the start of 1998, my college students were discussing the fiery sexual passion of the Monica Lewinsky-Bill Clinton affair that had just broken in three-inch headlines on the cover of *The Washington Post*. They were predicting that Hillary Clinton would wait until the end of her husband's term as president, then promptly file for divorce. Fifteen years later, the Clintons remain a married couple with their own private artillery of strategies that have kept the relationship from exploding. Though we do not know their secrets, we can safely assume that one of them is not the constant wildfire sex they may have known in their youth. They share history and a deep friendship Sara Wilson refers to, and a whole hell of a lot else no one will ever know about.

I do know when I speak to wives Hillary Clinton's age, they tell me that they would rather be settled into their old marriages, however imperfect, than be embedded in a young marriage, with newborns who never sleep.

The honeymoon is over quickly, as you are about to find out.

PART TWO

~

THE HONEYMOON
IS OVER

CHAPTER 3
SEX AFTER BABY

Newlywed bliss is snuffed out swiftly once the
squawl of an infant replaces sex as your new
wake-up call—24/7.

—Iris Krasnow

During the six-month visit for my first pregnancy, I had already packed on forty of the forty-seven pounds I would
gain. My obstetrician, Janet Schaffel, told me my spirit seemed
"radiant" but that I should be mindful of the scale. I told her I
knew I was bovine, but for some reason, even in these XXL
sweatpants with a hole in the butt, I was feeling pretty sexy. The
string at the waist was long gone, as the bulge alone held them up.

Dr. Schaffel's response: "Enjoy it while you can."

I was one of those women who thought sex was pleasurable
during pregnancy, deep, shuddery, and delicious. Actually, I
loved almost everything about being pregnant until the swollen
last couple of weeks—the bursting C cups, the gorging without

guilt, and a taut belly that undulated in August as I sat on Delaware's Middlesex Beach. All four births were in November and December, so August was the marker when I was still in that blathery state of joyful expectation, in a bikini that looked awful but in which I felt magnificent. The heat of summer compounded with the sense of occupying a new body made sex feel really different and really fun.

Other prepartum friends moved into spare bedrooms and were repulsed at the thought of even being touched. In his "All about Sex" column of June 14, 2010, in *Psychology Today* online, Michael Castleman, author of *Great Sex: A Man's Guide to the Secret Principles of Total-Body Sex* (Rodale), refers to several studies that demonstrate the diversity of responses to sex during pregnancy. As was the case in my sampling of expectant girlfriends, some women found the bloom within to be a turn-on, while others' libidos were flattened.

Castleman reports that men also experience a range of desire during the wife's pregnancy, citing a study conducted by Swedish researchers in which some men loved sex with a pregnant wife, while others had no interest, particularly during the bulky final trimester. One of my male pals, Louis, now approaching seventy, remembers the times when his wife was pregnant with their two children as some of the best sex of his marriage.

"You and your partner are totally bonded through that child during this time, so sex is all about love, love, love—which is really sexy," says Louis. "It is sex like no other sex because, though not conscious or intellectual, the loving on those nights and days comes with the feeling of creating new life and family. You can't match that fullness at any other time of a relationship."

Pregnant women with high-risk conditions such as placenta previa or incompetent cervix are not able to freely indulge in intercourse, and are appropriately counseled by their doctors.

But for those mothers-to-be who are gestating healthily, there are added pluses to being plus-size.

"A common response to sex during pregnancy was better orgasms," writes Castleman in his *Psychology Today* online column. "Many pregnant women reported the most intense orgasms of their lives. Some women who had never had orgasms had them." Late pregnancy orgasms were actually associated with a lessened risk of premature delivery. This is astonishing and positive news, but any pregnant woman approaching her due date knows that the last stage of pregnancy are the cumbersome days when we least desire sex.

Levels of testosterone may also affect libido during pregnancy, when there is a significant rise in the male hormone in females: two to four times nonpregnancy rates. Scientists are fixated on testosterone as a substance that may drive sexual desire in both genders, a topic to be addressed further in later chapters.

Whether it was heightened testosterone or sleep-deprived mania from the failure to find a comfortable prone position, sex was great while I was huge. This was heightened by the fact that I had zero self-consciousness, and we got to create some innovative postures. A different and larger body brings on a different and larger response. I felt voluptuous and Rubenesque, not yucky and fat. That is, until a wide-eyed baby boy came out and busted apart the Rubenesque hots, at least for several weeks. Newlywed bliss is snuffed out swiftly once the squawl of an infant replaces sex as your new wake-up call—24/7.

I know that many of you reading this are decades past that crazy time of leaky breasts and babies wailing and the strained and strange overhaul of a marriage that occurs once the family goes from two to three. Yet this was a passage necessary to dissect, as pregnancy and childbirth are a pivotal period in which those traits that make us sexual beings, our brains, female organs, and hormones, are torpedoed and whirled around like no time else.

"For as many as 67 percent of new parents, the transition to parenthood is accompanied by sharp declines in relationship quality, significant increases in relationship conflict, increased depression and psychopathology, and decreased quality of the parent-infant interaction," cites a research abstract titled "Bringing Baby Home" by renowned love doctor John Gottman and Alyson Shapiro. Gottman's 1999 bestselling *Seven Principles for Making Marriage Work,* coauthored with Nan Silver, remains one of the most effective guides to sustaining intimacy in a marriage.

I could have used the marriage guru Gottman when we were the parents of four sons under the age of three in November of 1993—three of them breast-feeding. It was wild and snarly for a while there, and decidedly unromantic. Cleaning up poop and pee and crusted peas took precedence over getting down and dirty in our own bed.

"Mystery is critical to romantic love," writes anthropologist Helen Fisher in *Anatomy of Love*, the timeless bestseller published in 1992. "This violent emotional disturbance that we call infatuation (or attraction) may begin with a small molecule called phenylethylamine, or PEA," a substance in the brain that arouses feelings of "elation, exhilaration, and euphoria."

This can't-eat-can't-sleep high is the reason young singles may become addicted to the fleeting bliss of hooking up. What those bed hoppers will find out if and when they opt for monogamy and commitment—and parenthood—is that romantic infatuation is not biologically sustainable. Ask any mom in the first weeks after delivering and in the first years of marriage.

One of the most content wives I ever interviewed was a woman in her late sixties named Dee from Los Angeles. Her revered husband of forty years had recently died, and she spoke wistfully of the 1950s, when brides and grooms entered marriages naive, and not jaded. Dee's central message is to marry when your heart is aflame with infatuation and not when the elation has fizzled. In other words, strike while the lust is hot, and not after real life and real challenges set in.

"My generation married young and generally did not have premarital sex, let alone live together before the wedding night," Dee started out. "The way things are now, a prolonged period of living together and physical intimacy before marriage, that takes away the initial excitement of the first couple of years of marriage. It was so exciting when we got married and could sleep together! That new toy can sustain a marriage for the first couple of years until the babies are born, and then the thrill about the babies takes over.

"Now couples have eaten dessert first, and the excitement is dwindling just as they are getting married," continues Dee. "Many marriages are on the brink of tedium right from the start; couples are already somewhat bored with one another. Then the babies come and it's a total disruption of the parents' already fragile interaction. In our time, when you got married and became intimate for the first time, there was this sexy, wonderful discovery of each other that could last for years."

As the prowling singles in my chapter on hooking up proclaimed, postponing sex until the wedding night is not likely to become a trend. But Dee's story does contain a warning that is timeless and true: Familiarity lowers the temperature of romance.

According to Helen Fisher's assessment of the natural evolution, and the anatomy, of love, the normal duration of infatuation is two to three years. Significantly, the two-year mark in marriage is one of the prevalent junctures for divorce, a time when love is morphing from the lustrous infatuation stage into a wobbly, tarnished union, particularly if you throw a newborn into the mix.

In this chapter, you will meet women in fledgling marriages, with young children, who were not virgin brides but deeply in love at their weddings. They are working to sustain that "sexy, wonderful discovery of each other" Dee talks about. This while confronting roadblocks to intimacy that strike well beyond generic complaints such as "he snores like a jackhammer." Christine Hall and Carmen Calvo address immobilizing postpartum depression and the struggle to push through a common new-mom lament of feeling more attached to their babies than to their mates. Two children later, Jordana remains besotted in lusty love with the college boyfriend she married five years ago, and she confesses some of her sexy tricks.

They are unique in their responses to juggling marriage and hormonal swings and babies, but united in their mission to work hard at negotiating tough grown-up issues that impair newlywed intimacy. The work is essential if the marriage is to endure.

Studies on postpartum depression are numerous and vary in precise numbers, but overall it is estimated that between 15 to 20 percent of pregnant women will experience some severity of depression and anxiety. In Carmen's case, the symptoms were wicked. She had recurring catastrophic fantasies that her first-born son was in mortal danger, such as being mauled by animals, and a swooping depression that suppressed her spirit, "like a heavy, dark cloak."

To ward off another immobilizing bout of the blues, she ate her own placenta right after a second son was born. This process, conducted under the supervision of a licensed therapist, involves drying the nutrient-packed afterbirth and placing it into capsules to be ingested by the mom in the first weeks after delivery.

This process, called placentophagy, is a mainstay of ancient

Chinese medicine and is believed to boost emotional health. January Jones, who plays Don Draper's ex-wife Betty on the AMC hit *Mad Men*, credits eating her placenta, which all mammals do except humans, for her rapid bounce back to the TV series following childbirth.

While placenta encapsulation is not FDA-approved in the United States, the practice has become more widespread, with effusive endorsements from Hollywood moms like Jones, Mayim Bialik, and Alicia Silverstone, and from the growing legions of supporters of holistic medicine. Definitive research on the consumption of afterbirth is still in its infancy in the United States. Yet scientists do know that the gelatinous slab, which measures about nine inches long and one inch thick, is packed with restorative hormones associated with alleviating stress and depression.

Carmen Calvo found this treatment to be so effective that she became a Certified Placenta Encapsulation Specialist herself, and now operates a thriving practice out of Baltimore, named The Nurturing Root. "Since I work with a lot of bleach and blood, I usually go to work casually like this," says Carmen, in jeans and a white chef's jacket over a T-shirt that reads PLACENTA CHEF. Indeed, her style of kitchen duty may not be touted on The Food Channel, but it is impressively extensive: sanitizing the sink and stove, steaming the afterbirth, drying the contents, and then stuffing them into capsules.

An earthy beauty with a sensible Anne Hathaway haircut and no makeup, the thirty-three-year-old Carmen is now surefooted in her role as mother, wife, and healer. As she describes below, she has come a long way.

CARMEN CALVO

Shortly after we were married in May of 2009, I found out I was pregnant. And during that first year of marriage, we hardly got out of bed. We were so in love and so excited to be married. I was pregnant and we were just so happy.

I was overwhelmingly naive about the impact having a baby would have on my marriage. After our first son was born, my body was no longer my own. Not only did I not recognize it, with the hanging belly and swollen, sore breasts, but I had an infant attached to me almost every waking moment. The stress of colic was difficult to deal with, and not being capable of soothing my own baby was heartbreaking.

The first week or so postpartum, I was elated. I was certainly love drunk with my new baby and with my husband. However, after the new-mom high wore off, I began to experience postpartum anxiety. I was terrified to tell anyone what was happening out of fear they would think I was crazy or unfit. The anxiety wasn't a constant, but when it came over me, it was a heavy, dark cloak. It was consuming. I would have vivid visions of terrible things happening to my son. These visions would appear out of nowhere and make my heart race.

I saw things like our dogs mauling my son while he slept peacefully in his swing. I saw him falling nine stories off our condo balcony while the three of us were away for our first vacation together. I saw myself falling down a flight of steps and landing on top of my newborn. Eventually, the anxiety subsided, but I never told a soul, not even my husband, until very recently.

When my second son was born fourteen months later, I didn't have the same anxiety or postpartum mood imbalance due to placenta therapy. However, I can't say that intimacy was a priority. I was running at maximum capacity both physically and emotionally. By the time I prepared dinner, and my husband came home from work, my emotional bank was completely sucked dry, leaving him nothing. I was giving all of myself emotionally, and especially physically, to my babies, and sex was the last thing I was thinking about once the sun went down. I was being touched all day long and didn't want anyone's hands on me by the time the kids went to bed. Not to mention, I was tired. So very tired.

Like many couples, sex after baby wasn't a frequent occurrence. It simply wasn't a priority for me those first few months. Sex can be scary for a woman who just gave birth, even six weeks later. Fortunately, once we started again, it not only felt fine but—and I can't attest to why—it is better now, more than ever. Things feel deeper and more intense, and physically, it is generally more enjoyable since having children.

Looking back, there was a lot of resentment in my marriage that first year with two kids. I resented my husband for not being around much due to his schedule. I felt like I was the sole caregiver of our children and didn't feel very supported or appreciated. I felt boring, frumpy, and was often lonely.

Conversely, I think my husband resented me for not appreciating how hard he was working to make ends meet for our family so that I could stay home. I would ride him about not spending enough time with the family while he felt pulled in a thousand different directions. We had the same argument over and over for a year. To put it simply, we basically argued about who worked harder, who was more tired. Sadly, we both felt misunderstood, which led to feeling disconnected at times. I felt my identity as an independent woman was swiftly being taken away.

I used to be an interesting person. I used to be able to talk about books and film and art. I used to go out and socialize. I had hobbies. And now, here I was at home, constantly changing diapers and breast-feeding. All that remained was that I was a mom. I was extremely appreciative of the privilege of being able to stay home with my babies, so I felt guilty for being lonely, and feeling enslaved.

In hindsight, I was being hard on myself during that time. Back-to-back pregnancies, two breast-feeders, a new marriage, postpartum blues, not contributing to the financial well-being of our family, and wrestling with my identity is a lot to endure.

Our culture fails women by not talking about the reality of the postpartum experience. Generally, women are unprepared for how difficult it can be. We are told we should be elated, floating on Cloud Nine. And when women don't feel that way in those difficult first few weeks postpartum, they feel shame and guilt, so they don't talk about it. They bottle it up and silently suffer. Postpartum mood disorders are nothing to be ashamed about. It doesn't mean you don't love your baby or love your husband. The more we talk about it, the more women will feel comfortable seeking the support they need.

When I was five months' postpartum with my first son, I discovered I was pregnant again. With a newborn and toddler, I knew I could not afford to feel so anxious again. So I looked into natural ways to avoid the postpartum mood imbalances and stumbled across placenta encapsulation. After a lot of reading, I learned that women who had placenta encapsulation experienced a lot of benefits. I researched how it gives moms more energy, can aid with lactation, helps the uterus contract more quickly, restores mom's iron levels. I hired someone to encapsulate my second son's placenta immediately after birth, and my experience was so vastly different that I felt called to help other women recover more easily from childbirth.

Being a new mom is hard enough; no one should have to go

through the hormonal crash after birth that leaves many of us constantly weepy and overwhelmed.

Shortly after my second birth, I began the journey of becoming a Certified Placenta Encapsulation Specialist and started The Nurturing Root in 2011. Most of my clients feel they have the energy now to get them through their day despite the lack of sleep at night. It follows that placentophagy also increases libido. With more energy and a better mood, there is a higher likelihood that a couple will regain intimacy much sooner after childbirth. Some of the best testimonials I have heard are from dads who say they can tell a difference when their wife has or has not taken her placenta capsules.

I know it worked for us. I was hesitant to resume sex because I was afraid it would be painful and uncomfortable—which it is at first, but for me it's now better than ever. I was also worried it wouldn't feel the same or be as enjoyable for my partner. It's also difficult to be in the mood for sex or to feel sexy when you are usually covered in spit-up and haven't gotten out of yoga pants because none of your clothes fit. Now that the hectic infancy period is behind us, we are eager to connect as a couple again, with more alone time together, which is so nice. There was a time when we were so busy taking care of babies, we both failed to nurture our marriage. We were in survival mode. We are a couple again.

Carmen's fear about how her partner would react to her post-partum body is a very real factor in how quickly and successfully a couple can snap back to, or even surpass, previous sexual fitness levels. In a study published in the September 2012 issue of *The Journal of Sexual Medicine* titled "Exploring Women's Postpartum Sexuality," authors Lauren Hipp, Lisa Kane Low, and Sari van Anders found that the way in which a new mom senses her spouse's response to her body postpartum is a decisive guide in how their sex life will resume. In plain speak, as in all intimate relationships, it helps to think the other person is hot for your body, even when that body has become just a bit more ample and imperfect.

As the authors conclude: "Women who perceive themselves as attractive, including to their partners, report higher levels of sexual enjoyment, frequency of sexual behavior, and less sexual pain. This study supports women's sexual health by encouraging health care providers to discuss resumption of sexual activity in terms of social and relationship context instead of determining readiness purely by physical healing."

At all phases of our development, it is often a woman's mood and mind-set about the status of her relationship that is her compass toward, or away from, intimacy, a fact underscored in later chapters featuring older wives. Like Carmen, Texas psychologist Christine Hall also lapsed into a dark mood and depressing mind-set that affected all aspects of her life after birthing her first child. And, like Carmen, she morphed from a weak state into an emboldened healer with a specialty practice in perinatal and postpartum mood disorders.

Standing nearly six feet tall, Christine, forty-four, has straight sandy-colored hair and bright green eyes and is wearing sweats, having just come from a jog through her Austin neighborhood. Hearty and happy now, the black postpartum cloak she shared with millions of other new moms has long been tossed away.

CHRISTINE HALL

I had never been in a state of depression before. Yet when my son was born, I felt really lost and incredibly irritable. Here I had this baby that I loved so much and wanted to protect, but I just felt like crap. I was just so, so sad, then I would cry, and when I tried to communicate my emotions, no one understood what I was trying to say. And I had really dark feelings of "I don't want to be here anymore." My husband was working six to seven days a week, so I had little support or chance to take a break and take care of myself.

I didn't want my husband anywhere near me. Intimacy fell by the wayside—I felt I had nothing inside of me to give to him. All of my obsessive focus was on that baby, and I had to make sure that baby was okay and safe. I breast-fed constantly the first year, and holy shit, it's hard stuff! Breast-feeding was a great bonding experience, but I couldn't really enjoy it because of my emotional state.

My husband was really patient during our sex standoff. I think he was really getting it that I just couldn't be the sexy wife right now. A lot of women come into my practice who have husbands that don't get that the primary job of the boobs after birth are to nourish the baby. Whether you're pumping or nursing, most of my clients do choose to breast-feed. And many husbands look at the boobs and say, "Oh they're mine, and I want them back."

The state of feeling overwhelmed, for me, became so bad that I was almost suicidal. My second son was probably six or seven months old. I remember standing in the master bedroom at home, and just feeling so depressed. My husband was working in his home office, and came into the bedroom and expressed concern that I didn't seem right. I tried to deny it at first, but then I started crying and told him that I felt so overwhelmed that I couldn't get my bearings.

Even though out firstborn was sleeping through the night by that time, I still felt so exhausted and lethargic. I wanted to just stay in bed, and would become irritable each time I had to nurse or change a diaper. One day during the height of this depression, my husband grabbed me, held me tight, and told me that he and our sons needed me and loved me. We then talked about calling my OB to discuss medication, and also to call a therapist. I went on a low dose of an antidepressant called Lexapro, and began therapy, and the turnaround was amazing. I expressed concern to my OB that the baby would be exposed to the Lexapro from the breast milk, but he assured me that it was one of the safest antidepressants to take at the time. Within a week of taking my first dose, I felt clearheaded and energetic. I no longer wanted to remain in bed and stare at the wall, and the irritability was completely gone. And because I am a psychologist, I knew about all the studies on depression that can take hold for women after babies are born, so I was assured that I wasn't alone.

I admit it was a little odd being in therapy. As a psychologist seeing a psychologist, you don't want to seem too crazy. If you reveal too much about your life, the psychologist may never refer clients to you in the future. It can be a double-edged sword.

I made the mistake of choosing a man for my first psychologist and quickly realized, after a few visits, he couldn't really understand what it was like to have a baby sucking at your boob 24/7 and other feelings of being a new mother. Once I really started looking into depression among postpartum women, I did see that the support system for those women is lacking. Most people just assume that new mothers are blissfully happy to have a new baby! That's what it's like in the commercials, right?

I did not have a support system—my extended family all live out of town. My mother passed away when I was twenty-five, so I didn't have anyone to prep me on the reality of what it was going to be like to have a baby. And my stepmother never had children. She and my dad had come into town to be with us at the birth. My dad came into my room, tenderly patted my head, and I started crying. He promised me things would get better as time went on and as the baby got older. I remember thinking, *How the hell do you know? You didn't squirt a basketball out of your body.* But he was right.

A few weeks later, my sister flew in from Arizona to be with me for a week and to give me a break. I remember feeling so much relief when she arrived. She took the baby from me, played with him, helped get meals ready, did laundry, and gave me time to take long, hot showers. When she had to go back to her family, I stood at the top of the stairs, watching her leave, crying and thinking, *How the hell am I going to take care of this baby? I can't do it by myself!*

Women can really help each other by talking openly about their feelings after having a baby, and by being receptive and nonjudgmental when a friend comes to you and asks for support. Instead of focusing on how to be perfect, we should be focusing on how to be vulnerable. When my second baby, a daughter, came along four years later, I made it a point to rely on my girlfriends and husband more. I monitored my moods each day, and learned how to take deeps breaths and really, truly sleep when the baby slept. By monitoring my emotional state and relying more on others for support, I made it through my second postpartum period just fine.

One of my first steps in working with women who have postpartum depression is to meet with the husband. I always want the spouse's perspective, simply because Mom is discussing only one side of the situation and the spouse can offer his view of what's going on with her, with him, and with the newborn.

With these joined conversations, I can usually get the spouse on board to be more of a household help and take some of the stressors away from the mom. Again, based on my own postpartum blues, I know how important it is to help the mom share responsibility for the baby.

And if I can't get that transformed behavior from talk therapy, and the mom still comes in and looks really haggard and is feeling depressed after six to eight weeks postpartum, I say, "Maybe we need to talk about medication—you're at an impasse and you're not moving forward."

Just within the last year, my daughter turned four and our son is turning eight, and we are rediscovering ourselves sexually. We're coming out of the big time where your kids are all-consuming. Now we can go off and lock the bedroom door way more than we ever could in the recent past. We can take our time and explore each other again, and remind ourselves what it was like when we were dating.

And so it's a wonderful transition as a mother as your family also transitions. Your kids become more independent, they can get their own juice out of the fridge. So you're kind of ready for sex—you're like "hmm, I want this again."

Women suffering from perinatal and postpartum mood disorder have no sexual desire; they do not want anyone to even touch them in an intimate way. They can barely contain whatever is going on inside of them, let alone deal with sex. They are overwhelmed like I was with anxiety and depression, worrying that they are failures as mothers, and feeling guilty that they are feeling depressed when they should be feeling joy.

And when these moms are finally at a point where they can relax, the last thing they want right away is for their husbands to nudge them and say, "Hey, how about it, honey?" Then that really causes a lot of distance between the couple, because the spouse is thinking, "All right, the OB said no sex before six weeks. You're all clear, let's go!" And the new mom is telling me, "Oh my God, I can't do this yet. I am still fat and often sad and I am not ready to have anyone close to me!"

But there is hope—I'm at a really good place now. You go from not feeling sexy at all and trying to get across to your husband, "Hey, these are not your boobs right now," to feeling "Hey, I'm ready."

Many new moms don't want sex because they've been torn or cut from front to back. And who wants to have a penis come near there when you recently pushed a watermelon through a water hose? I remind new moms that sex doesn't always have to involve intercourse. Sex during this time can involve supportive intimacy: touching, caressing, kissing, talking, holding each other, and masturbation. The new dad likes these variations of sex, too. He finds comfort in knowing that he still has a connection to his partner, even though he realizes he's taken a backseat for a while.

This advice from Christine to reinvent old patterns of lovemaking as a way to stay sexually interested—and interesting—is echoed in nearly all of the interviews I have done with women who have managed to stay married way past their pregnancies. In fact, most of the senior citizens still with original partners who spoke to me for this book listed sexual chemistry as a primary ingredient that contributes to the relationship's longevity.

With a healthy sex life comes other marriage builders, like open communication and more willingness to forgive. When couples make intimacy a priority, as problems arise, which they always do, they can find solace in each other's arms, an escape that is primal and relaxing—for at least eleven minutes or so. One of my closest girlfriends, married for thirty years, has sex with her husband every Wednesday. When I told her that scheduling sex so precisely drains the spontaneity out of the act, she laughed and assured me the mystery is still there: "Because we never know what time on Wednesday we are going to end up in bed!"

Some more shrewd advice comes from an octogenarian wife named Betty, in a sixty-two-year marriage that produced eleven children: "I'm not always in the mood, but I decided a long time ago if he wants it, I would just lie back and enjoy it. Usually, I end up enjoying it enormously."

Jordana has been married only for five years, but she already knows Betty's secret to harmony-ever-after—to lie back and enjoy it. You have just heard stories of brutal battles with depression after baby arrives. Jordana is on the other end of the spectrum, effervescent as she recalls that "magical time" when she and her husband Jake, her college boyfriend, managed to take lusty breaks while their two babies took their naps. Above the laughter and shrieks of her two children, now ages two and four, Jordana talks about experiencing hormonal swings but never forgetting that sex is a surefire pickup for a tired new mama and a papa feeling neglected.

Born in Israel of Persian Sephardic parents, the buoyant Jordana has shoulder-length brown hair striped with flame red, a match for her fiery and forthright character. She attributes the ongoing peaks of intimacy in her marriage as "the reason we are still together."

Surrounded by stacks of diapers and toys in her Staten Island home—but still a Hot Mama in leggings and a cropped jean jacket—hers is a story of love, sex, babies, and priorities with this central message: Remember to show at least as much passion for your partner as you shower on your children.

JORDANA

For Jake and me, it was truly love at first kiss; it was everything at first sight. In college I just loved and still love everything about him. We had amazing chemistry, amazing sex; we were bonded in our religion, and in our family traditions. It was everything all at once for the first time in my life. We still have this amazing chemistry.

People always ask us how we are so connected and sexually charged after two kids and being together for so long, and I find it quite simple. It may sound trite, but we live to laugh, eat, play, and make love. This makes us able to handle anything, and the best part is that we handle it together. There are, without question, moments of stress and horrible arguing, but basically in those moments you have to work to bring things back to basics. Remind yourself that you need only these necessities in life—sex, food, and love.

I met Jake at nineteen, and it felt destined from the start. We couldn't keep away from each other in the sexual sense. We were so young when we met as freshmen in college; few were seeking Mr. Right with whom you will spend the rest of your life. Yet something about my connection with Jake was instant, and it felt like we had gotten to the top of Jenga the moment we met.

I was whole with him. I was safe with him, and I was strong with him. He never tried to make me smaller. He always thrived in my personality and still wants me to be the loud, full-bodied person that I am. During our young relationship free of marriage and parenting, we scoured the world, enjoying sex wherever we were. We were the couple that snuck into club closets when we were overwhelmed by our sexual desire.

Jake really helped transform me. When I went to college, I

knew I had the power to attract men. I felt comfortable with my sexuality, but I didn't want a commitment.

He was the first person I wanted to surrender to.

I know that we will be in love forever. We both come from very strong families with long marriages. We both know the power of sensuality, of physical touch. I think he is beautiful, and he thinks I'm beautiful. He thought that when he first met me and I was twenty-five pounds heavier, and when I was sixty pounds bigger during pregnancy.

Jake and I got practice in college having to be quiet during sex, which you have to do with children around. Here you are in a dorm with a roommate, and you have to learn how to have sex silently. But that kind of sex is so passionate and connected: you are in a twin bed, and your lips, eyes, mouths are smashed together, along with your bodies crammed up on the wall. You have no choice but to be as intimate as humanly possible.

We managed to resume our sex lives soon after having babies. Much like sex during college, there was always someone else lurking in the room, waiting to interrupt the moment. With babies, it is hunger, vomit, poop, piss, or tantrums. And when we can steal a break, we get this primal encounter that brings us right back to our passionate beginnings. We sneak into our room, giddy with the thought, "Yes! We will get laid!"

In June 2007, doctors told me there was a 75 percent chance I wouldn't conceive, and if I did, it would likely be ectopic because of my endometriosis. Then I got pregnant two months after the honeymoon without any intervention. I did have pregnancy problems both times and was put on bed rest, but the babies came out perfectly healthy, both by cesarean.

After a C-section, obviously it is difficult to get right back to sex, but we did right after the six-week mark. Yet even for a very close couple like us, intimacy after childbearing was not easy to achieve. A child would wake up hungry, gassy, pissy, anything at any moment definitely challenged our intimacy to the core, as did my body healing. Plus, my boobs after I had the babies and started breast-feeding turned into almost a size G!

We had so much fun with my big boobs—one day my husband got caught in the moment and forgot that I was nursing and practically breast-fed from me, for which I slapped him and said, "Never go near my boobs till I give you the go-ahead again!" As a new breast-feeding mom, I just didn't want that sexual connection. Then I had to take a step back and realize that the only reason I have been able to have these beautiful children came from this man and from a place of love.

So I made it a point during that first six months of our baby's life to make sure there was a supercharge of love and energy in our relationship. And those moments when sex would happen were extraordinary. My parents live forty-five minutes away, and my mother is the person who makes it possible for us to connect so incredibly as a couple. She has taken on child care for countless date nights, weekends away, and even vacations so that we don't lose ourselves in the daily grind.

One memorable night, we went back to the restaurant where we got engaged. Drinking wine, we relived our passionate history, even the volatile fights. After all the reminiscing, we ended up having sex in the car right next to my kid's car seat. It was absurd, and I loved every second of seizing that moment! My rule is that if my husband instigates sex, even if I'm not in the mood, I get myself in the mood just because of how much I love him.

How do you keep having great sex surrounded by babies? The answer is that you have to make sex a priority. I don't let a week go by without having sex. The second you let a week go by, it becomes two weeks, then a month. I have so many girlfriends in new marriages already in that sexless place, and that brings much resentment. It's a horrible way to start a marriage.

I tell them that even if you are in the worst mood ever, after some good sex, you are able to articulate what you need and open up; you become a better person for yourself and your partner.

For us, we started our relationship when I was so young, and from the beginning it was wildly sexual—why should that go away? Relationships certainly evolve, but having sex, and the fun memories that come with it, is satisfying on so many levels.

Until I got to college, I had no idea that self-confidence had anything to do with physical presence. I thought self-confidence was something solely from within that reflected your character. I still feel that way, but I also know that confidence has everything to do with my perception of my body and my sexuality. When I was twenty-five pounds heavier, with huge boobs, curves, and a surprise serving of adult-onset acne, I still always felt like hot shit. Feeling you are beautiful inside and out without question leads to good sex.

I tell my girlfriends that maybe if you aren't having a passionate marriage, it's because you don't feel passionate about yourself.

Jordana is proof beyond the studies that say it is true that self-love and confidence sure as hell do make a woman feel better about her partner and more eager for intimacy. I am not saying you can ever resurrect prenuptial enchantment or your prenuptial weight. But what I do know from my own twenty-six-year rollicking marriage and from hundreds of seasoned wives is that sex is a great getaway, and in a marriage, you do not have to go far to find it.

It is summer of 2013 and I am at my annual visit to obstetrician Dr. Janet Schaffel, whose waiting room I have been in, paging through new mom magazines, many times during the past quarter-of-a-century. An unflappable five feet two, Dr. Schaffel speaks in a slow, even-toned voice that has soothed me through gestating and birthing four children, which included one emergency C-section. After the exam, I show her a photo of my four strapping sons, who were slithery infants in her hands what seems like a month ago and not a lifetime ago. They now range from six feet one to six feet five, and shave. We recall together those days when the twins were born, joining brothers who were two and three and how my postpartum visits would include some crying jags.

In my late fifties with wrinkly eyes and wiry gray hair, I tell her all is calm, too calm, really, with no kids and a big house occupied only by me and a thin husband. I share some of the laments and victories I heard from postpartum women and ask her if their symptoms and syndromes are emblematic of the several thousand birth mothers she has cared for in her thirty years of practice.

A graduate of Brown's medical school who trained at Northwestern, Dr. Schaffel reveals that she herself had postpartum depression with both of her children. Here is more from the good doctor whose Women's Ob/Gyn Physicians practice is among the most popular in the Washington, DC, area.

DR. JANET SCHAFFEL

I would say 95 percent of my patients have no interest in having intercourse at six weeks, which is the time doctors tell them they are cleared. Women are exhausted. Given a choice of sex or sleep, she'll take sleep. The body is basically self-preserving;

it can't afford to get pregnant again just yet, so it shuts down the ability and desire with no ovulating and no libido.

Sex can be painful, as breast-feeding and vaginal dryness go hand in hand. The woman may be fearful that her vagina is different physically, and is concerned how her partner might respond. Basically, new mothers are not happy with their bodies. Breast milk is everywhere.

There can also be a lot of stress and conflict in their relationship over the newborn. A partner may think he isn't getting enough attention, or the mother may think he isn't helping out enough. Then the breasts are no longer as erogenous as they were before pregnancy. Breasts are a source of life for your baby, a source of recreation for your partner, and a mess for you. Your nipples are sore. You leak.

The societal expectation is that this is a wonderful and blissful time. You see the vignettes of the nursing mother, calm and rested, and she has makeup on. Who has time to put makeup on? New mothers barely have time for a shower. This sets up such unreal expectations.

Of course it's never the same after you have a baby. Your body is not the same. Your outlook on life is not the same. Your relationship is not the same. On top of emotional issues, there may be insecurity about the vaginal opening being too large or too tight from the stitches.

A lot of women think about how the man's view of her vagina may have changed, having seen a baby come out. Women do talk about this, and some choose to keep the man at the head of the bed so he doesn't watch the actual delivery. Sometimes this is because they are worried he is going to pass out but also for what he might think about her vagina. Amazingly, the vagina manages to expand to allow the baby out and usually goes back to normal, but that takes time.

A lot of women also have incontinence of urine immediately after a delivery, and sometimes it lasts for quite a while. You may pee every time you laugh.

While we promptly treat postpartum bleeding and other delivery complications, one that we do not immediately address is pelvic support issues. This includes problems controlling the passage of urine, gas, or stool. These usually get better with time and when hormone levels return to normal. We usually wait at least a year after the woman has delivered her last child. At that point, if a woman's symptoms don't respond to time and pelvic physical therapy, she becomes a candidate for surgery.

This is an indicated surgery as opposed to some of the elective gynecologic plastic surgical procedures being done today, such as labiaplasty, which is a reduction in the lips. Except in rare instances, we do not perform this procedure. This can be a dangerous elective surgery; it can result in scarring and pain with intercourse.

It sickens me that women fall prey to some idealized, airbrushed version of the vulva as shown in pornography and sex magazines. The message is that your vulva should be perfect, not too long, not too floppy, not too dark, and of course with no hair.

There are occasional cases where there is a very large labium that needs correction because it becomes a problem during sex or when wearing tight pants. It is reasonable to have surgery for this, or, for example, when the vaginal opening is gaping and sex is not satisfying for both partners.

We have a fair number of gay pregnant couples. Their issues are similar. The women have to adjust to their new roles in their relationship, and suffer the same exhaustion and physical changes as heterosexual women. I do find, though, that they are more sympathetic regarding the resumption of sex post-partum. The woman who was not pregnant and not breast-feeding has to figure out her role as the "other mother" and caregiver.

I think the most important thing I can tell postpartum women, really any woman, is not to feel she has to have sex. It's your relationship, and there is no standard quota—do what works for you. No one is keeping track of your sex life but you. Some of my patients haven't had sex for years, and they tell me "we're both fine with it." On the other hand, for the major-ity of couples, sex is a really important part of a long-term relationship.

You have to communicate about your sexual needs—don't ignore the 800-pound gorilla in the room when there are prob-lems. You have to talk about it and you have to work at it. Work-ing at sex doesn't sound very sexy, but it is necessary. There is a fascinating phenomenon we doctors who treat women have found—the more you have sex, the more you want it. We don't know why, but this appears to be the case.

A healthy sex life is good for every aspect of your life, as-suming it's voluntary, emotionally and physically safe, and with the right person. Sex is good for your self-esteem. Sex is aero-bic exercise. It's good for blood flow. So have sex. With the right person. In the right circumstances and on your terms. It certainly strengthens a marriage, and people in long-term rela-tionships live longer and in general are happier.

"On your terms" is the takeaway from my chapter on sex after pregnancy. There is no standard expectation or rule of how much sex to have or not to have during pregnancy and after baby arrives. Women respond all sorts of ways, from hiding under the covers in tears to a full-tilt, full-breasted attitude of "bring it on." I purposely gave you some dark stories because they end in a hopeful light. And how about that Jordana? A testament to one of my own mother's favorite sayings: "Where there is a will, there is a way."

My unsolicited advice: Every pregnant woman is sore down there from pushing a baby out or being sliced open. Postpartum is a time to explore "adventures in outercourse," the subject of the last section of this book, in which older women dish about great sex without intercourse.

CHAPTER 4
SEX AFTER HIS ILLNESS

It took my husband's brain tumor to really cut my
heart open and expose all the love in there.

—JULIA CROWLEY

We have heard from young women on the expected issues
that arise when new marriages are compounded by pregnancy and babies. Now I present two stories of postpartum moms
who had to barrel through unexpected obstacles far more severe
than hormonal imbalances and sleepless nights. The arrival of
their children coincided with their husbands' medical emergen-
cies. Richaela Stevenson's husband of six months returned home
from Afghanistan, to a new daughter—and missing a leg. After
battling years of infertility and painful treatments, Julia Crowley
was finally able to conceive and carry a pregnancy to term.
Shortly after the birth of her son, her husband was diagnosed
with an inoperable brain tumor.

Both women speak truth to the power of this cliché: What does not kill you will make you stronger.

If Richaela can surmount the obstacles of a new marriage and a new baby while keeping the romantic embers stoked, anyone can. She met her Marine husband, Derek, while he was based at Camp Lejeune near her North Carolina hometown. She was a waitress at the Texas Roadhouse, and he came in for dinner with a few of his buddies. After two years of dating, they got married at the courthouse in Jacksonville, North Carolina. Three weeks later, Derek was deployed to Afghanistan. Richaela was twenty and Derek was twenty-two.

In December 2010, one month before Derek was scheduled to return home, he stepped on an Improvised Explosive Device and lost his right leg above the knee. Derek was flown to Walter Reed National Military Medical Center in Bethesda, Maryland, where he was still undergoing rehabilitation more than two years after the injury.

To add to the bedlam of this transition, Richaela gave birth to their daughter, Madeline, early on in Derek's treatment. She wrote me a letter, after reading *The Secret Lives of Wives*, for advice. The subtitle of the book is *Women Share What It Really Takes to Stay Married*, and she expressed that she needed to find out how— right now.

I met her in a coffee shop near Walter Reed, and during a long and tearful interview, Richaela described stressors she is saddled with at the age of twenty-two that most wives never face in a lifetime.

Born to a German father and African American mother, Richaela is thin and striking, with tawny skin and high cheekbones and huge brown eyes outlined in kohl. As she plays with her thick black ponytail, twin swallow tattoos appear over her collar. "The swallows mate for life, so that's why I got them," she tells me.

Another tattoo on her arm is imprinted with MADELINE above a clock displaying the time her daughter was born.

RICHAELA STEVENSON

My mom was a Marine, and as I grew into a young woman, I wanted nothing to do with the military. I especially did not want to be a part of deployments and constantly moving. Then I met Derek, and he was so sweet, and we were such good friends. And here I am—married to a Marine who lost a leg during his first deployment.

When this first happened to Derek, I felt helpless. I had a new baby, my mother lived six hours away, and Derek couldn't get away from his severe depression. Other military wives of amputees who lived in our compound spoke down to me because I look like I'm sixteen. I just felt helpless, like I would never get my husband back, and I felt awful about myself, no friends and no outlets.

Finally, after many small arguments with Derek and one huge falling-out, I packed my stuff and drove alone with my daughter back home to North Carolina. I cried the whole way home because I knew it wasn't what I wanted. I wanted to just have my husband back to his old self of being the motivated man who cared about his job and family. I also knew that, given his medical situation, it would be a long time before this could happen.

I sat on Topsail Beach, my secret retreat near my home, and decided that I didn't want to give up, but I needed some kind of real advice. Who could I turn to? Most of the young married girls I know divorce in the first years as soon as things get tough. I realized I had to find someone who had been married longer than twenty years.

I wrote you when I was at this really low point and I had stumbled upon *The Secret Lives of Wives*. What I got from the book is the secret for a wife's happiness is not to bow down and serve your husband, like a preacher might tell you to do. I learned that to be happy, a wife must have her own life, her own accomplishments, and her own glory apart from her husband. That advice was like a ray of enlightenment! I realized that one huge problem in my marriage was that I was relying on my husband way too much. And he was understandably in a really bad place.

So I went out and got a part-time waitress job. I wanted money of my own, and it felt good to go to work, and no one knows about me or my husband. When I'm working tables, I am my own person. For a while, I had felt like I was just a wounded warrior's wife. Finally, I was Richaela, and people would ask me normal questions like "Did you see this movie?" instead of "How's your husband? Did he walk today?" Once I got out there again, I became so much more optimistic about the marriage.

The day we got married, I felt so happy to have a partner in life, somebody I could talk to about anything. I just thought about how lucky I was that I got to have the rest of my life with Derek, who quickly became my best friend. He left for overseas twenty days after our wedding. We didn't have a honeymoon, but instead, we drove all around the country visiting his family and friends in preparation for his deployment. I was living with my mom and already pregnant, and Derek would call me once a month, but we could only talk five minutes at a time. He was part of an infantry with seven other men in his camp.

Derek's job was to be what is called a point man—he was the first person to bust into a building with a gun and check around to make sure things were clear, that no one was in there, sweeping for mines and IEDs.

Marine deployment is seven months long, and after serving in that job for six months, Derek was about to come home in a couple of weeks. Then it happened. They went into a building and had pretty much swept the whole place for IEDs. But as they were getting ready to leave, the sergeant told Derek to go back in and check on one last section. He did it, and he heard a click go off, and that was it. His left leg was burned and his right leg was gone through the knee. He was awake the whole time, never blacked out, never went into a coma or anything.

They found his boot but they never did find his leg, so there was no possibility of reattaching it.

I remember where I was exactly when that call came in: I was in my mom's bedroom, and we were watching the news, and they were talking about snowstorms in New Jersey. Derek's mom lives in New Jersey, and I was thinking maybe I should call her to see if she was okay. Then I got a call that showed up on my phone as a long, weird bunch of numbers. I didn't think it was Derek, because when he called, there would only be six digits, so I ignored the call, thinking it was a telemarketer.

The phone rang again, same number, so I picked it up and it was my husband. It was the day after Christmas, and I was so happy to hear his voice because he only got to call me once a month. I was like "Oh, cool, what a great Christmas gift!" At first he sounded fine. Then he asked me to sit down. I was thinking maybe he just wants me to be comfortable because I was pregnant and maybe we were going to be able to talk longer than five minutes. The last thing I thought of was anyone getting hurt.

Then he says, "I'm coming home. My leg is gone." Just like that. I freaked out, and he kept telling me to chill out and to calm down because he didn't want me to go into labor. "I am fine," he kept saying, but of course nothing was fine. This wasn't fine.

God, it was scary when he first got to the hospital. My husband is five feet eleven, and he was down to 111 pounds. He had always been slender, but when he was deployed, he weighed 170. Because of the extent of his injuries and the treatments, his face was sunk in, and he hadn't shaved and his beautiful, thick dirty-blond hair was just going crazy. And the smell of that floor in the hospital I will never forget. It smelled like antiseptics and blood and sweat and cleaning supplies.

Derek would say things like "Will you still want to be married to me and make love with me even with my bum leg?" He was really scared because we are so young, and most people our age are out doing active things. Before this happened, Derek would skateboard, play basketball; he was a runner. And he just thought, *I would want to be out there being active.* I assured him that him not being able to run around is fine with me, because I'm not very active. I don't care for hiking or that kind of stuff.

Seeing him for the first time freaked me out, but I didn't let it show. He's still my husband. And I was not turned off to him sexually, but we couldn't be intimate for a while. On top of his leg injuries, he has what they call TBI, traumatic brain injury, and that's really frustrating for him because he likes to be right all the time and he has a horrible memory now. And he also has severe post-traumatic stress disorder, which means he gets very angry.

So all this adds up to the fact that he gets very depressed. He sees what his other friends who aren't injured can do, and he wants to be able to do those things, too. Simple things. Like when my daughter's godfather picks her up and walks around with her, that upsets Derek. Anytime Derek holds Madeline, he has to be careful there are no bumps in the ground because if he falls, he can't catch her.

His way of coping was to start playing video games. When

I dated him, Derek never played video games. We were always out of the house, going to the movies, going to the park, driving around. But he was sucked into this game I hate called *World of Warcraft*, and he wouldn't leave his computer all day, playing it for hours and not getting anything else done. He wouldn't go to his physical therapy.

At some points, I felt like leaving the marriage. I felt like he was an absent partner. I'd ask him to go outside and join other couples who were having a barbeque, that we could eat hot dogs and hang out and feel normal. He wanted to stay in a dark room in front of his computer. But then, as he began to work through his injury, he started to shake off some of the depression. As he got stronger, I was able to feel again how much he loved me and our daughter. This man made it through one of the worst things that could happen to a person, and watching him change really changed how I felt.

When he first got hurt, we didn't really have much sex for a long time. It just shut off. For the whole summer of 2011 through the summer of 2012, we'd have sex once every few months. There was a point where I was sleeping on the couch because he wouldn't get off the computer all night. The light would keep me up, then I'd have to wake up early with the baby. Sometimes he'd wake me up at 3:00 A.M. to have sex, and I'd say, "No, I'm tired and this isn't fair to me, to wake up and have sex with you, then two hours later I have to wake up with the baby!"

It was hard to become intimate again. He'd want to have sex, but with the pain in his leg, he couldn't bear weight. Once we finally figured out how to do it, every time we'd finish, his leg would jolt with pain. His orgasm triggered that pain. It made me feel really bad because he would say, "I want to have sex with you," but it would hurt him afterward. I didn't want that to be his memory of sex.

Now his leg has become more able to bear weight, and we are able to have sex in any position we want without him getting uncomfortable. And over time, his leg has become less sensitive and now when he has orgasms, he doesn't feel pain anymore. Honestly, we don't have sex in long sessions anymore like we used to because he just gets tired more quickly. I don't really mind. At least I have my husband!

Madeline is now two years old. And while our sex life is not back to what it was before this happened, it feels normal to me. He's still my husband. His face is the same. He has these amazing blue eyes. I love this guy and I know how fortunate we are compared to other guys returning from war.

There was a man we met at Walter Reed who lost both of his legs and his penis, and his wife was going absolutely crazy. They were very young like us, and both really took a dive into depression. There are many, many guys we met who have much worse injuries than Derek; their faces and hands get deformed, they lose both legs.

I would hear some of those wives talking about how they were hanging around with other men because they couldn't have sex with their husbands—or didn't want to. I've never felt that way. I am married to a sexy and loving man. You come to realize that love in marriage comes from so many other things than what our bodies can do. Although Derek can do a lot on his artificial leg.

He has a few legs, but his favorite leg to wear has a carbon fiber socket which fits over his stump like a glove and holds his leg in place. Inside, there's steel and titanium with a hydraulics system that makes the knee move. He can walk anywhere on that leg. He goes up and down stairs and hills; it is very lightweight and battery operated. It charges overnight, and can stay charged for four days! Derek told me that leg cost roughly

$80,000. Fortunately, the government paid for all of his legs and the necessary accessories, such as socks and leg liners.

Life is a lot better now because we moved to North Carolina and are living with my parents and fourteen-year-old sister, Graciela, who can help us with Madeline. Derek is retired from the military and is enrolled in college, and he wants to get his bachelor's degree in computer science. He has a service dog he loves, a German shepherd, Zooey.

Zooey is learning commands beyond sit, stay, and heel, such as pressing the handicap button on doors at stores, picking up things off the floor for Derek, pulling him up stairs as if she is acting as a second railing. One thing I think is really cool is that Zooey will learn how to sense his anxiety levels. If we are in a crowd, like the mall or an amusement park, she will sense Derek's anxiety and, depending on the situation, she'll make a barrier between him and the people with her body or push her way through the crowd to make a path for him to walk through.

The sensing of anxiety is really important to both of us: Derek's PTSD means that he still gets aggravated at almost anything. Traffic noise, crowds, being around strangers, his memory issues, and his physical limitations are all things that bother him. Once, he accidentally dropped his silverware on the floor in a restaurant and wouldn't finish his food because he was so upset. Times like that make me feel helpless because nothing I do or say makes the situation better. When his PTSD spikes, it's never good for me. If we are alone, Derek will yell and swear, and sometimes throw things.

If we are in public, he tries to hide his anxiety by clenching his fists, grinding his teeth, focusing on the ground, pulling his hair or becoming completely silent. He describes PTSD as "feeling like my head is going to explode." And he still has nightmares about Afghanistan almost every night. In some of those dreams, he is stepping on IEDs or he's getting shot, his friends are dying or getting blown up. If he has an especially bad dream, he will spend the day angry at everything.

Our marriage, considering everything we have been through, is surprisingly stronger than it has ever been. We are about to move into our very first house we have ever lived in as a married couple—it's about fifteen minutes from the beach. We argue way less now that we are out of the hospital setting and Derek is removed from the strain and pressure of the military. I feel like I am finally starting the part of married life where we can enjoy each other. We enjoy sex. We enjoy freedom. We enjoy our baby.

It's only a leg. I've seen far worse.

Richaela's realization of how fortunate the couple has been compared to the injuries she witnessed at Walter Reed is corroborated by journalist David Wood, who won a Pulitzer Prize in 2012 for his *Huffington Post* ten-part series *Beyond the Battlefield: Rebuilding Wounded Warriors.* A seasoned war correspondent, Wood is an exquisite writer who unveiled the agonizing path to rebounding in romantic relationships for soldiers like Derek, missing limbs, and other warriors who come back with mauled genitals—or none at all.

Wood reports that more than 1,500 Americans have lost a leg or arm in combat in Iraq or Afghanistan, and hundreds of others have multiple limb amputations. An additional 1,500 warriors endure genital wounds, a consuming fear among those about to be deployed. Within the rapidly advancing field of the regeneration of organs, led by Dr. Anthony Atala's team at the Wake Forest Institute for Regenerative Medicine, doctors are making big strides in their ability to fashion human parts for transplantation. The regeneration of human penises is a top priority. So far, the Wake Forest doctors have regenerated penises that have been successfully attached onto rabbits, tiny genitals that have blood vessels and nerves that allow them to become fully functional. The rabbits were able to get erections and to get females pregnant, producing normal babies. Dr. Atala's team is now focused on the regeneration of genitals, and this research is progressing quickly with assistance from an $85 million federal grant to target their efforts toward lower abdomen battlefield injuries.

The attainment of this important goal appears hopeful: The Wake Forest doctors have already engineered bladders and urine tubes in the lab that have been successfully implanted in patients. They are also currently working to develop replacement tissues and organs for more than thirty different areas of the body, including cartilage for ears and noses, bones, muscles, heart valves, pancreases, kidneys, and livers. Dr. Atala's pioneering work was cited in *Time* as one of the top five medical breakthroughs of the year in 2011.

"Injury to genitalia has been identified as a significant problem facing military personnel," Dr. Atala told me in an interview. "While this is still in the experimental stages, we have had success with other organs and are hopeful and hard at work for similar success with genital regeneration."

A pediatric urologist, Dr. Atala began this area of research to treat male babies born with abnormalities of the genitals. In recent years, his research lent itself to helping wounded warriors, which he says "has become so meaningful for us. Because you are repairing not just their physical health but also the patients' self-image and their relationships with their loved ones.

"We are also working on the regeneration of extremities—another common casualty of war. All war injuries have a devastating effect, but certain organs obviously have a higher impact psychologically. Genitals, of course, are so central to a sense of manhood." Dr. Atala explains that the penises are restructured from donor organs and reseeded with the patient's own cells, eventually forming a functional phallus, which consists of a circular cylinder that holds three rods of erectile tissue, muscle tissue, and the urethra.

"For me, it's about making the patient whole again," says Dr. Atala.

Julia Crowley's husband, Rick, was a patient undergoing years of treatment for a brain tumor and seizures and is just starting to feel whole again. He did not lose a limb, but in the height of his illness, he did lose mental clarity, and suffered excruciating headaches and up to twenty seizures a day.

"Marriage is about the good, bad, and ugly—we made it through plenty of ugly," says Julia, thirty-two, who endured years of fertility shots. Then, when she finally birthed a child, Rick was the one who needed round-the-clock care—as did their new baby. His condition remained serious during the birth of their second child as well.

Julia is a successful independent sales director for Mary Kay cosmetics, dressed sharply, after a day calling on customers, in a blue sundress and navy-and-white-striped stilettos. She smiles brightly when delivering the news that as the couple marks their eighth wedding anniversary, Rick has not had a seizure in several months. Here is more from Julia on how she moved from the ugly into an "excellent and sexy" place in marriage with Rick, a high school history teacher.

JULIA CROWLEY

You know when your spouse gets really sick, I suppose it goes one of two ways; maybe some people want out. For me I realized what marriage really meant, that I was going to love him through good times and bad times. Something about him needing me made me want to commit again in a way that is both emotional and physical. As we celebrate our eighth anniversary, we are finally on our way to having a normal marriage. The intimacy is very strong, the commitment is unshakable. I think when I saw Rick at his most vulnerable is when I realized the depth of our love.

When I was pregnant with our second child, and had a two-year-old toddler, Rick started having dozens of seizures a day. The doctors discovered a tumor that looked like fingers wrapped through his brain, and because of those tentacles, it was really complicated to remove. So they decided to leave the tumor in because of its complexity, and also they weren't convinced it was causing the seizures.

To this day, no one really can pinpoint why he had multiple seizures daily, but by the grace of God and time and proper medications, right now those seizures have stopped. And the tumor is being watched to make sure it doesn't grow. Rick is slowly regaining his strength, though he has lost muscle tone.

But as his health would go up and down over the past years, honestly, there were often times that I struggled with keeping the desire up. The side effects of this tumor made it feel as if I was living with someone who has Alzheimer's. His recognition and memory would come and go. Some days he was fully normal, but then he would fall into a more detached state. When you have a husband who has a serious illness, and you have two young children, I have to tell you, you do not feel sexy. But I made sure that, unless Rick was really feeling sick, we don't go more than a week without time for some intimacy.

Throughout even the worst of this, somehow I grew more romantic about our relationship than I have ever felt. To explain, I have to take you back to the emotional place we were in when he got sick. Neither of us had admitted this to each other, but we had lost a lot of the connection in our marriage. We were fighting a lot, we were still having sex, but there wasn't a drive to do it that often. I had to take fertility drugs for years and I was exhausted. It took my sex drive away. I went from being a person who wanted to have sex a lot to someone who didn't want to have it at all.

That break in physical intimacy caused us to lose our emotional affection. There was very little romance, and I really started having doubts in my heart whether or not I wanted to stay in this marriage forever. Not because I was interested in someone else, but just a stirring within that something was wrong. I found out later that my husband was going through the same kind of feelings, because we were fighting a lot and not sharing any romantic time together. I went through this long phase when sex didn't feel good for me because I had to have so many hormone injections in my stomach. Our sex was for baby-making and not because we were feeling romantic, and that went on for two years before I finally did get pregnant.

Then Rick got sick, and that changed things really quickly for me in terms of realizing how committed I was to him. He was so sick and was put on so many drugs that I just had this force in me that I had to protect him, and stay almost glued to his hip. Within three weeks in the hospital, he had thirty electrodes and wires coming out of his shaved head, he was all wrapped up in bandages, and he looked so horrible. But something strange happened: My desire for him had never been stronger.

I remember looking at him and he felt so awful, and I said to him, "You have never looked more handsome to me." One day in the hospital, I actually crawled in bed with him, and we didn't have sex but it was the most intimate we had been in such a long time. Soon after he got home, I found out I was pregnant with my second son. Rick used to joke that his type of brain tumor was increasing his libido.

We both believe strongly in God and that He put this illness in our path to connect us deeper, and in a new way. Seeing my husband so sick and wired up like that made me realize he was my lifelong partner, and we became more sexually attracted to each other from that renewed emotional bond. Our sex life was mysteriously rekindled; I felt like we were teens.

There are still tough times; this is not easy for the spouse who is well. I do think he is healed, but the hardest thing for me emotionally is to get over our past years of struggle. His personality was so different; there were times when it would get so bad that he couldn't talk, and he'd almost look like a stroke victim. He knew what he was trying to say but couldn't get his words out, and his hand would curl up, uncontrollably. And he'd be in that state for four or five hours before he could communicate and understand you.

That was probably my biggest worry: Will he ever get out of this?

I know this image doesn't sound very sexy, but throughout the worst of times, I tried to focus on envisioning the healthy man I married. Something about him being so vulnerable was so sweet and loving to me. He was trapped in this body and wanted so badly to get to the other side.

I think back to that stormy time before he got sick, when we were having a lot of arguments and both thinking about leaving each other. But really it was in that hospital room after his diagnosis where we refocused our commitment and made a pact to be there for each other for the good, the bad, and the ugly. Ironically, it was in the heat of his illness when we got really romantic again—we had more sex when he got home from the hospital than we had in years.

He would say, "I don't know what drugs they are giving me, but I think they have increased my sex drive." This was also a time that, for the first time in our marriage, I wasn't on fertility drugs or I wasn't pregnant, so sex felt good for me again. So it took my husband's brain tumor to really cut my heart open and expose all the love in there. When he was looking so bad and feeling so bad, that is when I really rediscovered this passion. Usually you are older when you are forced to realize the true meaning of the marriage vows "through sickness and through health." I found out as a newlywed.

Julia and Richaela endured as newlyweds what most wives do not face until much later; that is, the challenge of retaining intimacy while caregiving for spouses who are ailing from the more common illnesses of aging, such as heart disease, prostate cancer, or Alzheimer's. (These subjects are covered in later chapters in the voices of older women.) While the gravity of physical conditions and the tenor of marriages are distinct from person to person, the lesson learned in all of their stories is that the vow "through sickness and through health" is a real test of, and testament to, true commitment.

The stories from Golden Girls are a reminder to young marrieds that the willpower to refresh and restore intimacy when it withers (along with other organs that wither) throughout life's passages is the distinguishing factor in who stays together and who ends up buying a divorce lawyer a new Jaguar. Making sex a priority with the guy you live with also protects you—and him—from wandering elsewhere.

CHAPTER 5
SEX AFTER INFIDELITY

*This affair woke me up sexually, and my sex life
with my husband is better than ever.*

—PAMELA

I am sitting in an oceanfront bar in Encinitas with my L.A.
friend Becky, savoring happy hour margaritas and the coral
dusk on the waves. At the table next to us are two middle-aged
men, their striped ties loosened, drinking Coronas from the bottle. They are laughing and craggy and tanned, grown-up California beach boys.

Becky leans over and says, "They are both wearing wedding
bands." She is forty-five, has been married for sixteen years, and
has one daughter, age fourteen.

"I wonder if they're happy?" adds Becky, removing her Kate
Spade cat-eye sunglasses for a closer look at the guys. "Maybe the
husbands don't think about 'Am I happy?' like their wives do.

"I only have two married girlfriends that are truly happy.

The rest of us are on the edge; sex has diminished or disappeared altogether. We think about leaving our relationships often, but I don't think any of us will end up doing it. The kids would hate it, and we don't know that what's out there is any better."

Becky is dressed in a pink polo shirt and white shorts. Her face is chubby and wide-eyed, accentuated by a recent brow lift. As she continues to talk to me about her midlife laments, I hear the voices in the piles of notes I've received from readers who have been married for between fifteen and twenty-five years.

These women are long out of the infatuation phase of marriage yet have continued to shuffle along. Along with the first years of marriage, the midlife mark is also a frequent juncture for divorce, when the combination of raising surly teenagers and a spouse's grating habits can up the level of wine consumption and the impulse to flee the house.

"Adolescents are not the only group who struggle with identity issues; many marriages also struggle during years twelve to twenty," says Nashville-based Ginger Manley, a certified diplomate of sex therapy, and an associate in psychiatry at the Vanderbilt University School of Medicine.

"Extramarital affairs and divorce are both quite common during this time. The proverbial bloom is completely off the rose. Each marital partner has been growing and changing in ways that often do not fit with the assumptions of the wedding day.

"Life is crazy busy at this time—careers are either flying high or stalled; all ages of children in the marriage have enormous needs," she adds. "What was new and exciting in the bedroom fifteen years ago is old and boring now. Sometimes it seems as though everybody in the family is seeking readjustment by acting out. Finding another playmate for sex or a relationship or both is easy. Occasionally after a fling, the straying partner may come back to the marriage, but forgiving and moving on within a marriage are tough decisions to make and tougher to live with."

I found out that those women making tough decisions about whether to stick it out or start over are a teeming population when my September 2011 blog titled "The Fine Line between Marriage and Divorce" became, and still is, one of the most viewed articles in *Huffington Post* history. In that piece, I relayed how my research and response to *The Secret Lives of Wives* resounded with ambiguity about achieving "'til death do us part." As I wrote:

"The biggest shocker is the number of wives in stable unions who frequently contemplate fleeing their marriages. These are not abused wives; they are women with nice husbands who give them orgasms and jewelry and stability. Yet many of these settled midlife women admitted they were slightly jealous of Tipper Gore, who gets to have a fresh start after forty years of matrimony with the same guy."

In this chapter, I talk to disgruntled spouses who sought solace in the arms of new and old lovers—not a hard thing to rustle up in the age of Facebook, flirty water cooler run-ins, the ease of travel, and Peter Pan boomers refusing to let go of youthful mischief making. After a thirty-year break, Pamela reconnected with her "first love, first everything" boyfriend from their Brooklyn hometown, which led to a blazing cross-continental affair. The fifty-three-year-old photographer cannot imagine divorcing her husband of twenty-four years, father of their five grown children. Nor does she plan to abandon the neighborhood boy, now an artist, to whom she lost her virginity and considers "my true soul mate."

For Lisa Abrams, the tables were flipped; it was her husband who strayed with a water-cooler romance. Lisa, forty-four, is a courageous superior court judge in Tucson whose husband's affair played out in papers and gossip circles all over Arizona, as he was also a high-profile city judge. The Arizona Supreme Court suspended Ted Abrams from practicing law for two years, and he is forever banned from the bench. Lisa survived the emotional fallout with a good psychologist and a new hobby of weight lifting. She is now buff of body and in a fortified marriage, made possible by a husband's shamed good behavior.

Then there is Gina, a public relations executive in Milwaukee, and the first story I will unfurl: She is fifty, five feet tall, forever blond, and still torn up about a lover who nearly sidetracked her from the altar. Three months before her wedding to a man she was not sure she wanted to marry, Gina started sleeping with a coworker, a man she had shared cozy lunches with since she started at the firm a decade earlier. Wrestling with the choice up until a day before the nuptials, Gina proceeded with the marriage and tried to force herself to forget the "one who got away" but failed on both fronts: The marriage was over within a year and even a hypnotist could not eradicate from her psyche the colleague, a burly suitor who moved out of state and severed ties once she became a wife.

This all occurred seven years ago, and Gina is now remarried and has a son with her second husband. Though when she reflects on that summer of love when she nearly axed her wedding—to be with someone who once surprised her with a white-cloth setup of lobster and champagne on a remote Lake Michigan beach—her black mascara streaks her cheeks.

GINA

I shouldn't have gone through with the wedding. I mean, I was madly in love with someone else. But you know, if you change one thing about your life, then you wouldn't be where you are now. And then I wouldn't have met this wonderful husband I ended up with, and I would not have my son.

My first husband was a man I had been dating for seven years, and in the beginning we were madly in love, too. We lived in separate cities, though, and he wasn't going to move to Milwaukee until just before the wedding. This man at work had been my friend, and we were always flirty with each other. Because my engagement ring was an emerald and not a diamond, I didn't mention I was getting married at first. Our lunches started to get longer and longer, and after one of them, we kissed on the way back to the office. That was April, and my wedding date was set for August.

Almost right away we started sleeping together and a month or so later, the day I mailed the wedding invitations, I told him, "Oh, by the way, I'm getting married. This is an engagement ring." Knowing we had only a short time together, that and the thrill of our misbehavior, only made our affair more exciting. This love and our lovemaking was really intense, really fun, and really romantic. My fiancé was also a great lover, but over the years, after law school, he turned into a dull conservative and was not that much fun to be around. He made me feel old, and the boyfriend was a Bohemian, loose and earthy and kind of wild. We were like naughty kids, the fun couple.

It was the best summer of my life. We were both just madly in love, and we'd sit on the beach for hours and just talk, or go for boat rides on lakes. Everything we did was fun; remember, we knew our time together was limited. One of my best memories is the night he walked me out to a hidden beach, where he had set up a lobster dinner on a little table covered in a white tablecloth. There was a cooler next to it icing a bottle of Dom Perignon.

After that, I got really torn up inside. I kept thinking, "I should be with this lighthearted guy, a kindred spirit. Instead, I'm going to be with a boring lawyer. Of course, the level of passion was because everything was so new. Sex was new and great. The way I felt about myself was new and great. With my fiancé, we had already been through so many ups and downs and fights and breakups, we were like an old married couple.

The magical affair lasted five months, up until days before the wedding, which would be attended by two hundred guests at a fancy hotel. Yeah, I was really a bad girl. The fiancé had moved to Milwaukee and I would still sneak out to be with this other man. One lunchtime, we ended up making love standing up in a bathroom stall at work. That's how bad I was.

Literally the week before the rehearsal dinner, we had this long talk. We were sitting on some rocks near the lake, and we both said we were definitely in love with each other. Then he admitted that, although he felt these feelings, the bottom line was that he wasn't planning on getting married anytime in the near future. He also told me not to call off the wedding on account of my love for him, that if I did call it off, it should be because in my heart I knew it wasn't right.

Well, I went ahead with the wedding. My biological clock was ticking. I was thirty-seven. The wedding gifts were rolling in. The relatives had plane tickets. I couldn't turn back, especially when I knew that my lover may never be the marrying type. I was right about that. A mutual friend of ours told me he just got married, at fifty.

Almost from the start of the marriage, it was pretty miserable. My husband had a really short haircut and he would put on a suit and tie and go to his law office and stay there for twelve hours. He came home tired and moody. Then I'd see my ex-boyfriend at work, and I would feel really sick inside, very sad, like I had made a mistake. One day, a couple months after my wedding, we were both working late. We ended up kissing and having some oral sex. He refused to have intercourse because I was married.

You know, in my heart I'm a good Catholic girl and I believe that you should do unto others as you would have them do unto you. The strong sexual feelings I still had for the other man, plus the fact that my husband and I were not compatible, made me realize pretty quickly that we would never make it. Thoughts of the other man became so consuming, I actually went to a hypnotist to see if she could get him out of my mind. I knew that longing was destroying my marriage. My mother had gone to the same hypnotist to stop smoking, and she stopped immediately. So I knew this hypnotist was really good.

I told the hypnotist my story and she said, "This isn't going to work for you unless you really want to let go of this man." And so she tried to hypnotize me and it didn't work; that's how much he had gotten underneath my skin.

As they say, time heals everything, but he lingers in a private place within me, especially in the summer when I am socked with memories. We were frozen in that beginning stage of love, when you are so infatuated with each other and having sex everywhere. But your fate unfolds the way it does because of those hard choices we have to make.

After the divorce, my work buddy and I slept together one more time, and it was both heartbreaking and overwhelmingly fun. Soon after, he took a job in Oregon and I have never heard from him again. I did check out his LinkedIn profile, though, and could easily get in touch with him, but I'm not going there. I have a husband and a child. But I looked at his photograph for a really long time. He still has thick, floppy hair, gray now and not black. But he has gotten pretty chunky, which is a good thing because it takes away some of the sting. He is casually dressed, and that is always a turn-on—after my first marriage fizzled, I swore I would never marry a man who had to go to work in a suit.

I have two girlfriends who were about to get married and wondered if they were doing the right thing. I told them if there is any hesitation, don't do it. I went into marriage with someone else on my mind, and it consumed me. I did feel like that other man was the love of my life, and still do in some ways. Though of course this husband that I married and gave me a child at forty-three is the love that gave me a life.

Gina's wistful recall of the one that got away I have heard from many midlife wives who are stifled by "what ifs" and sexy dreams of lost love. She was lucky; she has made peace with her fate and feels fortunate in the direction it has led. Her husband is a graphic designer who does not wear a tie, and together they made a healthy baby just before she entered menopause.

I will take you inside a lusty and longing obsession that still rocks the very-married Caroline "every single day." She has not slept with the old boyfriend since they broke up twelve years ago, yet the memory of their electric sex still jolts her out of the ability to be satisfied in the here and now. She relies on Zoloft to level the alternating peaks of joy and painful dives evoked by thoughts of him.

Caroline is a forty-three-year-old stockbroker in Virginia with a silken black ponytail, and decked in pearls and a crisp steel gray linen dress. She has come to our interview straight from work, looking and acting like a controlled and serious business-woman. Then, as she reflects on her boyfriend whom she still "feels closer to than anyone else on earth," her face melts into a wanton and faraway expression, as if she were possessed.

CAROLINE

I've got a loyal husband and four healthy children, so believe me, I count my blessings. But I'm telling you, this other guy, he is still in my mind and heart every day.

And so here I am, a mother and wife with a picture-perfect life, while inside I long for his touch and our passion. This is my dirty little secret: I have never, ever had a connection like this with anyone else in my life, male, female, family member, friend. ANYONE! I often wake up with a dream hangover about us, and it can destroy my day. I wouldn't have been able to survive this without Zoloft.

From our first kiss, I was done over, caught in a web of desire and the purest, most soulful tenderness that I've only read about in fiction, a web from which I will never be freed. I've been trying to catch my breath ever since. It's frozen in my mind as the perfect love—and has complicated my life. When he looked at me, it always felt that he wasn't looking at me, but into me.

For years after I got married, we were able to maintain our relationship on a friendly level; I would meet him for lunch, and we wouldn't touch, but we would just stare at each other, sharing life-altering stories that only he and I could understand. We talked about our mutual sexual awakening with each other, reliving all the places we made love, in cars, boats, golf courses, school, theaters, parks. We were like moths drawn to a flame.

I remember one night I was laid up on the hood of his car—phew! I almost can't breathe right now. Oh my God, it was more than just sex. We would then sit there for hours and just stare at each other. We could look at each other and know exactly what the other person was thinking. Always.

How can you shake memories like this, of a primal,

emotional, sexual love? I have slept with only four people and married one of them, but this was the greatest lovemaking for me. We'd screw sometimes four times a day. We couldn't get enough of each other. It was like a drug addiction.

I remember the day I told him I was getting married—He said, "Don't do it; marry me." I wanted both of these men, but the boyfriend was a rascal and not in steady employment, and the man I married started making money right out of college, and he pursued me big-time with flowers and jewelry. And here I am, years later, a married woman with children, still consumed with this unreliable turd who happened to be the best lover of my life.

We stopped seeing each other when I started having babies—he said he would never have children unless it was with me, and he never did become a father, although he did eventually get married. When he saw me pregnant with another man's child, he just went crazy with sadness.

So while I'm not having a physical affair with this guy, I feel as if it is like emotional adultery. He still lurks in my heart daily. It wasn't only the best sex I ever had. It was a total spirit connection between two people. As I'm telling you this, I can't catch my breath, I have butterflies, sweaty palms, my heart is beating so fast.

How do you keep this pink elephant out of this marriage? It's really hard. I feel him in me and around me constantly. My husband and I have an ideal life on every other level, but we definitely had more passion in our marriage before the kids came along. Isn't that the same situation with most everybody? The marriage starts out hot, then sex becomes routine. But I made the best choice in a husband and passed up on the best passion of my life. There is no question I chose a settled life over tumultuous love. But it still tortures me to this day.

I used to believe the primal abandon she felt could be found only in fiction until I heard lots of real stories, like Caroline's, of fantastic lovers that rival these juicy passages in D. H. Lawrence's *Lady Chatterley's Lover*. Keep your *Fifty Shades*—Lawrence gets the prize for depicting great sex. Here are some dispatches on the eruptions that take place when Lady Connie Chatterley sneaks off to shtup the groundskeeper of the estate where she lives, owned by her wheelchair-bound curmudgeon husband.

"It was a night of sensual passion; in which she was a little startled and almost unwilling: yet pierced again with thrills of tenderness, but, at the moment, more desirable. . . . Though a little frightened, she let him have her his way, the reckless, shameless sensuality shook her to her foundations, stripped her to the very last, and made a different woman of her. It was not really love. It was not voluptuousness. It was sensuality sharp and searing as fire, burning the soul to tinder."

Connie does not end up having it both ways. She chooses passion with a poor man over the lavish life of a lady, skipping out on her invalid, icy spouse and following the hunky grounds-keeper, whose child she is now carrying. Perhaps we would also pack up and move out if this is what we were heading toward, as she describes: "whirlpools of sensation swirling deeper and deeper through all her tissues and consciousness 'til she was one concentric fluid of feeling, and she lay there crying in unconscious inarticulate cries."

Yowzer!

Women seem to always have a hankering for men who are not afraid to get their hands dirty, who can fix things, and make things and are craggy. We are suckers for those sweaty alpha males who use tool belts and circular saws and claw hammers, and I am one of those women: I married an architect who is also a carpenter and woodworker.

Pamela has reconnected with her teenage love, an artist with weathered hands who forages for found objects and lugs around gigantic canvases. Although she is a very feminine woman, she thinks like a man, in compartments, which is evident as she coolly discusses her long marriage and new lover who is really an old lover newly excavated.

Pamela contacted me after reading a column I wrote for *Huffington Post* Weddings called "Can You Love Two Men at Once?" and told me, "Yes, you can!" And she does, a lovely husband and a long gone, resurrected lover. Her terse note tantalized me to learn more about a woman she calls "a wife with a secret life." I find a vintage hippie who stands nearly six feet tall, with bushy silver curls and decked in a caftan of Indian-print bedspread material.

PAMELA

I am blessed—believe me, I know—married two decades to an incredible man. We have grown children and grandchildren. So my story is not simple—I am sure there are myriad reasons why I have fallen off the fidelity wagon, but my journey to becoming an artist tops the list.

I always had a deep yearning for an artistic partner, which I knew I was sacrificing when I got married. I married a great guy, but he is a businessman, not an artist. When I made a decision to marry this man, I believed all the ingredients for a happy life were in place. I wasn't young, I was twenty-nine, and I was eager to have children. I also believed I was in love, although there was unfinished business with a former boyfriend who was more artistically bent.

At eighteen, I lost my virginity to that poet and musician, who was twenty-one. We lived in the same blue-collar, working-class neighborhood. He was the dreamboat of our high school, the coolest guy, and he was my first love and my greatest lover. He taught me about sex, and our lovemaking was amazing.

I was always a serious music lover and writer of poetry, too. Our shared interests made us a good match, but he was a wanderer, not really marriage material. Over the course of my marriage, I thought about looking him up but was too afraid to make the contact. However, I suffered from wanderlust and had a short-lived affair with a painter that alerted me to my own need to be with someone creative. The black hole of my soul was always taunting me, yearning for something more.

The unrest was my unfulfilled passion. I now have my own photography studio and I am a mentor to many other artists, young and old. My marriage became more satisfying as I have been able to pursue my artistic dreams. But I have always questioned the convention of spending a lifetime with one, and only one, romantic partner. I am curious by nature and love variety in food, entertainment, and all sensual pleasures—and in love relationships.

Last year, the yearning for a creative soul mate began to hound me again, like a dog in heat. I was invited to the wedding of the daughter of an old friend, and thoughts of young passion overwhelmed me with a desire to contact my old boyfriend. I didn't have to, as it turns out, because he was at the wedding, too. After that night, though we literally live a thousand miles apart, we have managed to start up again. I have seen him many times since then and have made love with him several times.

When we reconnected, we shared that we both had the same recurrent dream about finding each other again. This gives us both the sense that we are soul mates; he is becoming the rock of my life. The first time around, it was wrong for us; he was a stoner and didn't know what he was doing with his life. After we split up and I went out with other guys, I remember thinking what an idiot I was because he was the best lover I ever had.

I was always looking for him in other people but never found it, even in my husband, although we do have sex and the sex is good—but we've had to work on it.

For the longest time, I thought the mechanics were failing me. I thought we were a bad fit, physically. He just didn't penetrate the way I wanted—not a physical size issue, more like a depth-of-soul thing.

The first love was the right lover for me; our lovemaking flowed naturally. For me, the best lover in the world means it is someone who knows how to read me. There are just some men who are like that, though not many. We fit together perfectly, and although he has gotten pretty heavy, it doesn't matter to me. I never, ever thought I'd be attracted to a big, chubby guy, but I love this man.

I think about him all the time, and I wonder if I could be with him full-time and what would it do to my family. But I don't want to hurt my husband, and he doesn't want to hurt his wife—he has no children.

A secret life can be very affirming if it stays a secret. Actually, this diversion is helping my marriage. This affair woke me up sexually, and my sex life with my husband is better than ever. He didn't ask why, but he has definitely noticed my new sexual energy.

I like both my men and want to keep both my men. I am able to compartmentalize well. Since I've run my own business, I have learned to become more like a man, to think in categories. I have also gotten stronger about claiming what I feel is rightfully mine. The only person who knows about this is a seventy-five-year-old friend of mine. She called me years ago to tell me she was having an affair and needed to spill to somebody. I've kept her secret, and when I needed to tell somebody, it was her. It wouldn't be a shrink.

If I went to a therapist, she would say choose. I can't choose. I have this feeling that time will deliver some answers, because time always does. Both men have different smarts. The husband is business savvy, the lover is soul savvy. My marriage is a good one. However, there is the recurrent emptiness, the black hole of the soul. After relentless searching, my boyfriend came back to fill the hole—no pun intended. I don't feel guilty because I feel all humans deserve to be happy. I would never want my husband to suffer from my actions, but I do not want to suffer for my inaction.

I'm fifty-three, but with this love and artistic direction in my life I feel like I'm twenty-three, attractive, and in good shape. My husband is in really good shape, too, and is very handsome. The other man looks kind of beaten up by life, raw and worn. But he feels like an old and comforting Teddy Bear to me. We were both from the wrong side of the tracks; I was a bad girl and he was a bad boy—and I married a good boy.

I like having a lover. There are only a few people who marry their soul mates the first time around and end up blissfully happy. I get the best of both worlds: I have the stability and security of my husband, an intact family for my children, and I have the passion that I want and need in my life.

What I am living is not exactly fantasy or reality, but some place in between.

In response to my books and columns that give airtime to adultery and emotional affairs, I get letters accusing me of dishonoring holy matrimony. My coverage of infidelity may be offensive to some readers, yet I am a journalist and not a judge. My job is to share stories that are real and not rare about how some spouses manage to stay in lackluster marriages. Actually, for Pamela, having a lover has rekindled passion on the home front.

Whatever you make of wives entwined in double lives, call them heathens or sluts, they are claiming their own sexuality with the same unflinching machismo that has been stereotypically characteristic of males since Genesis.

Is a secret life okay to pursue as long as you are not hurting a spouse?

It is a timeless question that evokes a multitude of answers, from furious condemnation to "Whatever—it's their life, not mine." What I find, though, is when people tell me their twisted tales of sex and straying, a process that can take several interviews, they usually figure out for themselves what is the right thing to do—for *them*.

Even with the loosening of sexual mores in the United States, we cling to some of our old Puritanical laws that attempt to regulate sexual behaviors. There are still twenty-three states in which adultery was at last count listed as a criminal offense, including New York, Florida, Maryland, Illinois, and Arizona. In my next-door state of Virginia, sodomy remains on the books as illegal behavior. In some states, such as Idaho, Oklahoma, and Wisconsin, adultery is a felony—although it is rarely prosecuted.

Adultery laws extend back to the Old Testament, stemming from the patriarchal notion of tainting the husband's family bloodline when a married woman had sex with someone else and bore another man's child. The word stems from *adulterate*, which means to make something poorer in quality by adding an inferior substance.

While technological progress elevates human capability every generation, when it comes to sex and romance, some things never change. Despite blessed, tearful marriage vows, people veer from their promises, century to century, bumbling into situations that have shattered hearts and torn up dynasties, large and small. As human animals, we all need to eat and sleep and use the bathroom, and many people also feel a need to break rules.

Infidelity, frightening and invigorating, is an ancient human impulse to sample the forbidden fruit.

There are no accurate statistics on adultery because everyone lies about sex, but experts in the field of sexuality estimate that up to one-half of all marriages will at some point be struck. Affairs often remain clandestine and do not rock the marriages—at least not outwardly. Yet once the cheater is caught, or makes the choice to come clean, many marriages with deep roots and loyalty reconstruct as partnerships that are sturdier, more authentic and communicative, than before.

Marriage reassessment that sprang from humiliating honesty that played out in headlines and newscasts across Arizona ultimately turned Lisa Abrams's marriage into the "best shape ever." Lisa is also in her best shape ever. After her husband's sexual harassment charges were outed, and he was temporarily disbarred, Lisa went through severe depression and bouts of self-loathing. To cope with the mental agony, she became a bodybuilder, writhing through red-faced routines with major weights each morning at 5:00 A.M.

The Arizona Superior Court judge can now deadlift two hundred pounds and push-jerk one hundred pounds. Lisa met her husband, Ted, in 1993 when she was a law clerk and he was a public defender, and they were married in May of 1996. Their two sons are now ages twelve and fifteen, the cement and source of love that helped the couple forgive and move on—"although you never forget," says Lisa.

Lisa meets me after work at a Tucson sushi bar, in a soft silk blazer and a knee-grazing skirt that show off sharp shoulders and well-defined calves. Ironically, she has just come from a court case involving a divorce in which a woman charged her husband with adultery. She has great hair, short and floppy on top, with gold highlights, and the steely resolve of Hillary Clinton.

Instead of hiding this scorching period of her life, Lisa now speaks to groups about adultery recovery, with the goal of empowering other spouses with partners who "fell off the monogamy wagon," as Pamela put it.

LISA ABRAMS

When we met, I was twenty-four and still in law school at the University of Arizona. It was lust and love and still is—even after all I've been through. I have always been attracted to my husband. We were still intimate as a couple even during the affair—which I had no idea was happening. When I did find out, I had to go be tested for all sorts of horrible sexually transmitted diseases. Talk about humiliation! His actions affected me at every level, every fiber of my being, emotionally, medically, sexually, financially—there wasn't a part of me that felt whole for months and months.

I lost thirty-five pounds; I felt sexually unattractive. I'd been rejected.

To understand how this happened to our marriage, I need to start with what was going on a decade ago. In 2003, Ted was appointed to the bench as a Tucson City Court magistrate. Life was zooming by in a busy home with two young children, two parents with demanding careers—and four dogs.

Then in 2007, Ted almost died. He was hospitalized with strep endocarditis, an infection that landed in his heart, which attacked his aortic valve. He then had a bovine aortic valve transplant, full open-heart surgery. My husband was hospitalized for five weeks and on medical leave for four months. After the surgery, he was prescribed pain medication that he was becoming addicted to, OxyContin in particular.

Of course, when I look back on this time period, I realize that our marriage was on the verge of collapse and that I was terribly unhappy.

Ted slept a lot and he was irritable. I made a lot of excuses for his weird behavior when he snapped at the children. Once he went back to work, he started to go in really early and then he would go out to a live-band venue almost every night. I rationalized that this was okay; he liked music and I liked to work out in the mornings. So I just thought it was good for us to pursue our separate interests. In May of 2010, I was appointed to the superior court bench. I was deliriously happy, my children were healthy, our careers were soaring and were recession-proof incomes. I ignored the crumbling marriage going on before my eyes.

On October 26, 2010, after we put the kids to bed, my husband said, "Oh, something bad happened at work today." I thought he had made a ruling he wasn't happy with or there was an emotionally draining case in his courtroom. I never expected what I heard and saw next.

Ted pulled out a letter from the presiding judge of Pima County, the same judge who had appointed me to my position six months earlier. My husband had been placed on administrative leave, accused of sexual harassment and gross judicial misconduct.

I was stunned. Sexual harassment? My husband? Never! I am a graduate of Smith College—I wrote my case note on sexual harassment in the workplace. But his secret life very quickly tumbled out: He had an affair with a lawyer who practiced in his courtroom and had engaged in gross misconduct. He was using pain meds every day, all day, and he admitted that he was totally out of control.

The pain I felt is indescribable. That first night, I ended up at my best friend and law partner's home, racked with tears and vomiting—I had many, many nights like this.

Within a week, Ted was hospitalized at the University of Arizona Medical Center in the psychiatric unit. Within three weeks, he was in residential treatment in California. And I was left to pick up the pieces of our lives.

I tried to keep things normal for the children. My oldest son's Bar Mitzvah was January 2011 and I helped him do all of the preparation alone—and I am actually Episcopalian. I got the children to their extracurricular activities. I went to work every day without fail, listening to divorce cases and allegations of marital misconduct. I cried the entire drive to work and the entire drive home.

The newspaper articles came next, filled with allegations and half-truths, and excruciating to read. My private life was exposed for all. When your spouse is not faithful and you are rejected by the person who is supposed to be your biggest ally, it causes you to question every aspect of your life. If I wasn't a good enough spouse, maybe I'm a lousy mother. Maybe I wasn't sexy enough. Maybe I was ugly.

But I did my best to hold my head high. After Ted finished residential treatment in California and returned to Tucson, he lived elsewhere for several weeks while I decided what should happen next. Much to my mother's and siblings' surprise, my husband and I went into counseling to try and repair our marriage. They thought I would file for divorce as soon as the Bar Mitzvah was finished. But I truly felt that I owed my marriage more—that I had to fight for my marriage although Ted had not. I knew I owed this to my two beautiful boys.

My own mother did not speak to me for six weeks! Yet I knew I was stuck with this jerk for the rest of my life in some capacity—at least as the father of my children. From my perspective, therapy would allow me to express my feelings of shame and humiliation and to seek some form of closure—so that we could be the best co-parents possible should we decide to split.

Therapist Number One was a hairy fellow who spent a lot of time telling us about his relationship with his mother. After several months, he stated, "You know, Lisa, men would f–k mud." This led to a period of time in which I called Ted a mudf–er. Ha! I almost fell off a ski lift, texting "Mudf–ker!" This therapist got us through the first stage of anger, but we moved on.

Therapist Number Two was very clinical, judgmental, looked down his nose at us and made us feel awful about everything. Therapist Number Three—Fabulous! She literally embraced us and was excited to help us unravel the rat's nest of our marriage. She gave us action plans, reading assignments. She said, "I want you to succeed!"

And so here we are, two and a half years later. We are still in therapy and our seventeen-year-old marriage is totally different. We carve out time for each other, even if it's a trip to Costco. We make it a point every day to look each other in the eyes and be completely honest with each other.

Ted is sober from drugs, a critical component. He has repeatedly expressed his remorse, and taken responsibility for his actions. He is engaged with our children and they are thriving and excited to have their father back. He is their basketball coach and the go-to carpool dad. My mother now understands that I wasn't being a doormat, that it was the very calling of feminism and empowerment that gave me the courage to fight for my family!

I recently spoke on my experience at a meeting of the Association of Family and Conciliation Courts and there were two hundred people in attendance. I received a standing ovation. I started to speak out because I wanted to have my own voice as people were gossiping about me and my husband behind my back. I needed to show them that the person portrayed in the papers as a vile creep was the man I chose to make two beautiful babies with and I happened to still love.

I would not have been able to move on had my husband not expressed deep remorse for the pain he caused our family. If he had been arrogant and not sought treatment, this would have been a different story.

He looks back at this awful time and puts his head in his hands, and has cried. My marriage now, though, is better and more intimate than ever. We are in this with our eyes open. You try to forget and you try to move on, but have I forgiven him? I have on most days, but it is a lot to survive adultery. You start to question every aspect of your life. You tell yourself, "I wasn't sexy enough. I wasn't good enough in bed. I wasn't worthy. That's why he turned to other women."

My healing has been greatly helped by my physical accomplishments. I am getting stronger all the time. Really strong. I started doing CrossFit. I can push-press one hundred pounds over my head and deadlift two hundred pounds. I can do unassisted pull-ups and flip three-hundred-pound tires! I even completed the Tough Mudder: 12.5 miles and twenty-seven obstacles designed by the British Special Forces, including crawling under 10,000 volts of electricity and jumping off a two-story platform into frigid water!

As I became physically stronger, I became emotionally stronger and far more confident. I know it wasn't love he was feeling for this other woman—it was just sex. But I am still

healing and will be my entire life. Though I have started wearing my wedding band again, and I haven't called him a mudf—er
for a really long time.

What really helped me become intimate with my husband
again were both his expressions of genuine remorse and lots of
reading on the topic of affairs. Elizabeth Edwards's book was
great—she described the mistress as someone peering through
your living room windows and wanting your life.

No one else is getting my life!

I travel from Tucson back to a cottage in Leucadia, California, a rustic hideaway flanked by fig trees and palms that is my
customary writer's retreat. At the end of an eleven-hour day at
my MacBook, unraveling tales of midlife kvetching and infidelity, I take a split of J. Lohr Cabernet down to Grandview Beach,
to watch the surfers and the sunset and to stop thinking.

You sit on a beach and your whole life goes by.

A skinny woman in a bikini, with an enormous pregnant
belly, is walking with a shorter man whose right hand is on her
butt. Two kids who look to be in the nine-to-eleven range are
next in line, trailed by their mom in a purple tank suit, shouting,
"STOP! Wait for me!" The wine and the rhythmic curls of the
surfers are starting to quiet my mind, which has been gyrating
about sex and marriage. I flashback on our own wedding on a
snowy night in Chicago in 1988 and the birth of four boys in
rapid succession, who are now out the door.

I know from the work I do that if couples make it through
the first twenty years, through battles over babies and money and
teenagers and boredom, chances go way up of their marriage
lasting until someone dies.

We are at twenty-six—can we go fifty?

As if on cue, an elderly pair strolls slowly in front of me, feet in the water, pants rolled up, talking animatedly; they look to be around eighty. She is wearing a wide-brimmed straw hat and he has on a red USC baseball cap. They may be married, they may be widowed or divorced and linked through a senior dating site.

I start to rise from my towel, tempted to resume interviewing for this book, and ask them how long they have been together. Instead, I settle back against the cliffs and choose to go with my imagination: They made it through raising infants and teenagers and marrying off kids and are now doting grandparents. And while one or both of them may have deviated from their vows secretly or perhaps got caught, they are together today, and content on a breathtaking beach, arms around each other's waists.

And I just know they are still having sex.

Again, this is my wine-tinged fantasy that I hope is true yet may be far from it. I do, though, know a lot about the reality of how women deal with the pain of recovering from infidelity. Spouses who get caught must perpetually be in redemption mode, like Lisa Abrams's husband. And the wronged party never forgets; it is an ache that may be buried deep down, yet it never totally dissipates, and forever affects the ability to trust completely and to stop wondering, as Lisa did: "Maybe I wasn't sexy enough."

On the other side is the philanderer who manages to maintain a longtime affair and a longtime secret. Pamela is having it both ways for now, but she knows that in time, something is going to give; guilt will win out over the elation of an affair or she will ditch an old marriage and start over with an old boyfriend. Obviously if her husband finds out, the pain of guilt will be more severe, but the act of cheating in itself, even if no one knows, is something that burns within and does not let up.

"You have to look yourself in the mirror every day," says

Kate, a forty-eight-year-old married woman who just broke off a two-year affair.

"I felt like every time I was with this other guy, my mom was whispering in my ear, 'Don't do this, Katie. You've got a fine husband and kids at home.' Ha! And my mom had been dead for ten years. For me, it wasn't about the sex. I can get decent sex at home. It was about feeling like someone was really listening to me, without judging me. It was about being told how pretty I am—What husband of twenty years tells you daily how pretty you are? With this man I felt adored and appreciated. But then I would come home to my husband and children and just feel like a sham. Wherever I was, I was never at peace—because I was torn in half.

"Finally, a month ago, I got back home from a dive hotel where I would meet my lover once a week, and I just had a meltdown," continues Katie. "My teenage son was at the kitchen table doing his homework and my husband had left work early, surprising me with my favorite bottle of wine, for no reason at all. I ran out of the room and just felt so sick I actually vomited. On that day, at that moment, I realized I could no longer live with a cheater's heart."

Katie has decided to never tell her husband about the affair because "it's really over" and she believes while her behavior was wrong it set her straight. She said she was always angry with her husband for not talking to her more, complimenting her more, making her feel more appreciated. She also realized she had never asked pointedly for any of those things until one night after dinner:

"I said, 'Look, I need more from you. I need to be heard. Tell me I look nice. Make me feel special.' A funny thing happened. He said, 'Could you please do the same for me, too? I've been feeling ignored.' I had been ignoring him, of course, because my mind was fixed on another man. The result of us being vulnerable with each other is that we are talking more. And our sex is more fun. Affairs are just big fantasies. It's always special because you don't live with him every day. Well, that fantasy has fizzled for me because I realized my real life is pretty damn good. I'm lucky that I didn't blow this marriage before I gave it a chance. I hope God has forgiven me for cheating on my husband because I can never forgive myself.

"It's my dirty secret to keep, and it feels just awful."

CHAPTER 6
SEX AFTER DIVORCE

I won't settle until I am swept off my feet again,
wildly and with abandon. Not just sexually, but by
the whole package.

—MONICA

Katie feels awful about nearly destroying a marriage that
could be saved. But there are clearly times when it becomes more important to save yourself than to continue prop-
ping up a doomed relationship.

I am staring at a picture of Jane Fonda and Ted Turner when
they first went public as a couple. She reminds me of a racehorse:
sleek and defiant, her muscled neck held high, topped by a tou-
sled mane.

Turner's little smirk under his bristle of a white mustache is
triumphant. *I got her*, it says, as if he just caught the biggest trout
on his Flying D Montana ranch. Perfect, sexy, and regal, they

appear to be, in Christian Mingle lingo, God's match for each other.

Years later, on *Oprah's Master Class*, Fonda is talking about the pain of leaving the man she considers her "favorite ex-husband." The king of Turner Broadcasting started putting the moves on Fonda the day after her divorce from Tom Hayden was announced. Though they had met only once before, the ballsy suitor phoned a sexy stranger he admired to ask: "Is it true?" Turner's full-court press pursuit, conducted amidst the bison and bears on his nearly 114,000 acres of land, led to a decade-long marriage that consumed most of Fonda's fifties—and broke her heart.

"I remember when I was sixty-two and I had done something that was very, very, very painful and difficult," Fonda said in her Oprah interview. "I had left Ted Turner, my third husband, who I loved very, very much."

While divorce is a separation of a relationship, of a family, and of assets, for Fonda the choice signified a desire for wholeness. As she told Oprah: "I knew that I would die married and rich, but not whole." The heartbreak of divorce was familiar to Fonda, who has two other former husbands, Roger Vadim and Tom Hayden, fathers of her two biological children. As she writes in her memoir, *My Life So Far*, published by Random House in 2005: "On the night I turned fifty-one, Tom announced to me that he was in love with another woman."

Ever the unstoppable racehorse, with the tightest body and the most rebirths of any woman her age, Fonda is winning in the end. The Jane Fonda Center at Emory University, which she created with a lead gift in 2000, has emerged as a prototypical institution in advocacy and treatment for adolescent reproductive health. And at the age of seventy-five, Fonda revealed in an interview with the British *Hello* magazine that she is having the best sex of her life with her boyfriend of four years, Richard Perry.

In her January 2012 TedX talk on what Fonda terms "The Third Act," she compares aging to a staircase, an "upward ascension of the human spirit bringing us into wisdom, wholeness and authenticity." A daughter of Hollywood royalty, Jane Fonda is not a commoner. Yet I have found in the voices of women across class and race that a universal sisterhood shares a common heart: Women want to love and be loved, and we share an overarching quest to feel whole, integrating work, family, and intimate relationships. *Whole* is defined in the dictionary as "complete, including all parts or aspects."

On that staircase into wholeness, getting a divorce makes the climb more excruciating, you will hear in this chapter as ex-spouses discuss a passage of life that splinters history, families, and self-identities. But along with that heartache can also come relief and release. Ingrid discovered this when the first man she took to bed after her divorce—the first sex she had in six years—turned out to be an "incredible, affirming" lover, though their interludes at her apartment cannot take place until her seven-year-old is asleep. Cathy Meyer fled a sexless marriage with a man who humiliated her and was addicted to porn. Monica's husband was addicted to sex and money but was incapable of intimacy. Renee's husband drank too much and retired too early.

While each woman occupies her own notch on the scale of "Who suffered more?," as a group they possess some key unifying traits: After the hard punch of divorce and healing over time, they opened themselves up to intimacy again. By extracting themselves from unhealthy marriages, a process they initiated, these ex-wives demonstrated their unwillingness to be part of the silent pool characterized in this famous quote by Henry David Thoreau:

"The mass of men lead lives of quiet desperation."

These women's stories are about the courage to speak up and get out. However shattering is the experience of ending a marriage, they made the choice to be led by their deeply felt needs and not by fear of the unknown. Because here is what they *do* know—they can no longer tolerate a partnership in which there is no talking or touching or comfort or support.

When the music dies in a love partnership—a process that can take decades to acknowledge—the sexual crackle has generally long been dead as well. Then, finally, someone pulls the plug. I know this from hundreds of readers and interview subjects who left their marriages, and while the details of departures differ, these themes prevail: adultery, abandonment, and/or abuse that has left them in brittle, sexless—sometimes scary—relationships. Beaten down and battling over money and rights, then paying out enormous attorney fees, a desire for intimacy after divorce does not come easy.

Yet it does happen. And sex after divorce can even be way better than before.

I chose these women because they serve as a barometer of hope for any wife who has toppled over that fine line between marriage and divorce. You may identify with one of these stories and pull your own plug. Or you may realize that what you have, albeit not perfect, is far more tolerable than what these women endured.

Ingrid moved to the States a decade ago from her native Italy when her husband's tech firm relocated him to New York City. Although she was leaving her parents and homeland, she was "ready for change and adventure." Ingrid ended up having more change and adventure than she could have imagined. The forty-two-year-old mom of a second grader is in the final stage of divorce proceedings from a husband who turned volatile and who, by restraining order, can no longer come near their apartment. Breaking away from his aggression comes at a price: He has withdrawn any financial assistance for household expenses, and Ingrid has become a strapped single mom—so far, she owes her divorce lawyer close to $100,000 in fees.

Yet between full-time work at an ad agency, housekeeping, and shuffling her seven-year-old son to school, soccer, and Cub Scouts, Ingrid has managed to slide in some time for a secret, torrid romance—with the soccer coach.

Unlike older divorcées with empty nests, scheduling a social life is not easy for Ingrid, particularly when she cannot afford child care. Luckily for Ingrid, her little boy is in bed promptly at 8:30 P.M. and sleeps like a rock, giving her a window for home entertainment. Ingrid is a slim woman with delicate features and a lilting accent, who has found that the agony of divorce is soothed considerably when a nurturing lover is available for late-night dinners.

INGRID

When I got to New York and started to have my own career, my own circle of friends, my husband still expected that I would be there to meet 100 percent of his needs, and he had a lot of needs. I had more and more responsibility at work, I was taking care of our apartment, I had full responsibility for taking care of our child. All of this took a lot of time and attention, and my husband is not somebody who would give much help. He is not a giver. He is a taker. I would describe him as a black hole in which you give and you give, and it's never enough.

He wouldn't hit me, but he started in with emotional abuse. All of a sudden, I was too skinny, I didn't dress well enough. My cooking wasn't good enough. My job was bullshit. He was completely degrading of everything I am. I was very confused by this because in the past, he thought I did everything right. He went from complete respect, telling me I was smart and beautiful, to this degradation, and it got worse and worse.

He started to spend a lot of time with a woman from his work, and he would come home between two and five in the morning. This went on for two years. He would say, "Oh, she is just a very good friend." Meanwhile he was treating me like shit, and he was never home. Finally, I pulled the plug and initiated divorce. When he was served the divorce papers, he became threatening and volatile. He walked up to me and said, "You are going to regret this. I will put you in the grave." And these threats continued, really mean and scary. I got a restraining order, and now he can see our child only on supervised visits.

I was with my husband for twenty years, and during those first years, we were extremely close and very sexy. But the passion died down very quickly; we would have sex, but I never had an orgasm with my husband. I don't think he ever knew this because I faked it. He probably wouldn't have cared; our sex, like our life, was all about pleasing him. Then our sex life went down to doing it maybe two to four times a year, and that would be him getting on top of me and getting it over with, and that was it. In the final stages of our being together, he could not perform anymore. This inability to hold an erection coincided with the time he started to see this other woman.

So he moves out, I change the locks on our apartment, and I find myself at a crossroads. I'm completely void of emotion and sexual energy. I had zero desire, nothing. I was so occupied with divorce and caring for my son, the last thing on my mind was dating. Then Hurricane Sandy hits and floods our apartment, and we are relocated to temporary housing, where I don't have to pay rent for four months.

This was like a miracle for me. I had been so broke right after my husband left that sometimes I had no money to buy food for my child. Then all of a sudden, I had some air to breathe and some money to spend. I did things I hadn't done for months—I had my hair dyed professionally. I bought a couple of sexy outfits. My husband had put me down so much, I wanted to look pretty. And I could afford a babysitter so I could go out once in a while.

I had been taking my son to soccer practice three times a week, and to his weekend games. His coach is a handsome man. What I found most attractive about him was that he was very engaged with the children. He is about my age, and his son is on the soccer team, too. Nothing happened for months, but I am starting to feel really good about myself, and sexy again, and I'm noticing him more.

The team took a field trip to a museum and we were looking at one exhibit in a dark hallway. All of a sudden, I get this prickly sensation, like someone is watching me, and he is coming up behind me. We start talking, and I felt this connection with him; there was a lot of eye contact, just this really sexy energy. And I'm thinking, *What is going on here?* and then I notice he is wearing a wedding ring. And I'm like *Oh, good. He is married. I'm safe, nothing will happen.* But the next week, he invites my son and me to join him and his son at a restaurant for dinner, and he orders oysters and champagne, and it is definitely a flirty evening. So I'm thinking maybe he just feels sorry for me. I'm a single mom, in the middle of a divorce; maybe he is just being a gentleman.

Then I get an e-mail from him asking me to go out to see a Broadway show and I'm starting to see that, clearly, this man is asking me out for a date. I think of the wedding ring, but then I figure *Why not?* I have been very excited to be around him.

Maybe we can just be friends. The night was a lot of fun, we went to see *Jersey Boys*, which has great music we both related to, then we went out for a drink. We talked mostly about our children. He did not talk about his wife at all.

I saw him at a team practice a few days later and we made another dinner date. This time, he took me to a very dimly lit French restaurant, and next thing I knew he was holding my hand. After dinner, we sat down at the bar and he kissed me. At that point my internal cravings for sex are getting strong again. I was ready to be laid, quite frankly. It had been six years since I had sex!

We both went downstairs to the bathrooms and quickly it turned to all-over body touching, grabbing each other, hands in each other's pants. I pulled away and said to him: "You are married." He said, "Well, so are you." I said, "Not really." And he said, "Well, maybe I'm not really married either." That night we didn't sleep together, but we both knew it was going to happen.

I'm thinking to myself, *Do I want this? He is married. I'm still confused from this divorce.* But I find him extremely attractive and then there is this other voice that says, *Let's do this. I don't want commitment; I just want relief, release; I want to be f—ked."*

The next time we got together was at my house. I invited him to come to dinner, at 9:30 P.M. when my son was fast asleep. I told my son before he went to bed that his soccer coach might come by so we could plan their next parents' picnic, in case he woke up—which he never does. So he came over, we drank a bottle of wine, and he started kissing me again and we ended up in bed—before eating our dinner.

It was furious and intense and great; I was too nervous, though, to have an orgasm. But oh it felt great, having sex back in my life, skin against skin, the heavy breathing, the feel of a man. It was an amazing, amazing feeling.

I've been seeing him for a few months now and we just have great chemistry. He is very bold in the bedroom; he really knows how to ask for what he wants. He loves to watch a woman touch herself, so he started buying me toys I never owned, like a vibrator. He watches me use it and with the vibrator I started to have orgasms. He enjoys that tremendously. As I get excited, he gets excited, then after my first orgasm, I am ready for him to enter me, and I have started to be able to have multiple orgasms.

So here's the little problem: While this fun sex has been going on, I started to develop an emotional bond with him. We have been seeing each other at least once a week; he comes over when my son is asleep, we have sex, take a shower, then he leaves—he can never stay. I've noticed that I am going from feeling very high about us, to very low emotionally when I see that he is really not available. Or is he? We never talk about his marriage, though he has mumbled a couple of things that make me think it's not great.

But the thing I am really aware of is how hungry he is to have crazy and passionate sex that he doesn't get from the wife. And I'm hungry for this now, too. So I am the mistress, and it goes from feeling so great to feeling not so great. But, you know, I am also enjoying my independence to be out from under an abusive marriage to a man who was so demanding. And to be uncommitted for now.

So it's hard to explain. While I do have strong feelings for this other man, I am very aware that if he told me tomorrow that he is incredibly in love with me and that he would leave his wife, he is not the kind of guy I would want as a husband. No, because he is disloyal—he is cheating on his wife with me!

Then my emotions flip around, like last week, when I was feeling lonely and sad and empty. So I wrote him an e-mail that said: "This is wrong. You are married, and this isn't feeding me what I need. I need more than sex. I need to feel passion and love without limitations and without boundaries. Look, we are two adults. We had a good time. But this isn't going anywhere. I really hope we can still be friends, because we still will be seeing each other a few times a week."

He e-mailed back quickly: "I understand. You are an amazing woman. I want to be friends. No hard feelings."

But then the next Wednesday, I could sense that this man who is usually so self-confident and happy was a little bit down. He was clearly hurt. Soon I get a text message: "I would love to have one last night with you." So that "one last night," he brought me a necklace and a bracelet and of course, it was not the last night. I am still seeing him, really, whenever I want to. The sex is so good, and our chemistry is so strong.

So right now I'm like "What the f—k? Why not? Maybe this is what I need right now. I deserve this." Even though in my brain I know that he isn't the man I will end up with, I know that emotionally and physically this is something I need right now. I look forward to his e-mails; it is exciting when we plan for our next date. He makes me feel like a sexy woman, and who doesn't want that? Okay, then I hear the voice of the realistic side of me warning me that he is on my mind more than he should be. That I might be a little obsessed. And I don't want to be hurt again by a man.

So here's where I am now, and I have made it very clear to him: When I'm with you, I'm with you totally. And that's what I expect from you, too. To be with me fully in this moment. Then we both can have our other lives. In fact, I just went on Match. com, and I am starting to see some very interesting other men. But my soccer coach is still on the top of my list.

And the more I pull back from him, he starts courting me again vigorously. Recently he has been sending me philosophical love quotes, and we have some very nice phone sex. Then my instincts for craving him take over my brain, and he comes over again, 9:30 P.M., when we know my son is out like a light. Obviously, there is an incredible connection between us that I feel and he feels. I don't buy this shit that men can have sex without feelings. We both are feeling a lot of things.

I don't think I'm in love, but I do think we both know and feel there is love around us. And we both know we need this right now. It makes me feel like a woman again, sexually aroused, giving a man pleasure and getting the pleasure of knowing a man wants me. And having lots of orgasms! It makes us both feel fantastic. The good thing about this sexual affair is that it took that thorn out of my side, that "I need to get laid." Now as I am starting to date again, I will focus more on finding someone with whom I am compatible.

In the meantime, because I'm having such great sex, he is hard to let go. He has brought out my passionate side; I am going a little wild, with no strings attached, and escaping a hurtful marriage. I would recommend this feeling to any woman who is trying to get through a bad divorce.

Ingrid lived without sex for six years before she bailed. Cathy Meyer's sexless marriage went on for nearly three times as long. A tall and spunky redhead, Cathy Meyer is a divorce coach based in Nashville, who knows the subject of divorce distress intricately, from both sides of the couch. She was married for seventeen years to a Navy pilot who withheld sex and compassion but heavily laid on the humiliation. I discovered Cathy's inspiring and provocative voice when she published a blog about sexless marriages in *Huffington Post* Divorce. During a follow-up interview with Cathy I learned more about a sexual drought that many spouses are in but are too embarrassed to divulge.

The mother of two grown boys, Cathy speaks in a sugary Southern drawl about the demolition of her marriage, which caused her "to come apart in a million pieces." She has harnessed the strength gained from piecing herself back together again into a busy divorce coach practice in which she guides other women on the path toward regaining wholeness.

CATHY MEYER

All those years, I was trying to fix something in myself that was broken in him. I had to open a vein and let it all spill out before I could become a whole, sexual being again. You can't put a lid on this and ignore it, or else you will tear yourself apart forever.

I finally knew I was pushed over the edge when I woke up screaming because of a dream I had about this marriage. I felt like a war veteran having a bloody flashback.

Some people are okay to live and die without sex, but I am not one of them. For me, the need for sexual bonding with my husband was a very deep desire. And I know from the work that I do as a divorce coach that mine is a common cry. There are many, many women like me who internalize a painful, sexless marriage for so long, and they are relieved to find out: "I'm not alone. This isn't my fault. I deserve a loving, kind, and generous partner."

Our relationship began well. He was kind, loving, and highly sexual. He couldn't keep his hands off me. It was the most amazing sex I had ever had, and I was like *Wow—I get to spend the rest of my life with this man!*

I swear to you, the night we married, the sex stopped. Several things played into my husband's failure to form an intimate bond with me: He was molested as a child by a Catholic priest. He had a very domineering mother who was a devout Catholic;

her purpose on earth was to procreate. Sixteen pregnancies and eight live births are proof that she did that well. She failed miserably at actual mothering, though.

I, on the other hand, was raised in a household where my father's alcoholism was the main focus. A miserable way to live, but it taught me unconditional love. My mother, my sister, and I adored my father. We forgave him when he needed it and excused him based on his frailties.

My husband never learned to love; I learned to love to a fault.

He said he was too tired to make love on the honeymoon and he continued to be tired 90 percent of the time over the course of a seventeen-year marriage. We had sex four times a year on the average; very rarely did he initiate it. When he did initiate sex, he wanted oral sex or a hand job. He wanted me to perform sex on him, not to have sex with me.

I felt degraded, but internalized my hurt and anger. I really thought there must be something wrong with me. I kept trying to be better and better.

Outwardly he was an affectionate man. We held hands. We cuddled on the couch and watched television. But in bed he gave me five minutes to cuddle and when the time was up, I had to go back to my side of our California king. It was humiliating to live like this for all those years. I don't know how I came out of the marriage emotionally intact.

People would look at us and think we had a good marriage. We didn't argue. We had nice kids together. Everyone was shocked when we divorced. I was very unhappy about our sexless marriage but in the end, I didn't leave him—he left me.

We had not had sex for four months, and this one day, I was in the living room and he was on his way to work. He was a pilot and he was wearing his flight suit. Those suits zip up from the bottom or down from the top—talk about easy access! He started hugging me, then he reached down, zipped up, and pulled it out, in all its glory. I did what I had often done, gave him oral sex, and off to work he went—with a smile on his face.

Four months later, we had driven the boys to spend the night with their grandparents, and on the way back to the house, he reached in the backseat and pulled out a *Playboy*. I thought to myself, *I'm going to get lucky tonight!* I was so starved for sex by that time, I would have paraded other naked women in front of him just to get him interested in screwing me again.

We got home. I shaved, ran a bubble bath, and when I came into the living room, naked and ready, he was watching a movie on television. I lit a fire and lay down on a blanket in front of the fireplace. And he looked at me with this expression on his face that said *If I have sex with you, it will kill me*, a look of just complete and total dismissal. And every time before when he had dismissed me, I took it to heart, I made it about me and my worth. This time was different, though; this time I knew it was about him, not about me.

He got up off the couch and stepped over my naked body, and said: "I'm going to bed; are you coming?" I said that I would be there in a moment, then I rolled my naked body up in the blanket and cried myself to sleep on the floor.

The next morning, he got on the floor and he was trying to get inside the blanket with me and put the moves on me, and the lid blew. I can remember I was staring at the ceiling and I fell apart in a million pieces. I just started screaming, "I have spent seventeen years living this hell and for the love of God, you are killing me, you are killing me!" He got up, picked up his car keys, said, "I'm going out to get a Coke," and he never came home again.

Never. That was the end of it. He never stepped foot in our

home again; he sent a friend to get his things. Our kids were seven and fourteen. I was devastated. After years of sexual rejection, he deals me the ultimate rejection. He didn't just leave me; he left all three of us.

He gave me no reason for leaving, which left my head spinning and thinking the worst. *Maybe he is gay?* or *Maybe he is having an affair?* The gay question had crossed my mind before, but he had always enjoyed pornography in films and online, and his tastes were heterosexual when it came to porn. He also kept *Playboys* and *Hustlers* in the house, so I assumed it wasn't a gay issue, it was a Cathy issue. I figured I'm ugly as hell, fat as hell, and worthless as hell.

Rebuilding your life after a long trauma like this has been a slow process—one step at a time. My self-esteem was so low. I thought, when he walked out that door, it was final proof that I wasn't worthy of being cared for and loved by a man. I would often tell myself, "Maybe you are asking for too much from a marriage." But all I was asking for was intimacy and sex.

We have been divorced for over a decade and I've come to realize that my ex is literally the walking wounded. He didn't want a wife; he wanted a mother, someone to fix all his childhood issues. Speaking out on the subject has been a wonderful release, a purge, and a big part of my recovery process. I get dozens and dozens of letters from women and men in the same situation. It makes me happy in my divorce consultation practice that I can give them advice based on my own mistakes and failure to take action.

When we divorced I had not worked in fifteen years. I was a stay-at-home-mom, and a wife. He walked away with 87 percent of his income, leaving me to raise two children with the rest. It took me five years of getting my masters degree and building my own business to get to a point of feeling financially stable and able to pay the bills, help my sons with college expenses and to not fear losing my home.

It also took a long time to allow myself to have another relationship. We were divorced four and a half years before I ventured out into the dating field again. And while there were plenty of men who wanted a long-term thing with me, I found that I didn't want a committed relationship. I wanted to rebuild the sexual confidence I had lost during my marriage. It felt great to have sex again. It was fun!

Then I met a guy who I wanted more from than just sex, and we dated for a year. Then he died on me! I was devastated. But he left me with a gift: It is amazing what you can learn about yourself when romantically involved with a self-confident, emotionally healthy man. Since then, there have been other men who have lit my pants but not my soul.

Many women have a skewed reality; they think, *Oh, this must be normal in long-term marriages, not to have sex.* It is not normal unless both people are on the same page about their sexuality. Some need it, some don't. There is a plethora of ways to create intimacy with another human being, but sexual bonding is a primary way. I can tell you in my divorce practice that 99 percent of the time, the reason a couple splits up is from not feeling sexual or intimate, or not having sex at all. And when this has been going on for years, the majority of the time, someone is involved in an affair.

I have found that sex can get better with age—it has for me, oh my God, it really has. I have a deep appreciation for the power of orgasms and the importance of embracing my sexual needs as I age. I am very comfortable with my sexuality, considering what I went through.

As for my ex-husband, in case you are wondering what happened to him, he is going through another divorce.

I am not surprised that most of the clients in Cathy's divorce practice are sex-starved spouses who finally yell "Enough!" When it comes to choosing a lifetime partner, sexual attraction gets the relationship started, but the ability to stoke that flame over time into a deeper intimacy is the real ticket to marital survival.

Staying intimately connected, which is the magic of romantic love, takes conscious and consistent attention, even work. Over-scheduled and splayed between professions and family demands, we understandably forget to be intimate with a spouse, or to even *want* to be intimate. Someone is too tired. Someone is too grumpy. A wife is struck with the menopausal blues. A husband has erectile dysfunction from too much stress, or from his blood pressure medicine. During these dry spells, a couple can fall back on their emotional foundation to carry them through the slack in libido, which, hopefully, is temporary.

Along with that bond of intimacy, you also want someone who listens, someone whose opinion you respect. You want someone who makes you laugh and who backs away from an argument before it turns into a nasty fight. You want someone who is not too stubborn to say, "I was wrong and you were right." You want a teammate, not a control freak, like Monica married.

Monica's itch to move on also came as she neared the seventeen-year mark. Her marriage to a bossy, entreprenuerial and irresistible man had superficial luster but lacked the inner glow of real love. In their Florida community, she and her husband were the "It couple" who appeared to have it all. With black wavy hair and voluptuous curves, Monica is gorgeous and rich, earning six figures as a real estate broker. Her ex is also gorgeous and rich, earning seven figures as a developer. They threw Gatsbyesque parties in their penthouse apartment overlooking the Atlantic Ocean. Their idea of a quick getaway was four days in Morocco or Marbella on a private plane. Her engagement ring was a marble-size sapphire.

Unlike Cathy, Monica had sex whenever she wanted it—but it was sex on demand with a man she describes as a "sex addict who had no capacity for love."

I met Monica on a Southwest flight from Baltimore to San Diego. Dressed in blue jeans and riding boots, she whisked on board just as the doors were about to close and wedged herself into the middle seat of the row in which I was on the aisle. Soon after takeoff, I began pounding away on this chapter on my computer. Monica leaned over and said, "I am not eavesdropping, but I couldn't help seeing the words *sex* and *divorce* a lot on that page."

I told her I was working on a chapter on divorce in a book on female sexuality.

"Man, do I have some stories for you!" she responded.

Riveted after five minutes of conversation with this fifty-one-year-old divorcée, I flipped my laptop shut and we talked across the country.

MONICA

I got married at the age of thirty-three, and lived what looked on the outside to be a charmed life. Bob was handsome, sophisticated, successful, from the South, and eighteen years older than me. Friends referred to him as my movie star boyfriend.

But I married on the rebound. Just before I met Bob, I had just gotten out of a relationship with the first real love of my life. He was conservative and not ambitious, and I am liberal and very driven. Our lifestyles and interests were so different, but we just had this incredible chemistry, some of the best sex of my life. I met Bob at a time when I needed to get out of this pain. Bob wined and dined me all over the world. He pursued me so hard, and I realized it was time to start a new life—even though I still had a broken heart.

I ended up spending sixteen years with Bob—we had a lot of common interests. Our business successes and interests were aligned. We were both very much into the arts and culture. Our sons were the same age. We lived the life! We owned a penthouse apartment with five bedrooms on two floors and 1,800 square feet of roof garden. We had black tie parties that would go down in history. We were the It couple—but we were sexually incompatible.

No one loves sex more than I do, but he was a sex addict. He needed sex constantly. It was never a discussion if I had an exhausting week or an exhausting night that maybe I wasn't in the mood. With Bob, it was sex on demand. And he would get pissed off if I didn't want to do it—right from the start, I should have ended it right after what happened the night we got engaged.

We had an amazing dinner at this tiny Italian restaurant in New York City, with a $200 bottle of wine, and he pulled out this huge antique sapphire ring. How could I turn this down? I convinced myself that not everybody gets to be madly in love. I had an incredible lifestyle with this man. So while I wasn't wildly in love with this person, I was wildly in love with this life.

So we got back to our hotel; I was exhausted—after an evening that started with *Phantom of the Opera*, then a long dinner with martinis, wine, and champagne, I said, "Let's wait until the morning"—and he went ballistic. He yanked the engagement ring off my finger. It was shocking.

But I married him because, on so many other levels, he was stimulating to me. He has a great mind, and intelligence is seductive to me. But he had no capacity for intimacy. He just wanted sex, and that was not at all sexy to me; it's a turnoff. Yet we coasted through the years in grand style. It was an easy life after a broken heart.

Oh, did I mention that I am Bob's fourth wife? I knew the problems we were having could not be all my fault with that track record. We would talk about separation, but we stuck it out. I would justify it like this: Everybody doesn't get to be in love. We are good friends. We have joined our families together. And I would try and ignore the fact that we were both plain miserable. During this time, I was diagnosed with cervical cancer, and I am thinking that my body is never going to heal unless I leave this marriage.

He beat me to it. One night, Bob came home around 3:00 A.M. and he had this glazed look on his face. His lips were actually bruised, so I could tell that he was coming from a long make-out session. A few days later, he said to me, "I can't live like this anymore." Turns out he was having an affair, and he is still married to her several years later. I guess number five is the winning ticket for him, though I can't imagine she's not miserable, too.

He hired a bulldog attorney, so I got the biggest and meanest dirtball of an attorney, too. We went through really tough negotiations, and I did okay monetarily, but his girlfriend's requirement was that he would sever all ties with me. While this is going on, I find out the cancer is back. The doctors tell me I need to get a total hysterectomy, which I do, except I insisted they leave my ovaries in so I would continue ovulating.

Right after my last surgery is the only time I have spoken to my ex-husband since the divorce. He called to tell me he was sorry about not being there for me, in a really cold, brittle voice. Then he sent me a ten-page letter telling me how angry he was about all the money he had to pay out.

I cried and cried and couldn't stop crying. Eventually, I realized how fulfilling my work had always been to me, so I went back into real estate.

This is how I met the second love of my life, who owned the company where I was hired. When we first shook hands, I felt that energy, that excitement, when you know something is going to happen. Soon after, he walked up to me when I was leaving work and said, "Do you want to have a drink?"

That led to the most amazing love affair. I would line the walkway leading to my door with candles and put flowers all over the house. I would make beautiful meals and put on beautiful music. He would come in the door and hold my face and we'd start kissing and then make love. We were insatiable. When you feel like this, it erupts on a base, instinctual level. It comes from the tonal qualities of a voice, the scent, the vibration in the air—those are the sensory stimuli that move us into deep, soulful, sexy relationships.

What ended my affair is that the universe intervened with 9/11. I was in New York at the time, at a hotel on Fifth Avenue, watching the towers fall on TV. Everyone started to reevaluate their lives after 9/11 occurred, and for him, that meant there was no way he was going to leave his wife and family. People everywhere were clinging to their security, and realizing the fragility of life.

In a way, I feel lucky that lightning has struck twice for me. I've had two great loves. I am in my early fifties now, and my expectations have evolved. I will never again sacrifice myself on a spiritual and psychological level to a man like I did with my husband. I am looking to have an intimate connection with someone that goes much deeper than sex, and with someone who is not married.

Though dating at this age is a real challenge because you

are dealing with people who are fixed in their personalities, and likely hurting from other failed relationships. However hard it was going through a bad divorce, I find it exhilarating to be moving on a path of new self-discovery. I haven't felt this exhilaration since my twenties. I am open to having a serious relationship again, but it has to be the right combination of emotional depth and sexual chemistry. It has to be the whole package.

Though I am not looking to be saved by a man. I saved myself. I am financially independent and successful on my own.

As I am writing up Monica's story of a high-earning woman who doesn't need to be "saved" by a husband, a report came out that mothers are now the top earners in four out of ten households in the United States. These findings released by the Pew Research Center spotlight the breadwinning capability of the new female powerhouses, a cultural shift that demographers say is irreversible and rising. Yet money of their own in the bank, and the ability to feed and educate their kids without a second income, does not take all of the hardship out of splitting up a marriage. Many of the women I spoke to who are going through a divorce feel initially like Jill Clayburgh's character Erica feels, like puking in a garbage can, which she did in the 1978 Paul Mazursky film *An Unmarried Woman*, when her husband announces he was bailing. And my sources ride the same roller coaster of emotions that Erica endures—sadness, rage, confusion, depression.

What is different for today's divorcées is that Erica's affluent life in Manhattan was made possible by her stockbroker husband. Many modern ex-wives can increasingly fend for themselves.

Monica was temporarily weakened while going through her divorce but rebounded because she had herself to fall back on, in the form of a fulfilling profession and a hefty income. And when her self-esteem and self-identity were compromised, she had the self-respect to get out from under an oppressive male. Monica is an exemplary product of the Me Decade of women of the 1970s who gave that early shout-out to demand equality and respect in love partnerships. Actually, Erica does evolve in *An Unmarried Woman* as a whole person beyond her status as a wife, finding solidarity and direction from hanging out with other liberated women who make her realize her self-worth. (Her recovery is also expedited by the arrival of a sensitive and cuddly boyfriend, played by Alan Bates.)

The seventies, which spawned both women's liberation and no-fault divorce (wherein the dissolution of a marriage does not require a show of wrongdoing by either party) blew apart the staid 1950s model of marriage, when brides said "I do, and I will" and did until they died. This meant sticking with husbands who were bullies, gamblers, philanderers, lazy—or all of these things and more. Women had to stay put, through the most horrific of times and particularly when they had children to feed, for the husband was typically the sole economic engine.

Along with monetary dependence, our ancestors clung to their failing marriages as if they were sacred antiques to save face: Until the late 1960s, the D word was still a rare and embarrassing taboo.

Women now occupy more than half of the management and professional positions in the U.S. work force and make nearly a quarter of this country's six-figure salaries—increasingly out-earning their husbands. These growing numbers of wives no longer have to stay in toxic marriages because of financial security, nor be ashamed to say "I'm divorced." Lots of people get divorced for lots of different reasons; sex and money and abuse are often listed as motivators, grating and grating, until someone breaks.

For Renee, a fifty-five-year-old Midwesterner, that grating

came from issues surrounding sex and money as well as piles of junk and piles of bills that awaited her when she got home from eleven hours at the office. Instead of pitching in with domestic chores, she would find her retired husband drinking Scotch on the couch.

Beyond her reputation as one of her city's most popular internists, Renee is also known for her killer outfits, bought with an ample salary she makes as founder of a large medical practice. This hard-driving woman from a middle-class family built her business from scratch, out of ambition and need: Following her divorce her ex cut her child support in half. Renee strides confidently into a hotel bar in high-heeled Mary Janes, a tight black sheath dress and a cropped silver leather jacket. She speaks in a rolling banter that is husky and intelligent, reminiscent of Lauren Bacall. I met Renee at a party and was hooked when she introduced me to the guy she was dating after divorce—her pool man!

Her delivery is laced with self-deprecating laughter and sighs as she explains the imbalance that led her to dissolve a marriage that consisted of her, the sole breadwinner, versus him, the out-of-work spouse who preferred liquor to splitting the domestic chores.

RENEE

That's what made me so resentful about my ex. I would get home at nine at night, and the house was a mess. I stayed in this marriage, though, for twenty years. But I would say the marriage was not really good from the beginning, although we did produce two wonderful children together.

Alcohol was definitely the reason the marriage broke up. My husband's job shifted and his office was relocated to New Jersey. He commuted back and forth to our home, and our marriage was fine as long as we weren't in the same state. Then his company was sold, he retired at the age of fifty-three, then did nothing for the rest of our marriage. I waited for three years after his retirement for him to get a job, to get a hobby, to go back to school, to volunteer, to do something. It didn't happen. He just drank more and more.

Intimacy had long gone by the wayside. I had no desire for sex; it actually got to the point where he was repulsive to me. He made himself feel better by putting me down. He was verbally abusive. An example: He was very good at math, so if I asked him to help me out with the commission structure for an employee, he would do it wrathfully, like "You are an idiot."

Nine years ago, right after our daughter's thirteenth birthday, I pulled the plug. It got to the point where this saying was true: "I'd rather be alone without you than lonely with you."

For years after the divorce, I had no desire to be intimate with a man. My only desire was to be by myself, and I was happy by myself. I did join a club called It's Just Drinks, which is a version of the dating service It's Just Lunch, but I don't do lunch—I work. None of the dates was bad; the men were interesting and nice, but I didn't sleep with anyone. I had no sexual desire for any of them.

What turned my heart was when I found someone who was attractive, he kissed me, and that was that. Something I believed was dead inside of me totally came alive. I never thought I would feel this way again. And it was the pool guy—a grown woman's fantasy!

I didn't think much of him when I first saw him; he was a new pool man I had not met before. It was on a Sunday two years ago, and I was lying topless in my backyard with some friends. In walks this guy to clean the pool. I casually covered myself with a towel and asked him if he wanted to sit down with us and get stoned. We started talking and it turned out we were both invited to the same wedding for the following weekend.

So at the wedding, we met and we chatted and he asked me out. After the first date, we were sitting in my backyard and he kissed me. Two years later, I'm still with him—though things aren't as hot as the beginning, like all love affairs.

In the beginning, I was obsessed with sex. Oh my God, was I into it. I made up for everything I hadn't had for the seven years since my divorce. Oh God, it was great. I was comfortable with him and totally turned on by him; it surprised the hell out of me. What we have sexually I never had with my husband. I'm not robbing the cradle—this isn't a really young pool boy. He is a man who is only a few years younger than me.

I am definitely more accomplished than he is, but the relationship was just such fun and satisfying. We laughed a lot, but he was also sexy. What more could I want? Initially he was like living out that fantasy, screwing my pool boy. I thought the fantasy would go away, but then the relationship kept lasting. So here we are two years later and my feelings about the relationship have changed.

The sex is still good, but it is certainly not as exciting. I used to meet him at the door in lingerie, then I would attack him and be all over him. The honeymoon is over. You're going to lose that honeymoon fever with even the most beautiful and exciting person in the world. When you see someone most days and most nights, familiarity breeds contempt.

I don't see the need to marry him or to marry anyone else right now. I am substantially better off than he is, moneywise, better off than a lot of men I know. That can be intimidating to men, but this guy I'm seeing isn't going anywhere, it seems. After two years, he said to me, "I think we should be at another level." I said, "What level do you want to be at? Do you want to live with me? Do you want to marry me?" He said, "I want more of a commitment." I told him that I'm not seeing anyone else, I spend most of my free time with him. What more does he want? This is as committed as I want to be.

Many women friends are staying in their marriages because of money. I didn't have to. And I like that freedom: I am getting my needs for intimacy met without having to get into the day-to-day wife life. When my mother was unhappy in her marriage and I urged her to leave, she said, "I can't." She didn't have a profession. She couldn't sustain herself financially without a husband. From my teenage years, I always vowed that if I was in a relationship, it would be because I wanted to, not because I had to.

It's nice to have the companionship, to have someone to dance with at parties, to have sex with, but I don't need a man to survive. If I did, I wouldn't have left a marriage. But I am not like the many successful women I know who are married to men they are basically supporting, and they are okay with it, because the guys bring something else to the table and make them happy. The men help around the house, and they help with the wife's business. They are growing and engaging. My ex stopped growing; he refused to learn a new skill or go back to school. He became boring.

So this is what I am grappling with now: I am with a man with whom I have a great time; we laugh, we are compatible in many ways. But it bothers me that if I want to travel with him, he can't go unless I pay for it. I know this is an old-fashioned view even though I'm this modern woman. I don't need anybody to pay for me, but I have an issue paying for a guy. I've been coasting on this problem for a while and rethinking this relationship.

I know that as long as I'm seeing him, I'm not leaving myself open to meet someone else. And as my mother would say, I'm not getting any younger or cuter. But I figure when and if this relationship stops being fun and comfortable and good, then I'll find someone else. Or maybe I won't. I did find out after my divorce that I'm okay just being with me.

As you heard from the outspoken women above, a desire for intimacy and equality were the central goals in choosing dates after divorce. The week that I am concluding this chapter, the book *What Do Women Want?: Adventures in the Science of Female Desire* has just come out. Author Daniel Bergner impeccably reports on the nature of, and myths surrounding, female lust and libido, an engrossing read that also covers the expensive race to develop a Viagra-like pill for women. That women crave intimacy and sexual adventures is something I hear over and over, not only from those divorcing but from the newly married and the happily single. The notion of taking a pill to turn us on, however, has spiked a lot of controversy (further explored in an upcoming chapter) and not a lot of support in my kitchen cabinet of women nor in a larger crowd of women apparently.

"I am not hearing that women want Viagra," says Marge Coffey, a relationship therapist whose Washington-area practice is largely midlife and postmenopausal women, including many coming out of a divorce. "What women want is a partner who is sensitive and interested in having a reciprocal sexual relationship. If that partner is interested in sexually pleasing a woman, then she is turned on. She becomes aroused by what's going on in her head. I am opposed to trying to Viagarize women's sexuality. Viagra and other drugs in that category address the physical capacity for men to get and keep an erection. And a woman doesn't need that—she needs to be able to communicate about what she wants and she needs a partner with whom she can give and receive pleasure."

Here is more from Coffey, who has been a therapist for thirty-three years, on what women want and how best to go about finding suitable partners after divorce. She is now in a committed relationship, found through Match.com, but she was single for many years after ending a marriage that had lasted two decades.

MARGE COFFEY

Some women when leaving a marriage already have a bridge, either a sexual relationship that existed before she left the marriage or an emotional relationship that turns sexual once she is no longer with a partner. Many women express a sense of relief to be out of a conflicted and unhappy marriage. They are no longer questioning themselves whether they should leave, they are no longer walking on eggshells in a marriage. They have the freedom to be by themselves and not have to worry about interacting with a difficult spouse.

In my many years of practice I have noticed an increase in the amount of women who are less apprehensive about leaving an unhappy and unhealthy marriage. Certainly more women are financially independent or at least less dependent upon spouses. But even those women who are still very dependent on the income of spouses are more willing to make the break. These women fear that if they stay in bad marriages they will provide an unhealthy role model for their children, especially their daughters. They opt to even work a second job both for economic necessity and to provide a positive model to take responsibility for one's own happiness and stability.

Making the transition into dating again can be understandably difficult. I will ask the woman going through a divorce, "What's happening with your sexual needs?" Sometimes for her to move forward for sex after marriage, she needs permission from someone close in her life, a best friend or a therapist. When the person is in my office, I have already gotten a sexual history. Most people masturbate throughout their lives and when they are out of their marriage, that is a nice option for them to have. Hopefully, at some point they will also be ready for a new partner.

I think the dating sites are a fabulous way to meet people, reflected by the fact that approximately 90 percent of people meet new partners online in the Washington metropolitan area. You can go to the church social or National Geographic events to meet people, but you aren't likely to be as successful as you are online. I think Match.com is the best site for older women because the pool is larger.

It is crucial for women to give it a lot of thought and develop a strategy before they go online. Many women going through a divorce were married in their twenties, and things are very different now. They may have grown up at a time when women didn't have sex until they were engaged. Now a man can expect sex on the first or second date. How are they going to react? This needs to be thought about beforehand: How will she respond to the invitation for sex? Is she going to say yes? She needs to think about these things before she has that first cup of coffee because sex comes up quickly.

So in the first or second meeting with this person, there needs to be some discussion about whether sex is of interest to either one of them. She wants someone with whom she is sexually matched. Then at some point, preferably in the first few dates, there needs to be a discussion about being tested for STDs and HIV. Yes, and if they are planning to have sex, they should bring a copy of the medical reports. If she is a woman interested in sex but wants to wait a while before having sex, she needs to be clear that she is interested but wants to go slowly. When the woman starts the conversation about expectations, she has the power to set the sexual script for the relationship.

She needs to anticipate that he is going to be anxious when they do have sex, and she is going to be anxious, too. But his anxiety is going to be more obvious, in the form of erectile dysfunction. I believe there is a very specific strategy that decreases the possibility of the man not being able to perform.

She says to him, "I'm a little bit nervous about this. I haven't had sex for a while," or "I have only had sex with one person for the past twenty years. And I am not likely to be as responsive as I will be in the future because I am anxious and uncomfortable and a little bit scared."

She wants this to be a conversation that gives him an opportunity to acknowledge his own anxiety. And hopefully, he will be honest, too, and say something like "When I masturbate, everything works fine, but I am really scared that I may not be able to do what I want to do with you." She then says, "That is totally understandable, so let's assume that whatever happens tonight will be a beginning, a time for us to be close, and we will just see what happens."

The very important result of this exchange: If this is a woman who wants to have a good sexual relationship, she wants a man who knows she is not going to be critical about his sexual capacity. So by initiating this conversation, it's really a plan for the woman to get what she wants sexually, in addition to developing a communicative relationship. That discussion decreases his anxiety and increases her chances of having a satisfying sexual experience.

There is no age limit to the ability to enjoy sex. I have women up until their late seventies in my office who want to become sexual again. The oldest patient was seventy-eight. She had been in a long marriage, she missed many things about the marriage, and she wanted to have another sexual relationship. We had many discussions and she did find a partner whose expectations matched hers, and were reasonable. They were not expecting a two-hour marathon, but it is reasonable for her to expect some quality sex once she has told a new partner what turns her on. A husband learns over a long time what turns a woman on. That sexual script has already been written. A new sexual script needs to be written with the new partner.

In a new relationship, you need to ask him what he likes and tell him what you like. After a divorce, a woman can wait as long as she needs to before becoming sexual again. But there is no question that once it starts up again, a woman has the ability to be sexual until she dies.

What do women want? Women want sex, fun sex, quality sex, and not to be a receptacle. They want a partner concerned about their pleasure as much as his own.

You have heard a lot of voices in this chapter from women expressing what they need and want. So what do men want? I asked a man in his middle forties who has been divorced for five years and who has a packed dating life. His language is down and dirty, yet his tips—no pun intended—are a peek into the male psyche that could help a divorced woman, really any woman, embellish the sexual script she wants to write for her next act.

Frank is a forty-five-year-old copy writer for a Philadelphia advertising agency, and recently divorced from his wife of thirteen years. He is wiry and handsome and wary of the "STD landmines" in the dating field. Nonetheless, he is having a lot of sex, relieved to be "released from a bland marriage."

Since the couple split in 2009, Frank has had three serious girlfriends and many casual hookups. He remembers going after "hot bodies" in his twenties. At midlife, he finds that sex appeal comes more from confidence and a willingness to "ask for what you want in and out of bed" more than perfect physical attributes—advice that mirrors Marge Coffey's.

Here is one divorced man's story of dating in the age of rampant herpes and HPV—and looking for healthy, sexy love while sharing custody of a ten-year-old son with an ex-wife.

FRANK

Suddenly being out there with lots of new people makes you understandably nervous about how vulnerable you are to STDs. Before I become intimate with someone, I do ask them directly: "Have you been tested for everything?" This is the new accepted dating etiquette.

The only time I really freaked out was the first time I slept with someone with herpes. It's a controlled virus, and you don't have to panic just because someone has it. But it made me not want to go down on her, and generally uncomfortable being in bed with her. We broke up soon after sleeping together a couple of times, but it wasn't about the herpes; I just wasn't that into her.

A few months ago, I met a woman I was deeply attracted to, who had herpes, and our sex was very satisfying.

After I got divorced, I realized that women thought when I showed interest in them that I was just trying to get into their pants, that it was all about the sex. It was never about that. When I showed desire to have sex with them, it was a sign of how comfortable I was with that person, of the level of intimacy I felt. If a woman is at ease with herself, that is a turn-on. If she is insecure on our dates and later in bed, that is definitely a turnoff. If she is too eager to satisfy me at her own expense, in and out of bed, I get turned off as well.

I'm looking for someone who matches my energy level, and my enthusiasm for life. I'm looking for someone who also has the same comfort and confidence that I have in bed, so there isn't any weirdness and hang-ups between us. I didn't blow up my marriage to be in a relationship that I don't find fulfilling and full of growth potential.

The growth potential includes sexuality, too—being able to explore our sex lives in ways that are creative, adventurous, and open—something I was not doing in my marriage.

The way I view sex and intimacy doesn't apply to all divorced men, because I have a son. As a single dad, I think the rules and responsibilities are very different, which actually helps me stay balanced. If I were just an unencumbered divorced guy, I think it would be too easy to dip into the self-destructive behavior of trying to screw all women I date, all the time. But being a dad for two and three days a week makes me really appreciate my fun time and spend it wisely.

I do enjoy my freedom on those days off from child rearing. Every guy I know struggles with the issue of monogamy. We're just not hardwired as creatures to be monogamous for so many years. Women maybe, but not men. Fortunately, most men don't follow through on these desires. But I know many of my married guy friends are jealous that I get to have new sexual adventures. Several of them joke that they are vicariously living through me and ask me to share stories.

Once I had an ex-girlfriend come by unexpectedly while I was hosting a poker game. She gave me a blow job outside on my patio while everyone was playing cards inside. Later that same night, a different woman I had met at a dinner party the week before texted me and came over after the poker game was over. She stayed overnight. Nights like that just don't happen once you are married. On other occasions, I've had sex with one woman in the morning and then another woman that night.

Right after the divorce, I did have a period of broad experimentation—always using rubbers. There were some women I'd see about once a month. It was understood that we'd hang out, have dinner or drinks or see a movie, and then have sex. I loved the variety. I hooked up with young and older, Indians, black women, tattooed brunettes, and the occasional blonde. But after a while, you get tired of this rotation lifestyle and feel the desire to settle back down.

This is especially true as a single dad. I used to hook up with a beautiful mature woman who was a lot of fun, but she was only compatible with my single divorced persona; I knew she wouldn't fit well into my single dad persona, she was forty and did not have kids. And I knew there was never going to be a time in the future when I'd want her to meet my son. So I let that one go. I don't know a single woman who wants to hook up who doesn't also want to settle down. That's the danger of messing around with a lot of women.

I have to say, though, I'm enjoying this period of my life. One of the best things about being a divorced guy in his forties is that age range for dates is pretty wide. I've had good relationships and good sex with twenty-five-year-olds and fifty-year-olds. Women at any age are looking for three things in a man: attention, maturity, and success. I can't tell you how easy it is to meet women if you have these qualities.

Okay, here's another downside. There are a lot of single women out there who aren't on birth control. Even when it's determined that they are STD-free, you have to wear condoms. When I was in college, every woman I knew was on the pill. Not now—so many women are avoiding extra hormones because of fear of cancer. Or they are nearing forty, not married, and figure "What the hell if I get pregnant? I've always wanted a child." I've had several pregnancy scares and have had to deal with the morning-after pill once. Not fun.

I really prefer being with older women who are also divorced with kids. She usually has an IUD or another form of birth control, and we can be more spontaneous and not be fearful of unprotected sex. I believe I speak on behalf of all males—having the freedom to come inside a woman without a rubber is always the preferred route. Coming on the stomach or breasts can also be fun, but there's something primal and alpha about ejaculating inside the woman.

Sexual misfiring wasn't the main reason my marriage failed, but for a while, as we struggled to get along, it certainly was a symptom. Toward the end, before we separated, my ex was trying to make things better, so the sex got better. But for a while, we weren't having sex for weeks, and that's just too long.

This may sound sexist to women, but you have to make sure the guy is taken care of. It's really the most important thing in a marriage from the male perspective. My advice to all wives is make sure your husband comes three times a week. It doesn't matter how you do it. Hand job, blow job, intercourse. Get him off, often, and he won't be in any position to complain.

Also, a lesson learned from the divorce front is that variety is the spice of life. Don't get into the same predictable routine every time. Get creative. Surprise him. Jump in the shower and give him a soapy hand job. I once got a blow job while driving on the New Jersey Turnpike and barely managed not to slam into the truck in front of me. I hear from my married friends that women stop or avoid giving blow jobs after many years of marriage.

A woman likes to have variety, too, this I know after my postdivorce experiences. Out of all the women I've been with in the past six years, I remember all of their styles and that's the one thing I miss about monogamy. There's a certain way this one woman gave me blow jobs that I would love to experience again and again and again and again. One woman liked to blow me while she touched herself and made herself come. What guy wouldn't like that? Right now, I've started dating a slightly older woman with whom I have wonderful sex and wonderful communication. Do I miss these other women enough to blow up my current relationship? No way. But I miss the variety.

The point is that women need to understand that men like variety in technique, not necessarily variety in women, and that sex with one partner can get blah and boring. Boredom in the bedroom leads to a wandering mind, which leads to infidelity. So don't be boring! It applies for men and women, gay and straight. You have to mix it up. Try new things. Be open and trusting to do something sexually risky and you will end up feeling renewed.

As for my long-term desires, I've had my thrills. I've slept with a lot of adventurous women over the past six years. Sometimes I wish I could still hook up with them, but that's not realistic. You end up realizing that, over the long haul, what you need is compatibility and love. And part of my whole journey in this postdivorce life was to figure out what I need in a partner because I obviously didn't find it in my first marriage. But you can't figure out who you're compatible with until you get close to them. And you can't get really close to them until you have sex.

So my journey has been a search for the right kind of intimacy. Sex is the ultimate barometer of that intimacy. After all, you're naked and exposed. If either of you is uncomfortable in this scenario, you have a serious problem.

I know if this relationship turns into a live-in gig, I'll be faced with the same old issue again, of feeling that domesticity can absolutely kill the sexual energy of a relationship. I also know, though, from playing the field, that sex can still be hot in a committed relationship if you retain the mischief, the coy surprises.

I started this book by saying that my readers and audience members are preoccupied with two themes when it comes to their relationships—sex and change. Sex and change are certainly at the heart of what divorced spouses must deal with in their fresh forays into new romances. Next up, women share an even more complicated response to sex and change—when divorce leads not only to new partners but also to new partners of the same sex.

PART THREE

~

MIDLIFE MALAISE

CHAPTER 7
SEX AFTER COMING OUT

My relationship with Louise—this is absolutely the most attracted I have ever been to anyone in my life. I do not miss a penis.

—LINDA

I am signing books at a Mother's Day event in Los Angeles, and the woman who is standing last in line requests that I inscribe *The Secret Lives of Wives* to Linda and Louise. I ask her if this is for her and a daughter. She smiles and says, "No, this is for a wife and a wife—and I'm one of them."

We walk together through the hotel lobby to the parking lot, and Linda, svelte in a Diane von Furstenberg wrap dress, tells me that she was married for eighteen years to a man who was like an "overbearing Italian mother." They had two children together and an "okay relationship" with okay sex and okay communication. Nevertheless, her widening unrest rippled steadily with each passing anniversary.

When her husband's job took them from Pittsburgh to Pasadena, Linda, now separated by a continent from gossipy relatives and childhood friends, "became the woman I was meant to be." Soon after she and her husband relocated their family, Linda began a love affair with a woman with whom she is savoring friendship, intimacy, and a blended family of three daughters.

Linda and the other former wives in this chapter, Bon Kyle and Carol, have gone both ways in their sexual desires and serious liaisons. They are all currently in same-sex unions.

A marriage busted up over same-sex desire is hardly the deviance it was considered even a decade ago. As I write this in the summer of 2013, there are ten states, plus the District of Columbia, that now issue marriage licenses to same-sex couples. According to Gallup surveys conducted from June through December in 2012, the national percentage of U.S. adults who identify as lesbian, gay, bisexual, or transgender is 3.4 percent of the population. And a Pew Research Center poll conducted in March of 2013 found that nearly half of Americans favor allowing gay and lesbians to legally marry.

Indeed, hiding a closeted life behind a heterosexual beard is increasingly uncool, and unnecessary. With donor eggs, donor sperm, and rental wombs now a click away on the Internet, same-sex couples are now toting their own biological babies, in front-carrying Snuglis, proudly and openly. Interestingly, though, as gay assimilation is gaining ground, four new gay-themed TV shows, including *The New Normal* and *Partners*, got the ax after season one. This while *Mad Men*, set in the early 1960s with sexist gender roles, has a salivating cult following, five years straight. America is ready. America is not ready.

There *is* that other half of American citizens that still think homosexuality is a sickness or a sin and refuse to deliver eyeballs, which translates into ratings and advertisers, to same-sex couples sharing kisses and a bed on the screen.

For me, watching the 2008 film *Out Late* marked the moment I realized that coming out after marriage was soon to be as ho-hum as anything else people did after divorce. This documentary, with its tagline, "It's Never Too Late to Be Yourself," was produced by Beatrice Alda and Jennifer Brooke and examines seniors who knew they were gay but forced themselves to adapt heterosexual lifestyles. Each person spent decades in conventional marriages raising nuclear families, until romantic epiphanies yanked them into admitting their truth.

Sprung from the closet, these older folks are elated to be free at last. They spent their younger years in times when homosexuality was considered to be a psychiatric illness and even a reason to be institutionalized.

"In those days, you just didn't come out," explains Elaine Webber, who appears in *Out Late*. Webber was reared in rural Pennsylvania during the 1930s. She was always attracted to girls, yet at twenty-four, she did what society dictated young women do: Get married and stay married for more than half a century. Throughout a marriage she called a security blanket, Elaine endured an adulterous husband and experienced her own sideline fling with another married woman.

Elaine was uneducated and unemployed, and she needed a husband to support her family of two sons. If she left, "He could have taken the kids away from me," she said.

Linda had none of the same fears when she came out in a suburb of Los Angeles, and combined families with her partner in a shingled bungalow. She says it would have been much tougher to replicate her life in the blue-collar evangelical community in South Jersey where she was raised: "You can show my relatives and friends back there two women who raised a Pulitzer Prize winner, and most of them would still say we will all rot in hell." In her adopted hometown of Venice Beach, it is considered more outrageous to dislike fish tacos than it is to have two mommys. When Linda met Louise in 1990, the furor of her emotions made her certain that her intuitions as a child had been right all along.

LINDA

Since I was small, I always knew I liked women. But I followed the rules—the most important thing to my mother was that her only child produce grandchildren. I got married when I was twenty-five and my husband was thirty-eight. He was successful and smart and generous, so as a young woman, I got swooped in. He was the quintessential catch, and we stayed married for fifteen years and raised two children together.

When we started dating, I felt it would be dishonest not to tell him that I had been romantic with women as well as men in college. He responded as if it was no big deal. Once we got married, I would say that sex with my husband was satisfying.

My mother and father got divorced when I was six months old, and my mother remarried when I was five. In the 1960s, you didn't have a lot of kids with divorced parents, and my mother was very insecure and ashamed of this, and this made me feel ashamed. Her new husband was the sweetest guy, and he was like a father to me, but I still had a real father who my mother would say terrible things about. It was all very confusing for me.

So you can imagine, when she found out I was in love with a woman, how shameful that was to her. First a divorce, then a gay daughter! It was a shock for my husband, too. He couldn't believe it after he had never said no to me for anything; he served in the role of the perfect husband. But that caring, nurturing husband was like an overbearing Italian mother. It took me years to realize how controlling he was and how smothered I felt. Finally, I couldn't breathe.

During this time of transition, I met Louise, a gay woman with a daughter, and we became very good friends. Not lovers, just close friends. I admired her confidence in being open about who she was. She was one of the early activists for gay rights. At the age of thirty-five, Louise had a baby on her own with a sperm donor. This was twenty years ago, and not common yet.

As our relationship grew, one day my husband was noticing I was becoming more distant from him. Out of the blue, he asks me one day, "Are you gay?" I said, "Yes, I probably am." And he was just astounded. He said, "Then why did you marry me?" We talked about a lot of things, how appreciative I was of the good life he had built for me and our two daughters. I told him that for a long time I had felt I wanted a divorce, that he was so frigging controlling. What I didn't tell him was how relieved I was to realize I was gay, that I finally had an ace in the hole to get out of the marriage.

My relationship with Louise—this is absolutely the most attracted I have ever been to anyone in my life. I do not miss a penis. Now we're going on fourteen years together, and I am still so incredibly attracted to her. It really is a very intimate connection; we sleep very close to each other. Our conversations are intimate. She is one of the smartest people I have ever known, very self-assured, no tolerance for bullshit.

Louise is a very handsome woman. She has never worn makeup. Fashion means nothing to her. She is a minimalist, and

I love that. I, on the other hand, love to dress up. People have said she looks gay, but I think she looks like Jamie Lee Curtis, our dream woman. And she's very strong. Louise was a volleyball champion in college.

Right now, we have no plans to get married. Until gay marriage is legal in fifty states, giving all gays equal rights, we do not plan to have a wedding. Our kids constantly joke that we are a couple of unwed mothers. I don't need a marriage license to validate our relationship. There are a lot of married people who do not have the love, intimacy, and friendship that we have. In our minds, we couldn't be more married.

The downside is that with three daughters and two moms, there are a hell of a lot of hormones in our house. I don't worry which of our children will be gay or straight. I am pretty sure two out of the three of them will experiment. One of them did say to me recently: "I'm like you. I am attracted to both." Because of the shame I felt from my own mother, I have said to them that the most important thing you should look for in a person is someone who brings you happiness.

Loving a woman is easier than being with a man because there is no penis, and the power it stands for. When the man is in the house, he's going to assume the head of the household. When I try to explore it deeply in my mind, the woman-to-woman connection, it's not really about being sexual—it is everything. You get something so deep that is not possible with a man. In Louise, I have a mother, lover, sister, and a girlfriend.

There are still relationship challenges that are not unique to gays or straights. You still have two people coming to the table with different backgrounds and different values. I am frivolous. Louise is frugal. I want the girls to have nice clothes. She could not care less. She thinks I spend too much. So the same shit comes up that you would have in any live-in relationship.

Then there is the shift in desire. Someone wants intimacy more than the other. I used to want it twenty-four hours a day. Now Louise wants it more than me and I am just plain tired. So we have to work on the intimacy balance, just like I had to work on it with my ex-husband. Any time I got naked, he would climb on top of me. The difference now, and it's so wonderful, is that we easily work through problems; I have never felt more uninhibited or comfortable with anybody in my life. I am with a partner who makes me feel totally safe and free.

Before I met Louise, I never had a vibrator, and now I own more than one. It's been surprising to discover how creative and exciting my sex life could be.

During my marriage, I was content with our sex life, and I was loyal in our marriage. Then one day he got home, and I noticed that I had no interest to be intimate anymore. I liked not having someone controlling me, and physical touch was part of that. Louise of course was part of my ability to disengage from the marriage. I really pursued her very aggressively, like a crazy woman. I started to fall in love. I'm surprised she didn't issue a restraining order on me.

She said, "Look, you are a married woman. I don't get involved with married women." But the attraction was overwhelming and one day I said to Louise, "Listen, could I really be the only one feeling this way?" She said to me, "No. I think we could be perfect together." I used to always believe I was bisexual, but I don't think that anymore. I am a gay woman, and I'm very comfortable with that. And now I feel like I have a new lease on life.

At the age of fifty-three, I am living my life as a whole new person, and a whole person.

Linda's proclamation that "I am a gay woman" is not something I heard across the board when talking to wives who had left husbands and acquired same-sex partners. Several of those women who left traditional unions told me vehemently that they were averse to being labeled. You will soon meet one of these women, Carol, who strikes down long-held stereotypes that if you are not straight, you must be gay.

As a college professor, I can tell you this—the students know what is really happening, that there are subtle gradations to gender identification that do not fit neatly into two boxes. Do not call someone she or he if they refer to themselves as "ze." These are the proponents of the New Free Love, eagerly signing up for courses in sexuality and gender studies, a major that is becoming one of the most popular fields of study on campuses nationwide. We are certainly seeing heightened interest at American University.

I asked an American University colleague, Gay Young, associate professor of sociology, who directed the Women's, Gender, and Sexuality Studies program for a decade, about her area of academic specialty, which is becoming a mainstay of college curricula. Gay (who is in a *straight* marriage) was the force behind establishing American University's new minor in sexuality and queer studies in 2013.

DR. GAY YOUNG

In the academic world, we are seeing a deepening interest among students in how old sexual scripts and gender relations and expressions are changing. What seemed like fringe sexual practices to past generations are at the center of contemporary students' college experiences. Engaging in historical studies of sexuality and asking sharp intellectual questions that queer (used here as a verb) sexuality and gender, they under-stand that the relation between gender and sexuality is com-plex and about more than just identities like lesbian and gay. These fields of sexuality and queer studies are lenses through which to see possibilities for bringing about change in society.

Variation in sexual practice, as Alfred Kinsey and researchers who came after him have been telling us for more than fifty years, is a part of human "nature"—not an aberration. Although I have taught women's and gender studies courses since 1991, I have to admit the unabashed openness about sexuality among students sometimes surprises me. I offered a course on masculinities a few years ago, and at the end of the semester, the students empha-sized that while we did talk a lot about sexualities, I should have included material focused on BDSM (bondage, domination, and sadomasochism). I wasn't quite prepared for that!

Their interests are sending a very clear message: Young people are challenging heteronormativity, and they are en-gaged in queering the social world through widely variant vi-sions of the potential of sexuality and gender. Right now the norm of heterosexuality remains a major organizing principle of social life, but students today are denaturalizing gender and sexuality in ways that upend notions of heterosexuality as nor-mal. That process carries potential for profound reorganization of social relations and institutions.

Carol would be classified as part of the "widely variant vi-sions" that Gay describes. She is a woman of fifty-one who re-fuses to have her sex life affixed with a label; in fact it makes her angry when people do. Carol was in a fourteen-year marriage that produced two daughters and is now in a same-sex partner-ship of thirteen years. She has blond hair and probing blue eyes, and is wearing black jeans topped by a red drapey sweater. Along with her two college-age daughters from her marriage, Carol has a nine-year-old son with her female partner, who just turned forty and carried the pregnancy. She says she is attracted to both men and women, yet she testily warns *not* to call her a lesbian or bisexual.

CAROL

When people call me a lesbian, I balk. I've never thought of myself with that label, even though I've been with my partner for thirteen years. I was with my husband for fourteen years and during that time I never labeled myself a heterosexual. I am me, and I am with a woman partner at this point of my life.

Do I miss having sex with men? Yes. But comparing sex with men and women, although tempting, misses the point. I believe that my late-blooming attraction to women was a deep desire for intimacy. Women have been so much closer physically for centuries, and sexual attraction is a logical extension. As for sex with a woman, yes, there is a level of intimacy that might be hard to access with a man. But in the end, I believe it is more about one's own willingness to let go of what gender you love and focus on who you are loving.

My divorce hinged on my belief that I needed to be with a woman. Was this true? Did it mean anything bigger than where I was at the time? I have no answers. When I researched why this is, I came to understand that some women in midlife are looking for a deeper connection. Perhaps they have had long-term inklings of being gay but never acted on it, or become attracted to someone, or are motivated by others who have made similar moves. If my former husband had been more open to me exploring this side of myself and not been threatened, we might still be together. Who knows?

As for my life today, I am content and in love with my partner. Yet as a family it's not been easy for many reasons, most of them related to blending families where new patterns, expectations, and balancing needs becomes more complicated.

I brought older children to the equation and then my partner and I had a child together. One way it is quite different is in my switched role from primary mom to secondary mom in relation to the younger child. I've often felt like I was the "Dad" in that no matter how much you care, the bond between child and mother is tough to crack. In fact, I get Father's Day and my partner gets Mother's Day, and it's kind of strange but also fun.

As a couple, we are best friends. We share our deepest fears, vulnerabilities, and challenges and can talk for hours. For many women, this is a gift, since we love to process!

As for sex, that has faded into the background for us. We, like many others, have what in the gay community is called "lesbian bed death." This means cuddling takes over from a lot of sex, but the intimacy and friendship remains strong—at least it has for us. In the end, we know we can rekindle that passion. But right now, with a young son at home, we find comfort and gratitude in knowing the flame stays steady and warm in so many other ways.

Leaving a straight marriage in search of "a deeper connection" was expressed in all cases during my interviews in this chapter. The attainment of intimacy was spoken about, reverently, as a state that supersedes the physicality of sex. I admit that at times I felt jealous of what these women described. They get a two-way channeling of nurturing, mirroring, and support at the end of each busy day, in their Girls' Night In. I know of only a few marriages in which a woman feels she is getting the empathy and unconditional love from a man that she receives from her sisters, or girlfriends.

That is why we have Girls' Night Out.

Because it is my job to be nosy, I asked the women who left husbands to be with women if they missed the closeness of a male body, more specifically, the pleasures of a penis. Carol was the only one who admitted to harboring "fantasies" about having sex with males. The others I interviewed told me something that is really the crucial message of this book: The achievement of true intimacy is more of the mind than the body.

I have spent close to thirty-five years interviewing women on what they want and need—and are not getting. "Having it all" is a cliché that is overused and generally not true. Bon and Deb come as close to embodying those words as any couple I have ever met. They both left long marriages and have been partnered for eighteen years, and they are that twosome you observe and know instantly they "belong together." Tanned and hard-bodied in shorts and T-shirts, they are both wearing bandannas around their necks and dangly earrings and sunglasses. Bon and Deb radiate serenity, best-friendship, and a hotness that is palpable in their adoring glances and how they lean into each other. A part of them seems to always be touching.

After enduring prejudice and the pain of splitting up families, they are savoring a happily-ever-after phase in a new home in The Villages, Florida, where Bon is on a softball team and runs a women's swim program called Aqua-SHYNE, for "Stretch Heal Yoga Nurture Exercise." Deb is also involved in swimming programs, working especially with those who are fearful of the water, having experienced near-drownings.

Buoyed by love and exercise, the seventy-one-year-old Bon tells their story and her story of what it feels like to be what we all aspire to in love—"soul mates."

Bon Kyle

My former husband and I were never soul mates. We took care of each other in the best ways that we knew. We cherished our children, as they did us. We are as close now as ever, probably even more so. And my former husband and his new wife have a house in The Villages as well, and we get together often when they're here.

I never realized what the depth of the term *soul mate* meant until I met Deb. Within two weeks of our first meeting, Deb and I came to serious terms on the true impact of what it felt like to really fall in love. After eighteen years together, I am still blessed with a partner who loves me and honors me for who I am, and who we are together. I never have a fleeting glance at another woman or man. We are truly living the life of active teenagers as we settle into our senior years.

We don't have the red-hot sex life we once had, jumping on each other as soon as we walked in the door. Deb is very concerned about losing that intimacy. She has been the more sexual of us as a couple, but we still are very close. We're twelve years apart, me being the elder gal. It's a different level of attraction now, still very physical and intimate, yet with the soul mate properties even deeper now. Our friends tell us that the looks we give each other say *I want to gobble you up.*

Deb taught me to kiss, I mean really kiss with meaning. She loves to kiss, and now so do I. I really wasn't fond of kissing men, and it took me a while to really learn how to kiss a woman. I love to watch her dance, even alone in the house with her earbuds in. Without sounding too goofy, so many times we say to each other, "Uh-oh, it just happened again . . . I fell in love with you once again."

We still try to look good for each other. She loves it when I am very tan, which I am right now. I have lost twenty-five pounds recently. She calls me her "skinny bitch." But she is more the woman in this relationship. She does more of the cooking and cleaning. I'm the guy, I do the man chores. She will wear a sundress. I don't own any dresses, though I am adding some feminine touches to my look. I let my hair go curly, and Deb loves to mess with my hair.

I was outed in college, and it was traumatizing in 1959, when the Twist was coming in and no one was coming out. I was a freshman, and I was involved with a young woman who was a senior. She was the head dorm counselor, and when our relationship was discovered, she was expelled from college. My roommate told on us—she had known I was leaving our room in the evening to be with this woman in her single room. Many times, we'd just go for walks and talks. I realized I had an attraction to her but I thought there was something wrong with me. Sometimes it was 2:00 A.M. when I would sneak back into my own room.

The dean of women called me in and told me the allegations, that we were accused of homosexual activity. I was told never to see this woman again, that she was leaving the school. I was being allowed to stay, but I would have to go to counseling for the next year. It was a small private college in New England, so many on campus soon knew about the situation. At that time, I don't think I even knew the word *gay* or *lesbian*.

After this happened, my friend came to visit me over Christmas vacation from another state. I remember going to the movie *The Ten Commandments* with her and she told me that I wouldn't see her again after that visit. I was so confused and devastated. And to this day, I have not seen nor heard from her, ever.

During her visit, we sat down with my parents in the living

room and told them about our relationship. My parents were Southern Baptist. My mother was sobbing. My father courteously asked her to leave.

In 1992, over thirty years later, my husband and I went together to the nursing facility and told my parents about our pending divorce. Once again, Mother sobbed, as I did also. Daddy, in his eighties and ill, said, "Does this have anything to do with that girl you met in college?" We responded by nodding our heads yes.

It was hard to leave my husband because he is a great person, and had been so tolerant, trying everything to coerce me to stay. He told me later that he lived with the fear throughout our marriage of losing me to a woman. Of course I knew he loved me, and I him, just as I still do. Just in a different way. Thirty-three years prior, when I met him in college, we became friends during that painful time of my life. It did become romantic, as I so wanted to be normal, and it did feel right and good at the time.

We did some sensual things together—dinner by candlelight, cuddling on the couch, walking hand in hand—but there was very little premarital sexual activity. Although knowing about my incident with the woman, he still pursued our relationship, as I did, too. He was very entertaining, was such a gentleman to me, and was very good-looking. I wanted very much to be with him, to be with a man, to do what was considered normal.

Homosexuality was considered a disease in the medical books, so I was terrified for a while because I thought there was something seriously wrong with me. He broke through a barrier for me; it was a relief when I was able to form an emotional attachment with a man. I had several boyfriends in my teen years—always guys who could play ball as well as me, plow driveways during snowstorms, would let me play touch football. But rarely did I even kiss one.

My marriage was wonderful; the births of each child enhanced the joy. I was very maternal, nurturing and loving each one in special ways. Our very successful business—a private sports and fitness school for children and adults developed on our property—allowed me to have the kids with me at any time. Oh, yes, I was very happy and content. I had been so enmeshed in motherhood and the business; I didn't dwell on our lack of true intimacy. When our last child moved on from our home, I felt empty, lost, and lonely.

I became friendly with some younger women, and one night we went to a gay bar. I saw that I was still very attracted to women, and I thought: "Oh my God, what has happened? This is impossible. I have a family." I quickly fell for a much younger woman who was already in a relationship. As hurtful as it was, she ultimately taught me some solid lessons about accepting myself for who I was and to learn techniques to control my unimaginable guilt.

It got to the point where my husband and I decided that I had to move out of our home. He knew I was seeing women, and our marriage was in upheaval. I told the children one at a time, their reactions ranging from the adjectives *courageous* to *desperate*. There were tears to silence to screams as each of my four precious babies responded in different ways. I very pathetically ended each encounter curled into a fetal position, shaking in sobs. I perceived that the gay issue was not what impacted them as much as the fact that leaving their father meant the dissolution of the All-American family.

Within several weeks, I moved out of our beautiful five-bedroom home and perfect life into a one-bedroom apartment on the third floor, about twenty minutes away. After a few days,

I remember sitting by myself in the very small kitchen making pasta and salad and thinking, "I am okay. I don't feel lonely. This is the real me."

I started coaching gymnastics and track at the local high school, and the soccer coach said to me, "The mother of one of my players is going through the same thing as you. She is struggling with coming out and upset about leaving her family and husband. Would you ever share your story with her?" We met each other and this was Deb. We went out to a dinner that lasted three hours, consisting of each of us saying, "Me, too," and "I understand this, I've been through this, too," and "I know what you mean." It was a meeting of the souls. We had such similar situations with our very happy marital experiences prior to the pain and agony.

At one point early into our introduction to each other, Deb had mentioned that a group of women were going to a soccer game over the weekend. As I got there, I wasn't sure that I would even recognize her, and I was trying to remember exactly what she looked like. I look down the row and I see this drop-dead gorgeous woman sitting there in a Carhartt rust brown jacket. All of a sudden, that woman said, "Bonnie?" and it was Deb.

After the game, we went out to get wings, and it was one of those restaurants where you get crayons to write on the white paper tablecloth. We talked and we talked, and while we were talking, I looked over and noticed she was sketching the letter *B*. Leaving that restaurant was the turning point—she was walking to her car and I was walking to mine, and when I went to say good-bye, I reached for her, and my fingers lightly touched her cheek. "Maybe I will see you again." That moment, we both felt something powerful.

One week later, I was coaching gymnastics at the high school and I looked up and she was standing in the doorway in a black skirt and a red blazer with black pumps. She had stopped by to see me. I looked up and was just startled, and I felt "Oh, wow." We kept seeing each other, and our love very quickly was clear. This was in 1995, and we have not turned back since. I was fifty-five and she was forty-three. We had seven children between us—the youngest would live with us soon after that for four years. But I would say that meeting Deb at that time truly saved my life.

When I introduced Deb to my daughters, I said: "I want you to meet the woman with whom I'm going to spend the rest of my life." They asked, "Mom, how do you know?" I knew. We had connected in the deepest place. We were incredibly romantic. Our worlds just meshed. This is the person with whom you are certain, when I am down, she will pull me up.

We don't feel a need to be married again. We both had long-standing marriages, and we honor what we had. My former husband is one of our best friends. Deb and I had a commitment ceremony, and all of our seven children participated. It was held in our church with over a hundred family and friends. This is not a second marriage. This is a commitment of the heart and the soul. A woman knows what another woman wants. A woman knows the basic, inner, deep needs of a woman. We know each other's sensitivities. We know our hormone cycles. Women generally are more giving. Women are more communicative. My husband used to say, "You tell your girlfriends many more things than you tell me." It was true. We can bounce off each other. We let each other be exactly who we really are.

I remember the first time we totally outed ourselves to strangers. We went on a cruise a few years after we became a couple, and there were five other couples at our table, all heterosexual. The first evening meal, introductions went around the table. "Hi, I'm Betty, and this is Jack, and we're from Oregon, and we have been married for twenty-five years."

We were the last couple to introduce ourselves, and I said, "Hi, I'm Bon, and I've been married thirty years, and Deb has been married twenty-four years. This is our fifth anniversary together." People were like "OHHHHH, that's interesting." By the end of the night, all of us were laughing and just having these very effervescent conversations. All of a sudden, we were okay; we weren't really freaks. There seemed to be an unexplained aura the rest of the cruise as each night, couples would shuffle about to sit next to us. We were later described as "this really cool lesbian couple."

When I think about what I had to go through in college, and then again thirty-three years later, I am so thankful for the rights and freedom that young people have at the present. At our ages now—seventy-two and sixty—Deb and I are proud to be open and show others it is okay to have a same-sex relationship. We just happen to be two people who work and play well together, and love each other deeply and completely.

Hmm, what did I tell you? They have it all—or most important what feels like "it all" to them. They *are* in love. So are many straight couples who are featured in this book and have been able to make their relationships last.

"I'm in love." How many times have we heard this phrase from siblings and friends and offspring? Love, what is love? Writers and philosophers and analysts through the ages have tried to define this elusive, essential force that binds us and builds us as humans. I have spent more than half my life listening to people talk about wanting love, finding love, and losing love. I have no idea how to explain the unique combustion of chemicals and hormones and timing and mind-sets that form love and sustain love.

But I do know it when I feel it, and when I see it. I also know that love and intimacy take a lot of hard work; these states we hope will flow in our lives do not just stream effortlessly. This book thus far has focused on how people tackle that work at varying stages and ages of life, with lots of different takes and views, and ups and downs. At this point, the thread that binds all of the women I interviewed is their realization that a healthy self-esteem, and a healthy acceptance of one's body, helps greatly in the development of sexual health and fulfillment.

Next, I examine a group of women who must reconfigure their self-images and sexual functioning as they heal from the loss of their breasts to cancer, the parts of our female anatomy that gives nourishment to babies, and are fondling toys of sublime arousal to men and women alike. Boobs, headlights, honkers, hooters, Bonnie and Clyde—there are many pet names for those two soft hills, worshipped throughout time, that stick out from our chests and tell the world "I am woman."

How does a mastectomy affect a woman's sense of her femininity, and the structure of her intimate relationships? The women in the next chapter open their hearts and show how the real power of our sexuality and femaleness lies in our minds.

CHAPTER 8
SEX AFTER BREAST CANCER

I don't look at my breasts the same anymore. I used
to see vanity, and now I see my future.

—HEATHER BERGER

I am at an outdoor high school graduation party for my girlfriend's son Wade on a sauna-like Saturday night. A couple
walks in with their two young children, a boy and a girl. The man
is portly and tall, and his wife is small and wiry, with short Audrey
Hepburn hair. She joins me at the buffet, and we dig into fat tor-
tellini strewn with strips of parmesan, laughing how the heaped
pasta on our plates will be bad for the summer bikini season.

We introduce ourselves and ask each other about our jobs.
Sophia Michels is an assistant teacher at her kids' elementary
school. I tell her I am working on a book about how sex changes
after just about everything imaginable that can happen in a
woman's life.

"Like cancer?" she asks with an expression that is both winsome and pained.

Sophia shares with me that five years ago, at the age of thirty-seven, she was diagnosed with Stage III breast cancer. She had her left breast removed and reconstructed, then endured months of chemotherapy and radiation that left her weak and bald and frightened that she would not live to see her kids enter kindergarten. Today, Sophia is cancer free, her spirit is indomitable, and her hair is back.

"I was like the Warrior Woman after my surgery—I took up running and spinning and had this self-image of being really feminine and strong, which my husband found really sexy," says Sophia, who has no family history of breast cancer. "We had great sex while I was bald, and I never wore a wig. My husband was surprisingly turned on by my new look. It was like he got to sleep with another woman."

Joining Sophia in this chapter are other breast cancer survivors who share their own stories of channeling warrior spirits—Terry Rubin, a double-cancer survivor, and Heather Berger, who had an elective double mastectomy in 2008 to preempt the breast cancer that afflicted her mother and two aunts, one of whom died.

Sophia's doctor, Dr. Lorraine Tafra, also weighs in on a prevalent disease that will affect one out of eight American women and is now largely treatable with early detection. Dr. Tafra sees more cases of the disease than many other surgeons in the United States. The hospital where she is based is in a region of the Southeast that has a higher than average rate of breast cancer.

The cancer survivors I spoke to were diagnosed at varied stages of the disease and differ in their struggles toward recovery. Terry had to rebound twice, after a malignant lump was discovered in her left breast ten years after her right breast was removed. Yet I am struck by their similarities: They are all grateful and mighty, and have learned the hard way that it is the mind, not the body, that is a woman's most responsive sex organ. They also realize, though, that breasts historically mean something else to people who have not been through what they have endured.

"For most of us, and especially for men, breasts are sexual ornaments—the crown jewels of femininity," writes Marilyn Yalom in her 1997 book, A *History of the Breast*. Studying the eras of art history, we do know the extent to which our mammaries have always been exalted, and fussed over—from seventeenth-century Rubenesque nudes and the perky boobs of Marie Antoinette to the cavernous cleavage of Sophia Loren and the impossibly curvy Christina Hendricks, who plays Joan on TV's *Mad Men*.

We can flaunt our breasts with décolleté or hide them with demure button-down blouses. Our breasts, full and droopy or barely an A, feed our babies and attract our lovers. Soft and warm and erect with arousal, they stir up fantasy, lust, and orgasm. Nevertheless, we find out in this chapter that there is way more to a woman's concept of her womanliness than what historians and Hollywood have long considered her crown jewels. Here is what happens when breasts are no longer there, when you are "stitched together like a rag doll," as Sophia describes it, and are put back together again.

Tanned in a low-cut sundress, Sophia, forty-two, talks about life, kids, sex, and Tamoxifen with grace, humor, and some tears in a quiet corner of the graduation party and in subsequent interviews. Her tumor, caught late, was fast growing and already larger than a marble, lodged in her chest wall. As summer approaches in 2013, the chemo and radiation are well behind her, her marriage is intimate, and best yet, she says: "my children will know their mother."

SOPHIA MICHELS

I'd say that while I am not thrilled with the way my chest looks now, my plastic surgeon thinks of me as his poster child. Recently he bragged to me that he is so proud of his work, he has shown pictures of my breasts—headless!—at oncology seminars in China and Germany. I'm a worldwide sensation!

I was diagnosed in September 2008 with Stage III type B invasive breast cancer. I was only thirty-seven and had just had my first mammogram a few months earlier, which had come back normal. Then, that September, I was doing my monthly breast exam and I felt a huge mass in my left breast, about two inches in diameter. I am small-breasted, and you could actually see the skin pulling around the lump.

Having lived through a near-death experience eighteen months prior, I think I was somewhat fatalistic: As soon as I felt this mass, I was absolutely sure it was cancer. I had a late-term pregnancy in which the baby died in utero, and during the delivery, I lost a lot of blood—and ended up needing thirty-two transfusions. I was obviously scared about the breast lump, but I didn't fall apart because I thought that at least my children, who were then almost three and five, would be able to have some memories of me if the worst scenario came true. If I had died from the miscarriage, when my youngest was only fourteen months old, she wouldn't have remembered me at all.

It turned out that I was right—the ultrasound picked up one large lump and two smaller ones, and the biopsy showed them to be cancerous. Because the larger tumor was so big and my breasts were so small, the doctors were concerned that it was impacted in the chest wall. They decided to give me chemo before the mastectomy so as to shrink the tumors before surgery. It worked! The chemo shrank the largest tumor from seven centimeters to one and a half centimeters, so when I did have surgery, they didn't have to dig into my chest wall.

I lost my hair months before my actual surgery—in fact, it came out three weeks after my first dose of chemo. I had long beautiful hair at the time, so this was a big change for me and particularly for my kids. However, I had it cut short for a few weeks, and once I started chemo, I had the kids help shave my head. I had read that this would help them deal with my new look. When I was bald, I would have them put fake tattoos on my head, fairies and dinosaurs and butterflies, and they loved it. It made them more comfortable with their bald mommy, and it made me feel pretty in an unconventional way.

I decided not to wear a wig because I didn't want the children to think there was something so wrong with me that I had to cover up my head.

Strangely and surprisingly, sex was good throughout my cancer treatment. My husband was very turned on by what he called my "warrior spirit." He liked my bald head. It symbolized that I was fighting something. I had always been physically active, doing yoga, spinning, and soccer. But when I got the diagnosis, I started running as well and got really fit—he liked that, too.

Sex was really good for me during my recovery. Well, you can't have intercourse right after chemo because you are so toxic you can make your partner sick from all those chemicals. I even used a separate bathroom in the house the first couple of days after each chemo treatment. But after three or four days, you can do anything, and I found sex to be really good for me during this time. Chemo is hard on your body; they put you on steroids to combat the nausea and other side effects. I definitely had steroid-induced adrenaline. So I had a lot of energy for sex.

It was amazing to have my husband desire me: We hadn't

been having a ton of sex before cancer, with really small children distracting us. Then it was strange to go through this illness and surgery and have more sex. Breast cancer is a long journey: I went through five months of chemo, the mastectomy took six weeks of recovery, then I had two months of radiation, every day. Throughout it all, with the exception of those first weeks postsurgery, even during radiation, we had sex regularly.

My reconstructed breast is so much firmer than a natural breast, and it turned out to look higher than my other breast. My breasts had dropped from breast-feeding two kids. The asymmetry bothered me a lot, so I went back to my surgeon and he put a half-size implant into my right breast and lifted it so it is now an even match. I was surprised by how much better I felt after that seemingly small adjustment.

I have feeling in the augmented breast but not in that nipple or the reconstructed nipple. I am really sad about that. I used to be able to reach orgasm easily through breast stimulation, so that has been a real loss for me. I wouldn't say I am happy with the way my fake breast looks. It depends on my mood.

In the movie *The Nightmare Before Christmas*, there's a character named Sally who is a rag doll stitched together, and sometimes I feel like Sally. Most of the time, though, I feel strong. I am proud that I am a woman with lots of scars. Scars from two C-sections, scars from a miscarriage and an emergency hysterectomy, scars from breast cancer. My scars make me feel tough and sexy, like a real survivor.

I am thankful that I have a husband who desires me during the periods when I'm up and when I'm down. Recovering from cancer, I did have good sex, but I would often feel like I needed more emotional support—and I should have asked for it. This is a lesson I can pass on to other women in my situation. I created the problem, really, because in my efforts to be strong in front of the kids and to just keep going forward, I let my husband assume I was invincible. And he was so turned on by how tough I was, I didn't let myself be weak with him.

In retrospect, I should have told him the truth, that I was often tired. That I was scared the cancer would come back. That I was vulnerable and just needed him to hold me.

I've been on the drug Tamoxifen, an anti-estrogen therapy, for almost four years now, but I'm sort of a weird case hormonally. Because even after a hysterectomy and chemotherapy, and while taking this drug that generally causes early menopause and vaginal dryness, I keep having minor periods regularly. I guess after the hysterectomy with the stillbirth, I still had some uterine tissue left in there. My oncologist was amazed that I would still get a period sometimes, but I was relieved because, since I still had some hormones kicking around in there, my vaginal dryness has not been so bad.

But I have had other side effects: I have hair thinning and fatigue, and exhaustion does not put you in the mood for sex.

Here I had been a trooper through all those months of chemo and radiation and then I started taking this one little pill and it made me feel terrible. I hated it! More advice for women who are just going on Tamoxifen: The first year is the toughest. Your body definitely adjusts over time. For the first several months, I had some depression, which I'd never had before. The doctor suggested splitting the dose, taking half in the morning and half at night. It made all the difference in the world! It can be hard to stay positive if your medicine is working against you, but there are things you can do to get relief—and it can be as simple as cutting a pill in half.

I'd say my husband and I are lucky; we've been married twelve years, we are raising two young kids, and it comes and goes, but we are still intimate regularly. Though I do prefer to have sex with my shirt on, then he will say, "You do not need to do that. You are more beautiful than ever." But I feel sexier with my shirt on because it makes me think less about how I used to count on my breasts for sexual satisfaction—and can now no longer do so. I'm still amazed that my husband thinks my breasts are so sexy and attractive now. I'm working toward the goal of liking them that much, too.

Sophia is tentative about liking her new breasts, which is a fairly typical response to the adjustment that takes place after reconstruction. Heather Berger was the one woman I spoke to who is effusively in love with her reconstructed A size. And they are beautiful, astoundingly authentic. I know this because when I asked Heather to describe them, she promptly e-mailed me a photograph, of small, round, and perfect breasts that blend seamlessly into her chest and do not have the ridge found in many patients with implants. They are topped by dark pink areolas and nipples the color and shape of the real McCoys, crafted from tissue extracted from her inner thigh.

Heather's full-on love affair with her breasts can also be attributed to the fact that her surgery was prophylactic, not driven by a diagnosis and marred by side effects from drugs. The mother of three from Idaho did not have breast cancer, but two aunts did—one of whom died—and her mother is still battling the disease that metastasized into other organs and bones.

Three years ago, Heather chose to have a double mastectomy to ward off what could lie ahead for a woman with three kids under the age of seven and a family history of breast cancer. She was a diligent and proactive patient who was tireless in carefully studying her options. Heather is also unafraid of medical casualties: She serves as a senior airman in the Air Force and works in the operating room as a technician alongside the surgeon in the Air National Guard.

Heather's long, charcoal-brown hair is windblown from a motorcycle ride. She loves that bike, and finds that she is more adventurous than ever, "now that the black cloud of cancer has been lifted from over my head." Heather's choice is one we will be hearing of more often in the aftermath of a recent court ruling that will precipitate a drop in the oppressive price of testing for genes that indicate a propensity for female cancers.

In June 2013, the Supreme Court unanimously ruled that isolated human genes cannot be patented. Since the early 1990s, Myriad Genetics has held the sole patents on the tests for the BRCA1 and BRCA2 genes, which, when present, raise the risk of developing breast and ovarian cancers. This will give other laboratories the opportunity to administer those tests, and with increased access, the costs will drop. Immediately after the ruling, executives of one company, DNA Traits, part of Gene by Gene, Ltd., said they would offer BRCA gene testing in the United States for $995 which is less than a third of the current price.

HEATHER BERGER

In 2008, I went to my doctor for my annual ob-gyn exam, and we talked about my two aunts having breast cancer—this was before my mother was diagnosed. My doctor brought up the possibility of having a prophylactic double mastectomy, which at the time was a new concept to me. She suggested I talk it over with a genetics counselor. I walked away thinking *This is crazy talk—I am only thirty-two and I would never remove my breasts just because of a family history of cancer. My mother didn't have cancer, so why should I worry?*

Fast forward a year and a half later, and it's December 2009.

I'm getting ready to go to bed and I feel a lump in my breast, and it kind of burns. I knew my mom had cysts that had to be aspirated from time to time, so I didn't give much thought to it.

Then, after Christmas, my dad called and he was crying. He said, "Your mom has breast cancer. And it's Stage Four." I immediately loaded up the kids and drove a hundred miles to their house. She had it bad; the cancer was also in other places in her body, her bones, pelvis, shoulder area. Of major concern were her vertebrae, being so close to her spinal cord.

They wanted to start treating her aggressively. She began radiation immediately, followed by hours of chemotherapy infusions, and she is still on oral chemotherapy today.

While all of this is going on, I go back to my ob-gyn, and she sees that there is definitely a lump in my breast. She was troubled by what she saw on the MRI, that it was not only one cyst but multiple cysts. She basically said I would have to be monitored every six months by MRIs for the rest of my life because of my family history. I could not handle that emotionally or financially—my first MRI cost more than $2,500, even with health insurance.

It became a huge cloud hanging over my head that followed me everywhere I went. I would look at my kids and be sickened at the thought that they might have to see me go through what I watched my mom go through. That whole experience just tore me up. It was a huge decision weighing on me. My breasts were very much part of me sexually, for my own self-image and during lovemaking. But aesthetically, I wasn't happy with them, so I was open to this.

I decided I would start interviewing different doctors and get their opinions on my choices, given the family history. Finally, thank God, I landed in the office of a very kind and well-regarded surgeon who specializes in mastectomies. I brought my husband into the discussion and we came away knowing that I was making a rational decision, for me, and for our family—I wanted to be there for my children. And here I was, a healthy young woman, not stricken with cancer. At this point, the ball was in my court, whereas later I might not have control. I did get tested for the BRCA gene, and the results were negative. Even with this information, just knowing the history of three close female relatives, I felt very confident about my choice.

I went under the knife July 7, 2010. The night before my operation, I didn't want my husband to touch me. I wanted to be alone with my body and not have the feeling of my husband touching my breasts as the last feeling I remembered of having them. I was crying the next morning and I asked him to take a picture of my chest, so I could remember what they were like.

I had chosen to have expanders placed in immediately after my mastectomy to start stretching the skin for the implants. So the first look I got at my chest was of two four-inch incisions where my breasts used to be. I was happy with what I saw; the incisions were precise and clean. Following surgery, I went in every two weeks and the doctor would stick a needle right into my chest to infuse the saline solution into the expander. It was definitely strange—it reminded me of a scene in *Pulp Fiction*. It didn't hurt because I had no feeling in my chest, though I am fortunate now because I have regained more sensation in my breasts than I thought I would. Then, after four months of expanders, I had silicone implants placed in.

I'm three years in now with my new breasts, and they look fantastic and feel very soft. The doctor took a skin graft from my inner thigh and grafted it onto my new breasts to make a nipple. They look so real, it is astonishing, except for a couple of tiny fading scars.

I don't miss my breasts like I thought I would. Especially

every time another friend is newly diagnosed with breast cancer, I really don't miss them. The surgeon removed every bit of my glandular tissue—my risk of cancer is down to 2 percent, whereas before, I had a nearly 50 percent risk. I understand I may get cancer somewhere else in my body during my lifetime, but I am sure it won't be breast cancer that beats me.

I worried how my husband would feel sexually toward me. After about four weeks, we started to get intimate. I literally shook the entire first time after surgery, nervous he wouldn't want me.

At first, he was afraid he would hurt me. Finally, I placed his hands on my chest and showed him that it was okay. He knows that I may not be able to feel it everywhere when he touches my breasts, but he is definitely sexually aroused by them, and he likes to play with them.

For me, unless someone brings up my surgery, I pretty much forget about them. I just see them as great boobs that are now a part of me. If they look like boobs and feel like boobs—they are boobs! The life expectancy of these implants is about eleven years, and then I'll go in and get another great pair. My life expectancy is what counts. I didn't give cancer a chance.

I don't look at my breasts the same anymore. I used to see vanity, and now I see my future.

According to statistics compiled by the National Cancer Institute, 232,670 women will be diagnosed with breast cancer in 2013 and of that number, 40,000 will die of the disease. The incidence of advanced breast cancer among younger women has increased slightly over the last three decades. A report published in *The Journal of the American Medical Association* cited that advanced cases climbed to 2.9 per 100,000 younger women in 2009, up from 1.53 per 100,000 women in 1976—an increase of 1.37 cases per 100,000 women in thirty-four years. There were 250 cases in a younger population per year in the mid-1970s, and more than 800 per year in 2009. The study is based on information from 936,497 women who had breast cancer from 1976 to 2009.

Although the increase is small, the finding is disconcerting because breast cancer in young women tends to grow and spread more quickly, and is linked to lower survival rates than in cases involving older women. The five-year survival rate for patients with breast cancer that has not metastasized is 93 percent. In women thirty-nine and under whose cancer has spread, survival rates drop to 31 percent.

According to information disseminated by the American Cancer Society, about 2,360 new cases of invasive breast cancer will be diagnosed among men in 2013, and 430 of those men will die from the disease. Male breast cancer is about one hundred times less common than in females, dropping to a lifetime risk of about one in 1,000 men, a statistic that has been fairly stable for the past three decades.

Breast surgeon and oncologist Dr. Lorraine Tafra has seen the full range of breast cancers, contained and aggressive, in young and old, in men but mostly women. She is founding director of the Breast Center at Anne Arundel Medical Center in Maryland. This region of the country has elevated rates of breast cancer, the impetus for many inconclusive studies that have examined its inhabitants' diet, heavy in fish and seafood from the Chesapeake Bay pollution blasts from nearby Baltimore, and the transient female population centered around the United States Naval Academy.

With pale blond hair and decked in a red blazer and black trousers, Dr. Tafra, fifty-four, is a muscular five feet four. She regularly bikes and works out with weights in order to weather her typical sixteen-hour work days. Dr. Tafra greets me with a forceful shake with both hands, hands that have operated on some five thousand patients during her fifteen years as a breast surgeon. Considered one of the East Coast's leading breast surgeons, Dr. Tafra was in the first fellowship group at the John Wayne Cancer Institute at Saint John's Health Center in Santa Monica, California, where she participated in the initial development of the sentinel node biopsy for breast cancer.

Excising the sentinel node provides a specimen for more focused analysis and experimental studies that improves detection of axillary metastases.

"Women have twenty to forty lymph nodes under their arms, and to remove all the cancer, we used to take most of those lymph nodes," explains Dr. Tafra. "Frequently we found that there were no lymph nodes that contained disease. We learned from the studies that initially investigated the sentinel node technique that tumors tend to spread in a very predictable way, going first to only a few nodes. It is possible to identify and isolate those few sentinel nodes and remove just those instead of removing a large number, which is a much longer procedure and fraught with more complications. Today only a small group of women have to have a large number of lymph nodes removed."

Dr. Tafra's passion for her work stems from more than her pioneering role in the diagnosis and cure of a cancer that is the second leading cause of death in American women, next to heart disease. Her mother was diagnosed with breast cancer in 1990 and did fine until she developed a liver metastasis that took her life.

DR. LORRAINE TAFRA

Breasts throughout history have been considered a center-piece of a woman's identity; in feeding her babies, in her sense of sexuality, and in her sexual pleasure. Losing your breasts is clearly a huge transition to make, yet the response to that process varies sharply from patient to patient. It has been fascinating to me as a surgeon to observe how different each woman reacts to the diagnosis of breast cancer.

Some women make it very clear that their breasts don't mean that much to them. They have a small tumor in one breast, and they want them both off, quickly. They tell me, "I'm fine with this, my husband is fine. I never really liked them anyway." Then there are other women who tell me their breasts mean everything to them. They say, "Whatever you have to do to get rid of my cancer, do it—but I'm not having these removed. I'm going to my grave with my breasts!"

I've been in this field now for going on twenty years, and the evolution of surgical management has changed tremendously over these past two decades. We always used to have to do a mastectomy, and now we try to do less surgery. With sentinel node analysis and other new techniques, we can now determine what's going on with these tumors and what their possible future course will be. We can find out the tumor biology, which means how the tumor is programmed, and that can give us a good idea of this person's prognosis.

A good tumor biology means that the patient will usually do just fine; if the tumor biopsy and biology is terrible, we know we are going to have a more difficult time getting those patients' tumors to respond to therapy and that ultimately they will probably die of their disease. But you never know—all the cards can be stacked against the patient, and then they stroll in ten years out from treatment and are doing just fine!

A good biology is basically tumor cells that don't want to divide very fast and they don't want to move around very fast. In lay language, they want to hang out. Bad tumor biology would consist of cells that love to grow and want to go everywhere and do everything. These inroads in characterizing the tumor biology in our field give us the best idea possible on how to base our treatment schemes. For example, even with some of the worst tumor biology profiles, and where the cancer has spread, we might choose not to do surgery but just use hormonal therapies because of our intricate analysis of the tumor's composition and future forecast.

Most women now want reconstruction right away, but again we see a wide variance in patients. There are women in their sixties and seventies who tell me: "I can't wake up without breasts! Get those plastic surgeons to work right away!" And there are young patients who may be athletes, and/or flat-chested to begin with, who have no interest in reconstruction, a process that requires more time, and more healing. And more recuperation. We had one patient, a professional soccer player in her late thirties, and she was so happy to be rid of her big breasts. They slowed down her game.

Over the last decade, we've begun to do more immediate reconstruction. We used to remove the breasts and reconstruct down the line. Frequently, now the plastic surgery team is there right away to reconstruct at the time of the mastectomy. The other trend has been nipple-sparing mastectomy, which Angelina Jolie had. Before, we removed all nipples during the mastectomies and now we don't do that across the board. More and more data is accumulating that as long as there is no disease in the nipple area, we can leave the nipple there and take out all underlying breast tissue. This procedure involves a smaller incision and ends up looking more like the original breast. Yet the patient does lose sensation in the remaining nipple typically immediately after surgery.

The work of plastic surgeons now has seen huge improvements with breast reconstruction. There are different shapes of implants with softer textures, and surgeons can shape new nipples with tissue from other places on the body. There are also artists who have taken nipple tattooing to a whole new level. We also can use belly fat for breast implants; that specific technique is a microvascular flap, or a DIEP flap. There are definitely advantages to using the patient's own tissue; the breasts feel more like native breast tissue. Having breasts that look and feel as real as possible makes all the difference in the world to these women.

Every day, I am made aware of how far we have come in the field of women's health. I had one patient who was probably in her mid-eighties, and she had a new, younger husband, seventy or so. When she was diagnosed, she was very hot to trot to get implants right away. With added longevity in women, I will be seeing more and more of these older women who are sexual in their later years, and want those breasts.

While my work is very serious, I do get amused when I get that size A patient who has a teeny, tiny tumor that would do fine with a lumpectomy. But she'll go for bilateral implants to get the bigger breasts she's always wanted, and she'll say: "This is my gift to me for making it through cancer!"

It is very complex to answer the question Who gets breast cancer? It probably comes from a combination of genetics and one hundred other events and factors that have to go wrong to create a cancer that we eventually detect and have to treat. Yet there is no question that survival rates continue to improve.

Fewer and fewer patients are dying of their breast cancer. We're also not seeing as many recurrences in patients, and that's from a combination of things—finding smaller, well-behaved tumors earlier, and better overall treatments with hormones, chemo, radiation, and more advanced surgery.

Because women are aware of the importance of diagnostic testing, I'd say in the last ten or fifteen years, a good percentage of our patients present with very small tumors. And they can usually avoid the big surgery of removing the breast. Typically, when we combine radiation with a lumpectomy, we see the same cure rate as with a mastectomy. In years to come, I'd like to see oncologists offer more guidance for women on how to deal with their changing sexuality after breast cancer. Surgeons aren't trained to help them with those issues, and many women will have very real medical issues they will need to address. The chemotherapy will throw them into early menopause, and that poses very complex issues for a young woman in her sexual prime. Our extensive training as surgeons and oncologists typically does not contain training on how to manage sexuality issues that arise from the diagnosis or treatment of breast cancer.

Even if the physicians were doling out instructions on what to expect from sex after breast cancer, it is our girlfriends and cousins and sisters who have gone through this grueling process who are our best, most trusted guides. I hope you have felt as I have—that the voices of women in this chapter have enveloped us in a prescriptive girl circle in which the unfiltered truth about coping with the disease was bared. Along with their challenges, we learn from Heather and Sophia that there is sex after breast cancer—"surprisingly" good sex, at that. We learn from Dr. Tafra that scientific inroads are turning breast cancer from a killer into a manageable disease with a plethora of new cures.

All of these women feel determined and proud, like chieftains who are winning a battle. But it is not the addition of saline or silicone or new boobs from body fat that is the basic reason for their reclaimed sensuality and power. Rebirth after breast cancer comes from a spiritual reservoir that lies within all of us and is often not tapped until we are assaulted with illness or personal tragedy. The healing process is also eased greatly by having a supportive partner, as you saw in the above cases and as two-time cancer survivor Terry Rubin attests.

An accomplished runner since her early twenties, Terry trains even more vigorously since her cancer diagnosis, and now competes in triathlons. "I have a healthy body and the best boobs of my life," says Terry, a nurse in Denver who wears her gray hair short and her earrings long. After cancer, she is now a full 34C, transformed from an A cup. Clearly her best boobs and tight core enhance her self-image, but the biggest feeder of her positive outlook is the soulful connection she shares with her pediatrician husband, Jerry.

TERRY RUBIN

Throughout my journey with cancer, all Jerry and I cared about was that I would live. We overlooked my physical being while I was going through mastectomies and reconstruction and my bald stages. I still have no eyebrows or any eyelashes. But eighteen years after my first diagnosis, I am here!

I always had lumpy breasts and was told it was normal, so I didn't have my first mammogram until the age of thirty-five. It did show I had fibrocystic breasts but was told, "You are fine; there is nothing to worry about." I went in for my next mammogram when I turned forty, and this time the doctor didn't say, "Fine"— he said, "We need another picture." After the ultrasound, the radiologist came in and said, "I've compared your mammogram to your last one and there has been a significant change, and we need to have a biopsy. I am worried you may have breast cancer."

The minute you hear this, the roller coaster begins. I just thought, *I'm going to buckle up for this ride because I know it's going to go up and down, probably for a long time.* My biopsy showed that I had ductile carcinoma inset, an early-stage breast cancer. Because the tumor was very large, it prevented me from having a lumpectomy. On the mammogram, it looked like a starburst—it was scary. They scheduled me for a mastectomy with reconstruction.

The night before surgery, as I was taking a shower and getting ready to say good-bye to my left breast, I felt emotional, but that came and went pretty quickly. I didn't allow myself to dwell in that space of self-pity. Instead, I moved into that bigger space of gratitude—that what I was doing was lifesaving. I chose to have reconstruction on both sides after getting my breast removed in order to make them symmetrical, and I did go bigger. I am an athlete and I never had that soft, bosomy look, but now I do have more of a cleavage, which I love in a bathing suit!

Nine years after my first cancer, I found another lump in my right breast. First, I thought this was probably just my cystic breasts, but it didn't go away. A couple of months later, it was time for my mammogram, and then it was the same roller coaster all over again. Doctor comes in and tells me, "Don't get dressed, we need an ultrasound; I'm not liking how this looks."

This time, the diagnosis was invasive ductile carcinoma, and was much more advanced than my first lump had been. Since it was time for me to have my implants changed, I had another total reconstruction of both breasts. I went through long and debilitating chemotherapy. But once my hair grew back and I started working out again, I really felt like I had put breast cancer behind me. With two mastectomies, and no breast tissue left, I do finally think my doctors have taken breast cancer off the table for me.

Because I had such small breasts, they never defined my sense of feeling feminine. But I would say with my plastic-surgeon-made breasts, I even feel more feminine. Naked, it's a different story; I look like a road map crisscrossed with scars from many surgeries. But in that Victoria's Secret bra, I look cool and feel beautiful.

Cancer to me now is such a nonpresent part of my day-to-day existence. Rarely do I think about the fact that my breasts aren't natural. The devastating part of breast cancer is not the surgery—it's that if you are young, the chemotherapy puts you into premature menopause. If I had known everything about that when I was forty, I would have done a bilateral mastectomy right away, and I wouldn't have needed chemo.

Chemo accelerates all hot flashes, vaginal dryness, lethargy, and weight gain. Then I was put on Tamoxifen and another drug treatment, and the drugs made me feel absolutely horrible. Finally, I went to my oncologist and I said, "I'm done. These meds are making me feel awful. I want to return to my normal self." Going off Tamoxifen and the other drugs upped my risks for a metastasized cancer. But I was willing to take that risk, because the quality of my life is so important.

Here I am years later—I feel like a million bucks. I have one of the closest marriages of anyone I know, and our intense intimacy has little to do with sex. True intimacy is that recognition of your partner's soul. And while you have the gift of deepening that intimacy through sex, the heart of true intimacy comes during those moments in life when you get to be authentic and vulnerable with each other.

Cancer definitely puts you into that very real place. Our connection and love comes from being mates of the soul, and this is way above the physical body. Sexual attraction gets the ball rolling. But it certainly doesn't keep you there.

Some partners would have been turned off to be with someone who has had as many physical changes as I've had. My breasts are scarred, and when I was going through chemo, I looked sickly and I would violently puke my guts out. Chemo is a very dark place to be. Your partner during this process has to be somebody who is a spiritual mate and sees far beyond just your body.

Terry was shocked at her first diagnosis; she had not yet even celebrated her fortieth birthday, and no close relatives had breast cancer. Along with a clean family history, she had led a very clean life. Terry does not drink alcohol, has never smoked cigarettes, is a fitness fanatic, and has been a devout vegetarian for more than thirty years. That she would be struck with breast cancer exemplifies what Dr. Tafra said about the disease being a complicated mixture of inexplicable factors. It was also intriguing to hear Dr. Tafra relay how some women actually prefer to be without their breasts, a load they felt was too large or just plain meaningless in their sexual role.

After the interview with Dr. Tafra was officially over, I stayed with her to extract more information about her medical specialty, which is a window into so many aspects of womanhood—vanity and psychology and survival instincts and sexuality. She reiterates the fact that when her patients do opt for reconstruction, which most of them do, they want boobs that look and feel as real as possible, and not just for aesthetics but because "it affects their whole being." She tells me that many of those women end up with "Vinnie the Nipple Guy," a world-renowned tattoo artist based in Maryland who specializes in nipple artistry for cancer patients with newly implanted breasts.

Vinnie Myers's exquisitely detailed trompe l'oeil renditions of nipples have caught the attention of oncologists, plastic surgeons, and cancer survivors nationwide, and globally. Mideast millionaires fly their wives to him. He tops the list of tattoo artists that Dr. Tafra spoke of as "taking this art to a whole new level." But instead of working out of an artist's studio in SoHo or, better yet, the south of France, Vinnie's masterpieces come out of a strip mall in unincorporated Finksburg, Maryland, fifteen miles west of Baltimore.

Displayed on the walls of his 2,500-square-foot Little Vinnies Tattoos shop are eye-popping displays of what in the business is known as "flash," images for patrons to choose from to adorn their bodies. While other artists in his studio still do traditional tattooing, Vinnie's main focus now is nipples, all shapes, all sizes, all colorations. "It's not every day that you get to choose your own nipples," says Vinnie with a grin. Clients can literally custom-design their own nipples and areolas, selecting from a palette of dusty rose, suntan brown, and peachy pink.

He splits his time between Maryland and Louisiana, where he is the resident tattoo artist at the Center for Restorative Breast Surgery in New Orleans. While his training is in art and not medicine, he has developed an expertise in psychology. By the time women are in Vinnie's hands, they are at the end of a torturous and lengthy saga, and bursting with built-up emotions. They are eager to spill to an anonymous listener—"like you would do with a hairdresser," says Vinnie.

Here is more from the fifty-year-old artist known as "the nipple guy," with his big sideburns, and wearing his trademark flat-brim porkpie hat on his shaved head. Vinnie will not give an exact count, but he has "a ton of tattoos," one hundred hours' worth, discreetly strewn over his slender six-feet-four body— including a coy fish, a shamrock, and a sacred heart—none visible to a visitor.

VINNIE MYERS

The approach in nipple tattooing must be milder and less aggressive than traditional tattooing or there is a higher risk of healing issues and scarring. Each case is unique and the approach will be different for each woman, due to color and thickness of the skin, radiation effects, her type of implant, and the reconstruction results.

It is actually much easier to tattoo ladies of color than white, as the darker color skin is much more forgiving. The darker skin hides what we call "holidays," the little areas of skin that show through the tattoo ink. The trick to achieving a good three-dimensional effect is the proper use of shadows and highlights and a good contrast between areola color and nipple color. It really is pretty easy: I look at a picture of a nipple and I tattoo what I see. Well, it is easy for me because I have been tattooing for almost thirty years!

To get nipple tattoos, women need to wait a minimum of sixteen weeks; everything has to settle down and heal into place. And sometimes so much tissue has been taken away that they just can't be tattooed. And I have to deliver the bad news, hard to do; they don't want to hear that.

Aside from the artistic satisfaction I get out of my specialty, this really speaks to my compassionate side. My sister had breast cancer and I know what she went through. She is doing well now and has been cancer free for three years. I am happy to be helping women feel and look as close to their old selves as possible.

It is pretty amazing to witness the transformation you see when a woman comes into my shop. She is nervous; most of these ladies have never been in a tattoo shop. Then they sit down with me and just start talking about their experience with cancer. It's like sitting down with a bartender or a hairdresser. And they realize pretty quickly that I'm a good listener, and that I understand where they're coming from—because I have heard many of the same stories hundreds of time.

When you hear "You've got breast cancer," you are loaded with an eight-hundred-pound gorilla. You have to start making decisions that affect the rest of your life. And a lot of the decisions are being made when you are not in the best state of mind. Hopefully, you've gone to a competent surgeon who has enough experience and talent to give you the best-looking breasts possible.

Oh my God! I have seen as many disasters as success stories. My opinion on how I exercise my craft has changed over the past decade. I used to just look at a lady and say, "Wow, that's really a shame that you don't like the way you look; let me get to work." Now that I know what a great reconstruction looks like, I feel like I have to inform them what's available to them. I will suggest that they go back to another surgeon and get it done over. I have to be very careful to approach this with kid gloves because you can really hurt someone's feelings.

I hear some really horrible stories. I have women tell me that their husbands have left them over this, awful to hear. They'll tell me the guy will say, "I can't deal with this," then he's out of there. Oh yeah, this job is very emotional. I listen and tell them, "You will have another life! You're going to look great."

I had one lady come into my tattoo room and her husband sat in the waiting area. When I asked her if her husband would like to come back and sit with us when we did the procedure, she said to me, "Oh, no, he has not looked at me since I was diagnosed." It was really quite sad to hear.

I love doing regular tattooing and that's a field in which I can really show my artistry. This is more limiting as an artist, but the rewards are so much greater than skin-deep. These ladies have gone through such physical and emotional pain. The tattoo process takes about an hour and a half and when I'm done, the thing they say to me more than anything else is, "You have made me whole again." I hear that over and over and over.

I'm a guy and I guess I can't really understand how these ladies feel. Maybe it's like a guy getting his testicles cut off then remade with silicone eggs. Only the difference with guys is that nobody really would notice his fake balls when he is dressed. With women, the breasts are among the first things you notice. Somehow I think that it is not only important for the women to look good and feel good when wearing clothing but to look and feel good when they are not. It is very important to feel that you look normal or beautiful when being intimate. So while I'll never really get what they're going through, I do get how thankful they are when they leave.

Most of the women I see range from mid-twenties to mid-seventies. One woman I tattooed who was most likely in her mid-seventies said she used to have really lovely nipples and she wanted her new ones to be as nice because she was not finished showing them off. I thought that was kind of fun and funny.

The older ladies are just as excited as the younger clients.

Getting nipples for breast cancer survivors is a huge step toward their healing, to feel sexy again. I love being that person that tops off their new breasts and sends them out the door with hopes for a new beginning.

The two things women need to think about even though they are scared and sad when they get the diagnosis: Number one, once you are diagnosed with breast cancer, odds are high you are going to live. Number two, there are a lot of medical options. So instead of making a quick decision, start thinking about how you want to look, and work toward that end. Too many people may be with a surgeon who only does silicone or saline implants and they are going to push you in that direction.

Maybe you are a candidate for a flap surgery that uses your own body tissue, or for nipple-sparing surgery. Shop around, see as many doctors as you want to see, realize you are in control of this, not the first surgeon who tells you what to do. You've got some time.

I find that flap reconstructions—taking fatty tissue from another part of the body and rebuilding the breast from the harvested tissue—when done by the right surgeon, do look more realistic than the synthetic ones. The key phrase here is "done by the right surgeon"—if not, any surgery can look not so good. The flap results also are not as cold in the winter as the liquid-filled implants. They don't have to be replaced, they look and feel more like the real thing. That cancer could have been in you for a long time, so make sure you are taking some time to become educated about what's available and find the best person to do the work.

I know I'm not a doctor, but I am a well-informed tattoo artist and I have seen more reconstructed breasts than most people or doctors in the world. And I am passionate about sharing what I have learned. I tell the women who call me for advice: "Do you really want to go through more surgery and get nipple reconstruction instead of tattoos? Do you really want the high beams on for the rest of your life?" Most nipple reconstructions I see look like cinnamon buns and they are rarely realistic-looking. The only advantage is that you do get an actual projection, but you better hope the doctor gets it right or your nipples will always look like you're walking around in the frozen food aisle.

And many male doctors encourage their patients to get bigger implants. Go with small if you want to stay small. Realize you are in control of this.

People often ask me, "What does your wife think of your line of work?" I am married to a very understanding woman. Some of my other tattoo work is erotic; people want tattoos put in places near their private parts. What I do now isn't about sex; it's artistry that is taking care of a woman's emotions.

My wife understands what I understand: To most women, breasts mean a lot. And as horrible as it sounds, women don't realize what their breasts do mean to them until they are gone. They are the part of your sexuality that everybody looks at every day. And when you can get your breasts back, as close as possible to the ones you lost, the ladies are thrilled.

CHAPTER 9
SEX AFTER MENOPAUSE

My orgasms [after hysterectomy] didn't become less intense; in fact, they seemed deeper and they would shudder through my body longer.

—JOANNE

I first heard the word *menopause* right around the time I had to buy my first box of Kotex. A pudgy comedian on our small TV set was making a joke about his fifty-one-year-old wife who was on "man-pause" because of menopause. I checked out *menopause* in the encyclopedia and found out all sorts of scary stuff that sounded way worse than my menstrual cramps—hot flashes, depression, night sweats, loss of libido. Libido? Had to look that one up, too, and found out it is the basic human sexual drive.

That basic drive was just starting to give me flashes of hotness that felt very good—thinking "libido" came with a sticker end date was dismal news.

Decades later, I present to you an array of menopausal women, rid of tampons and fears of getting pregnant and enjoying new depths of pleasure in their intimate partnerships, with or without, rocket penetration. They are working through gynecological issues associated with the female aging cycle, such as fluctuations in desire, vaginal dryness, and vulvar pain, with remedies unheard of when the comedian on my TV in 1966 was dissing his man-paused wife, a woman at midlife who maybe just didn't want to sleep with *him*. I also include interviews with sexual health educators and medical providers who smash old wives' tales about the passage my mother called "the change," ranging from holistic practitioners who prescribe lifestyle changes to doctors who endorse hormones and female Viagra-like pills.

The dictionary definition of *menopause* is "the end of monthly cycles," a word with an etymology that combines the Greek roots *men* for "month" and *pausis*, which means "cessation." Some fifty million American women have reached menopause, at the average age of fifty-one.

Yet physically and psychologically, menopause means something unique to every woman, affecting lust and libido and "how dry I am" in stark variations. Some women literally glide right through it—so to speak—like fifty-five-year-old Lucille, who craves sex and is having lots of it with her boyfriend, who is younger by fifteen years. Others like Ilene, fifty-eight, are craving sex but not with her husband, who is out of work and has gained weight and is generally "a turnoff right now," she says. Then there are women like Lynn, sixty, referred to briefly earlier in the book and who is relieved that her menopausal dip in estrogen has dented her desire for intercourse, which has become painful with vulvar atrophy. The good news for Lynn is that her "zero libido" was well timed with her husband's drop in testosterone levels. She says their intimacy is soaring even though sex has disappeared.

"I am more in love with him than ever," says Lynn, whose longer story is unveiled later in this chapter, along with Lucille's. You will also meet Joanne, who is still "horny as hell" as she approaches seventy. She reveals details of peak sexual experiences after menopause, and after a hysterectomy, with a lover of seven years who recently died. I also include an interview with a fifty-four-year-old husband who offers his take on adjusting (well) to a menopausal wife who is "wildly sexual" and (not so well) to her "adolescent" mood swings, which remind him of his teenage daughters. On the subject of mano-pause, when testosterone dips, erectile dysfunction strikes, and the prostate grows, I turned to urologist Dr. Mark Soloway, who offers some surprising advice on treatment of prostate cancer that can dramatically improve a couple's sex life in the next chapter.

Overall, I have found that the women who do the best with their shifts in sexual desire and their functioning during menopause are the ones who have flexible and supportive partners, to whom they also happen to be attracted. You can see this played out in Ilene's story, of an unemployed husband who is obese, withdrawn, and sedentary.

I will start with Lucille, divorced, age fifty-five, a California girl with a full-body tan and a gleam in her hazel eyes. She lives with a former NBA basketball player, African American, age forty. Lucille lets loose with unabashed candor about needing and getting "fantastic" postmenopausal sexual and emotional fulfillment from her boyfriend of going on ten years—aided by hormone therapy. She laughs off the "cougar" label as she describes a partner who is "mature beyond his years."

LUCILLE

I met Johnny at a bar; he was thirty and I was forty-five, and we had a very hot first hookup. What I liked about him as the relationship progressed, aside from the fact that he was a fantastic lover, was that even though he is much younger, he is beyond mature for his age. The relationship, it is very solid. I feel very secure. And the sex is just great.

When I met him, I was coming off a divorce from a marriage of fifteen years. My ex-husband and I decided we weren't having any children before we got married, so we didn't have to split up a family. I was an only child and never had an urge to have children. My ex-husband used cocaine pretty heavily, and we did it recreationally together during the first few years of our marriage, but he could never stop. He also drank pretty heavily. Eventually, he stopped the cocaine, then started with prescription medications.

Meanwhile, it was assumed I would handle everything—organizing the house and taking on all the financial responsibility. He was drinking and drugged and job hopping. Our sex life had dwindled to essentially nothing and everything was spiraling downward. I didn't have a nervous breakdown, but I had a lot of physical reactions to the stress. I broke out in hives, had anxiety attacks, and finally talked to a psychologist—which led to my initiating a divorce.

It was not hard at all to start dating again. I had lived so long without sex and without a real relationship, I had really been missing it. My sex life with Johnny was quite good from the start. But it's even gotten better—the fifties for this woman have turned out to be really hot. Two years ago, I started using a testosterone cream, which I take along with progesterone. I wish I had started hormones ten years ago; they have been just fantastic for my postmenopausal libido. I also feel that hormones make me stronger—I'm able to work out harder; I spin and lift weights more consistently every day. I have had no serious side effects whatsoever, except a little bit more facial hair growth, and also heavier hair under my arms. I am blond and blue-eyed and not a hairy person, so this is new to me, but easy to handle.

I didn't experience a really intense menopause. I think this is because I'm so physically active, I may not have noticed the symptoms, and I never felt my libido was diminished. I went on hormones because one of my close girlfriends turned me on to them. She clearly looked and felt better, about herself and about sex. Once I started, I felt an immediate difference in my energy level and in my emotions and in sexual desire. I felt more balanced.

The older-woman-younger-man thing, we don't really talk about that. Johnny has always been very complimentary to me in terms of my sexiness and my attractiveness—he doesn't even bring up the fact of our age difference. To him, my age is just a number. To me, I think of him as much older because he is so wise beyond his years. He's just been great for me. And the relationship is very fulfilling; he really is an equal partner. Having existed without it for so long, I think intimacy is more important than most people want to admit. When I didn't have it, I buried myself in my work, and I think most people who don't have it make excuses like "Oh, I'm too busy to think about sex." Sure, there are people who are just asexual, but most of us, my God, truly need sex to feel alive. Now that the hormones are kicking in, it makes everything feel so much stronger. I can't even remember what sex was like before.

I have been drawn to black guys before. I dated a few back in college. But as for sex, there are white guys who are good in bed and white guys who are bad in bed, and the same goes with black guys. Of course everyone thinks their dicks are so big. Ha! Johnny has a nice-size penis, but it's not like a horse's or a baseball bat. It's a little bit on the upper end of normal.

We are very well matched emotionally and physically; I definitely can keep up with him.

Lucille's choice in taking hormone replacement therapy is saluted by some doctors and researchers who consider testosterone, which decreases steadily after age thirty in women, as the agent responsible for sexual arousal in women. Yet definitive answers on how testosterone and other hormones steer libido and other areas of female sexuality remain inconclusive and controversial. After talking to lots of sex educators and physicians and menopausal women, my take on hormones is that if your symptoms are intolerable—heat attacks that soak your clothes at work and unrelenting bitchiness and depression—hormones may be indicated if your doctor determines your body can take it. There is no absolute standard for best medical practice on this one. Historically, results of studies on the risk and benefits of hormones have yo-yoed on crucial questions such as: Do hormones help or hurt your heart? Do hormones decrease or increase the chance you will get cancer?

After years of hormones being touted as a boost for heart health, a 2010 study conducted by the Women's Health Initiative struck down that belief. The WHI results followed a major fifteen-year research program to address the most common causes of death, disability, and poor quality of life in postmenopausal women, which are cardiovascular disease, cancer, and osteoporosis. This research established a trend toward an increase in the risk of heart disease during the first two years of combination hormone therapy (estrogen and progesterone) among women who began therapy within ten years of menopause. A more marked risk was noted among women who began hormone therapy more than ten years after menopause. Analyses indicated that, overall, a woman's risk of heart disease more than doubles within the first two years of taking combination hormone therapy. On the plus side, research shows hormones safeguard against endometrial cancer in women with an intact uterus.

The jury also remains mixed on the benefits of testosterone in treating sexual dysfunction after menopause, although some doctors and some women, like Lucille, believe it to be a magical potion. The vacillating studies, the seductive pros and the frightening cons, the effusive recommendations from older girlfriends with dewy skin and rabbit sex lives—makes many potential hormone shoppers very confused. The only point of agreement in the field of female sexual health is: Talk to your doctor to find out the latest research and if hormones are right for you.

I am not on hormones, yet am always interested in knowing any shifts in the medical findings since the 2010 study. So to get the latest scoop, I called my own ob-gyn, Dr. Janet Schaffel, who, in three decades of counseling menopausal women, has been a close witness as Hormone Replacement Therapy ratings have shot up and down.

"Along with the studies on heart disease, we do know that hormones increase the risk for blood clots and gall bladder disease, and reduce the risk for osteoporotic fractures," Dr. Schaffel starts out. "There is debate on the impact of hormones on Alzheimer's, stroke, and breast cancer. We have lived with the confusion. When I came on board, it was just at the transition when estrogen was believed to make you feel wonderful and live longer. Then we found out estrogen also increases the risk of endometrial cancer. Next, we found out that if you pair estrogen with progesterone, you eliminate that risk for endometrial cancer.

"And so it goes with the research—are hormones good for

your heart, or are they bad for your heart? Do they cause breast cancer, or do they reduce the risk of reoccurrence of breast cancer? Are they good for mental clarity? What it comes down to is that every woman has to work with her health care provider to determine if she is a candidate for hormones based on her health profile and anxiety levels over this conflicting data. But here's an interesting anecdote: There was a study that looked at hormone use among female ob-gyns, and the percentage of those physicians who choose to take estrogen is extremely high. They felt the perceived benefits outweighed the perceived risks."

Joanne had a full hysterectomy at the age of thirty-nine after an IUD caused a chronic infection, throwing her into full menopause. She took estrogen for twenty years, then when she turned sixty, she became engaged in a "best sex of my life" love affair, dropped the hormones, and has never looked back. She says the hysterectomy that threw her into early menopause left her feeling "like anyone who thinks this dries up a woman's body is crazy. I was always up for sex." Again, a lot of the reason she was up for sex was because she had a sexy and adoring partner.

I met Joanne when I was doing a book signing in Florida, where she was dressed in a white cable-knit sweater and tight white jeans, and could have been forty-five and not her actual sixty-five. She lives in a beach town populated with ripped young surfers and a fervent bar scene. Her preference, though, to satiate what she describes as a "lifelong high libido" are partners her own age, a pool she admits are slim pickings since many of those prospects go for younger women. The man she calls the "love of my life," seventy-four-year-old Richard, awakened her to what is possible in an aging woman who has gone through a double whammy, a hysterectomy and menopause.

JOANNE

The myth is that a woman withers up after she gets her female organs out, or when she is menopausal, and I say "bullshit!" Talk to a hundred women and you may get a hundred different stories, but my drive certainly didn't lessen—in fact, it increased. I never felt unfeminine. It was the best thing that ever happened to me. The sexual act itself felt better. My boyfriend of twenty years certainly didn't complain.

Richard died a year ago at the age of seventy-four. You talk about a sexual man? He was the same in bed at fifty-six as he was at seventy-four—virile without Viagra. He had heart issues, so he was advised not to take ED medication, but he never had a problem getting it up. He was just an extremely sexy person; he exuded sex. Oh, I can't even describe it. He was just amazing.

Not to brag, but I've had great sex with all my serious boyfriends all through my life. And with those boyfriends, sometimes they'd disappear for years but we always reconnected; they would come around again for more. But Richard was the hottest romance I've ever had, and it's been tough to replace.

I have my original copy of *The Sensuous Woman*, and I re-read it from time to time. That book just kind of reinforces my own feelings that a woman should be as sexual as a man. I guess I'm lucky. All my life I was never one of those women who couldn't have an orgasm. It just came! Literally.

Richard and I would go away for weekends. He slept over most weekdays. I was really falling in love, possibly for the first time ever. His touch, his smell, his masculinity—everything about Richard was a turn-on to me. He made me feel like the most beautiful and sensual woman alive. I absolutely loved, loved him! The one problem with our relationship was that this was a man who was serially monogamous by nature, emphasis on serially. However, when he was with you in a relationship, you were the center of his world, and he would be faithful. I did this routine for twenty years with Richard—we'd be together, then we'd break up for two or three years so he could be with another woman, then he'd come back to me.

He loved the chase. He loved the wooing, the courting, the capture. Once he got his prey, it would last two or three years before he would meet someone else whom he'd want to sweep off her feet. Then when that got old, he'd come back to me—always, he returned to me. And I'd date other men, but there was no one else like Richard.

In bed he was so adventurous, nothing was off-limits. Out of bed, Richard was equally adventurous. We would do hot air balloon rides. I went white water rafting and mountain climbing with him. So I took him back whenever he came back to me; I was powerless to say no to this man. He was just a real Romeo.

He kissed great. He had a nice body. He never let himself get fat. He had stamina. He loved to love. That just says it all. When we took our big trips together, I always wrote something in my diary. The other day, I was reading through it and I found this: "I'm in love with this guy and having the best sex of my life—at sixty. What more could I ask for?"

I won't let myself believe that this is the last of my hot lovers. I'm way too young to give up on good sex. But I know I lost perhaps the best I'll ever have in Richard. His death is still very fresh in my mind, though it's been nearly a year. He didn't show up for work and his son found him in bed, dead, of a heart attack.

And so died my hot love affair. The good news is that my appetite at the age of sixty-five is stronger than ever. Don't listen to anyone who tells you that after menopause your sex life will be horrible. I'm here to tell you the other side; sex is more of the mind than of the body. With that freedom from the fear of getting pregnant comes the ability to really let loose and enjoy everything about the sexual experience. My orgasms didn't become less intense; in fact, they seemed deeper and they would shudder through my body longer.

I took estrogen for about twenty years after the hysterectomy, but when I stopped taking it, my desire never waned. Just recently, I started dating again. And even if I don't find the whole package like I did with Richard, I know I'm going to find a good sexual partner. I need that. I've got lots of mileage left. One guy I went out with recently was ten years younger and sex with him was great. Believe me, I can keep up with these guys physically, but for a relationship to last, they need to be able to keep up with me mentally.

That's the key to successful sex—it's got to be a mental match. I used to melt from Richard's touch, but so much of our lasting connection in and out of bed was about the meshing of our minds.

Joanne is one of the fortunate women whose hysterectomy did not alter her sense of femininity or her appetite for sex. As with breast cancer, much of the psychological impact of a hysterectomy comes from dealing with the loss of a body part that defines womanhood. Because the reasons for the surgery vary, whether the patient presents with gynecological cancer, irregular bleeding, fibroid cysts, or infections like Joanne's, it is impossible to make general assumptions about sexuality after hysterectomy. Radical hysterectomies to cure severe cancer cases and other conditions can result in nerve damage and numbness of the vulva. Chemotherapy tends to cloud a person's overall sense of well-being, which can reduce libido. Radiation can cause bleeding, burns, and stricture, or a reduction in the width of the vagina. Despite the trauma of the surgery on the body and often the mind, some studies do mirror what Joanne is so pleased about, that sexual satisfaction was magnified post-hysterectomy, particularly with the lift on the psyche when a cancer is removed.

Enhanced pleasure can also come from the freedom from risk of a late-life pregnancy, unless the ovaries are left intact. A healthy menopausal woman can have sex whenever and wherever—since the kids are also likely out of the nest. (I did not do a poll, but I presume there is a big jump in kitchen sex after the age of fifty.)

Overall, since orgasm is largely clitoris-dependent, without other complications, most women should be able to resume full-on sexual enjoyment, minus a uterus. This is hopeful news as we age because chances are high that one of us will go through this. Hysterectomy is the second most common major surgical procedure performed on women worldwide, and almost one in three women in the United States have undergone a hysterectomy by the age of sixty.

SEX IMPROVES AFTER HYSTERECTOMY trumpeted headlines in health sections of newspapers and medical journals to announce a landmark study conducted with thirteen hundred women at the University of Maryland Medical Center. After the surgery, high percentages of women reported that they were having more sex, better sex, and more frequent orgasms as well as a dramatic reduction of pain during intercourse.

Other longitudinal studies conducted on thousands of women over the years have compared risks and benefits of vaginal, laparoscopic, and abdominal hysterectomy. Conclusions generally find that postoperative infection rates are higher for women undergoing open abdominal hysterectomy than those having laparoscopic or vaginal procedures. With smaller incisions and a less invasive surgical mode, the length of hospital stay and period of healing are also reduced.

While sex may improve, the choice to get a hysterectomy, if not a medical emergency, needs to be scrupulously thought out. Because something really bad could happen as well, such as perforation of other organs, more bleeding, more pain. If you do not have severe gynecological symptoms or cancer, explore other alternatives before going under the knife. There is progress with technology using lasers to heat and shrink uterine fibroids, which are among the most common reasons women get hysterectomies. And there are holistic routes to explore for pelvic pain, as documented in the interview below with nurse practitioner Deborah Nichols.

With women increasingly living into their nineties, a botched hysterectomy you get at sixty can result in suffering for the next three decades of your life.

I have just talked a lot about physical aspects, but I am remembering this essential line from Joanne about the key to successful sex—"It's got to be a mental match." She relays how she used to "melt from Richard's touch" but that it was the meshing of their minds that made their connection last. Like Joanne, Lynn discusses a love affair that reaches below the sensations of the skin. Unlike Joanne, Lynn is placidly content with a menopausal turning point that has put her in a place where she has no desire for sex, and has no desire to get back that desire. This is because the act of intercourse has become so painful, she is not urgent to tinker with her libido.

Lynn's first marriage in her early twenties, which produced one child, was sexually satisfying throughout their fifteen years together. Her second marriage in her middle forties was also very sexy for years—but she claims now is even "more intimate" without that body heat. Lynn has short white hair and luminous blue eyes and a peaceful acceptance about her life without sex that reminds me of my friends who have turned into spiritual beings after Alcoholics Anonymous drained their booze.

LYNN

I have always loved sex although it is increasingly becoming a thing of the past. My vagina has shriveled up, and sex is painful. Apparently, since I didn't deliver any babies vaginally, mine lacks the elasticity that others have. It isn't a huge problem for Ron as his testosterone levels are bottoming out and we're really content holding each other, kissing and cuddling a lot. He's still very romantic and intimate, but the act of intercourse is on its way out.

We've been together for sixteen years. When I met Ron, it was extremely sexual; we were having sex three and four times a day; our record was five times in one day. We were starved, both of us, for loving attention and physical intimacy. So it was hot, hot, hot for a few years. Then the norm became once a week, then twice a month, and now in the last couple of years, nothing. But that first phase when we were like rabbits, it lasted for about five good years.

As in most relationships, that initial euphoria just can't last. But we continued to be sexual until things really took a turn when I hit menopause four years ago. What happened was that I just dried up. There was very little lubrication, and at the same time, my desire started to wane. Ron was very accepting because his drop in libido kind of matched mine—he had a real drop in testosterone.

My gynecologist explained to me that if I had never had a vaginal delivery, the opening to my vagina is small, and without lubrication it's like a dry rubber band. And if you put something in it that's too big, it could tear those tissues. So being tight and dry, intercourse became very painful. A year ago, we were trying to have sex and I just couldn't do it. My doctor told me to try oil-based lubricants, like coconut oil, and that helped get me lubricated enough, and get it in, but afterward, I felt like I had a burning fire down there. I had to waddle; I couldn't even walk normally.

We had many tearful discussions—I was sad, and I still am sad. We have all the cuddling and hugging and kissing, and all that's wonderful. But I miss the intimacy of intercourse that you just don't get any other way, that intimacy of being joined as one.

The estrogen suppositories I took did help in keeping things moist and I have moved on to the dilators, these five graduated plastic penises that fit into each other like those little Russian dolls. You start with a small one, then you move up to the Wilt Chamberlain model—nine inches long and two inches in diameter. It's enormous.

I do not like them! Ugh! You have to lie there in bed; each one goes in for five minutes; you are moving through the five levels, watching TV, watching the clock, with these plastic things in you. It's too much work; I'm about to quit using them— I call them my vaginators. And even if they are helping to stretch the tissues, I just don't care. The desire isn't strong enough to make it worth the effort. My libido is so zero. I am having sadness over the loss of intimacy, but I don't have any real desire to have sex.

So it's a catch-22—I want to want to, but I just don't.

While this was happening to me, Ron saw his own doctor, who told him his decline in libido coincides with his decrease in testosterone. He is now applying testosterone cream. I offer to give him blow jobs but he's like me—he's not that interested in it and I'm not interested in him doing oral sex on me. We're just not hot and heavy enough to both head south.

Yet this is a man I am more madly in love with than when we were having sex five times a day. The more I've gotten to know him and shared life experiences together, I just know how fantastic this man is. On an emotional level, we have an incredible bond. He's my best friend. We have a spiritual connection that is strong and growing. There are just no more feelings of wanting to jump on each other.

When I think of the loss, it isn't intense grief like "Oh my God, I wish our sex was like it was when I was thirty-five." It isn't something like a huge missing element in my life. It's more like a memory of something, a thought like *Wouldn't it be nice to have that again*. We haven't talked about Viagra because of the libido issue; there is no desire. The last time we had intercourse was New Year's Eve 2011, and that was a success, but not something we have tried again. This no-sex state for us would be a much different issue if we didn't both feel this way. But I think, on a scale of one to ten, my libido is about a zero and his is probably a three.

I can't imagine it could be like this for most people, but without sex, this relationship is so solid. Sometimes I feel I should push it with my vaginators, like an exercise program where I force myself up to the size five Chamberlain model. I could do this religiously for a month and see what happens. But I don't have the inclination or motivation to put in that effort, and Ron hasn't encouraged that.

So I'm out the forty dollars that it cost for the dilator set sitting there out of use. I'd rather spend time with my husband hiking than lying around alone for forty-five minutes with these gadgets up me. We hold hands, we cuddle, we kiss—we are very romantic for people our age. And we really are in love. There is just this one nonfunctional area of our relationship, which I know is a major area. But it's just not that important to us right now.

I spoke to my gynecologist about it, and she said, "There

are a lot of women in my practice not having sex anymore and they are perfectly happy in their marriages. So you don't have to do it. Don't stress over it. You have a quality marriage without it." And that was reassuring, although I do think, *I'm too young for this*; I didn't think it would happen in my fifties. I don't even masturbate anymore; I am just not missing having an orgasm. I'm very fulfilled in so many other ways.

I have had a lot of time in this new phase to think about what sexuality really means. I realize that, with us, our hotness for each other was never just sex, it was love sex. There was always a spiritual component to sex that was way more than I have ever had before in my life. Ours was very connected sex. We had eyes-wide-open sex without hiding anything. Now I still have that honesty and intimacy, on a deeper level.

Lynn and her husband are giving each other what each other needs, sexy and compassionate loving without passionate lovemaking. As the interviews throughout the book have consistently revealed, it is women like Lynn, whose libido and interests are aligned with her spouse, who are able to form the tightest relationships.

Ilene is in the best shape of her life, physically active, and her libido, unlike Lynn's, is ripe and raring to go. Her husband is overweight, out of a job, and getting heavier and more sedentary with each passing day. Needless to say, they are at an impasse in intimacy.

Ilene is a tax attorney from Indiana who just celebrated her twenty-fifth wedding anniversary. She is fifty-six, the reigning smash server in an adult volleyball league, and has been taking hormones for the past three years, coinciding with the onset of an "unbearable menopause." Ilene also has an enormous sex drive, and no impulse or desire to unleash that desire onto her husband, who, has gotten "fat and lazy and generally unattractive."

A staunch Catholic who misses sex immensely she says she still "would never cheat on my husband," the father of their three sons. Yet Ilene feels stuck and sad and doubtful about the chances of a revival of the cozy romance the couple once shared earlier in their marriage when, as she puts it, "He was passing on the fettuccine Alfredo and getting his ass out of the house."

Here is more from Ilene, dressed in short shorts and a tank top that show off an impressive athlete's build:

ILENE

Here I am closer to sixty than fifty, and I am at my physical and emotional peak right now, working with a personal trainer, I can fit into my high school jeans. And I've been taking hormones since the start of menopause to alleviate some really bad night sweats and mood swings, and I do think they have helped me keep my weight down and give me more energy.

My husband is obese, and because he is on many medications for his various illnesses, including high blood pressure, that come from being overweight, he can't hold an erection. I feel like saying, "Look, buddy, if you passed up the heaps of pasta at dinner and stuck with salad, you'd lose weight. Your blood pressure and cholesterol would go down. You would have more energy. Then maybe your dick would get hard."

He tried Viagra and it did work, but honestly, I'm just not that into him. He's a turnoff to me right now, this at a time when I am totally interested in having a fulfilling sex life. I am on an upswing in my life and in my health. And our timing is wrong; my husband is on the decline.

When menopause arrived, I was hit hard and I took control right away. Along with horrible hot flashes and sleep interruption, there was a noticeable increase in irritability, bitchiness.

Things that wouldn't have bothered me did bother me, with a quick anger response or a sudden sadness. I went to my OB and talked to her about the gamut of hormone replacement therapy and how the studies showed mixed results. She told me that hormones could heighten my chances for breast cancer and they could diminish my chances for colon cancer. I told her I'd rather have breast cancer than colon cancer, and I've been taking a combination of estrogen and progesterone ever since.

I think they are great. The only side effect is that I feel better; I don't have hot flashes. My mood is much more balanced. I sleep through the night. My coping mechanism for the everyday shit that happens in our lives is much better. With exercise and just feeling really settled in my career, I do my accounting work part-time and I'm self-employed, I am feeling right now a sense of personal well-being. This could be a really good time to have a healthy sex life.

But I have no sexual attraction for an out-of-work husband who is an emotional eater and rapidly gaining weight. I have to admit that even before menopause, our sex life had taken a dive. He had just lost his job and I had to work overtime, so between insane hours on the job, raising children, and dealing with a depressed husband, being intimate was a tough place to get to. And he had so many other health issues associated with being fat, sex was really not happening often, and when it did happen, it wasn't happening well.

He has hypertension, high cholesterol, sleep apnea—he sleeps with one of those breathing machines. And all of these things are associated with being overweight, plus lately he has developed a heart arrhythmia. So he's got to be on a lot of drugs, and instead of listening to doctors who tell him to diet and exercise, he is in a slump. He doesn't move much.

Right now, he is starting his own business and we'll see how this goes. He's been out of work for the past eight months. The way I respond to all of this is that I get determined to get even more fit; I want to be there for my children, and for our future grandchildren. I worry that he will not last long at this rate.

So, recently, I was at a birthday party for a seventy-year-old neighbor, and she looked just great and her husband looked great. She said, "I've got this personal trainer." I asked for the phone number and now I go to that trainer three days a week. Since I can't control my husband's health, I've really taken my own health to a new height. I know we lose muscle mass as we age, but I'm determined to keep that tone and energy level going. Our volleyball team was first in our league last year.

Exercise for me, with this emotional downturn in my marriage, is very therapeutic. I am doing this for myself and for my family; I don't want to be in my seventies and have a stroke and have to be pushed around. Keeping in shape really staves off menopausal symptoms. I've always been an athlete and exercise helps cure all ills, and it is way cheaper than a therapist. And because of the way I look and feel, I am feeling much more sexual than ever. I have not lost interest in sex one iota. Do I get any? No. So that's kind of the tension. I'm interested and ready to go and my husband is not. Even if he was, it's me who is not interested in him. And every five pounds he puts on, which keeps happening, we are further away from restoring any semblance of intimacy.

And I am angry about this. A big piece of him not taking care of himself is going to affect me. Because he's going to be the one in a wheelchair, and I'm going to be the one having to push him around. And I'm going to resent it because I will remember that there was something he could have done about it and he refused to do so.

I could have an affair, but it's not in me. I don't want to violate our vows, though this tears me up. Because on the other hand, having intimacy, which is an important dimension of a marriage, has disappeared because of his negligence about his own health. I know there are a lot of people living in sexless marriages, but they stay put because they have great families. We have a great family, so I say to myself, "Okay, this is what I got right now." I'm already resigned to being a young widow who will be able to have romance again someday. My parents are still relatively healthy and they are in their middle eighties.

You know, you can't stop someone from ordering the fettuccine Alfredo and the wedge of lettuce piled with blue cheese and bacon dressing, then going for a huge dessert. It is so frustrating because I know if he lost fifty pounds, he would be able to get off nearly all of those medicines. Let's put it this way: The way I feel now is that if something does happen to him, I may not be calling 9-1-1 so quickly. I say that today, but then I remember. He is the father of my children. We are a family. I do love him. But I feel like I'm living with a brother.

This break in communication that comes from anger and frustration can be the last straw that separates marriage from divorce. Ilene, though, will likely stay on the betrothed side of the fence, because she is gaining personal fulfillment from her own pursuits. And as she states in the end, she does love the guy. As she also predicts, at this rate, she may have a second chance at a love relationship that incorporates intimacy.

Listening to forthright and divided voices during the two years of research for this book, I have had a lot of time to think about what sexuality really means in a committed relationship. As you have read, the definition of the word holds diverse meanings for each individual. I hope that within this wide array of stories, you have found someone who makes you feel you are not alone. And that you have realized there is no *normal* when it comes to an individual's sexual temperature. If you are like Lynn with "zero libido" and are ready to surrender into sexless bliss, that is not abnormal if it feels right to you. But if you do desire to have more desire and have a partner you desire, too, there are numerous treatments that lube and relax and get you more pumped up for sex, from holistic regimens to hormones to hard-core drugs in the making.

As I write this, millions of dollars are being spent by pharmaceutical companies to perfect pills to treat sexual dysfunction in women, including one being called the female Viagra. My neighbor in Maryland, Dr. Andrew Goldstein, has been involved in a dozen or so different trials with these drugs geared toward helping women with low desire, decreased arousal, pain with sex, and vulvovaginal atrophy. Dr. Goldstein predicts that one or more of these drugs will be FDA-approved and on the market by the time you are reading this book.

You may have seen Dr. Goldstein discussing female sexual stimulation with the mesmerized hosts of *The View* in January 2010. He developed his niche in the field of sexual health when he joined Johns Hopkins Department of Gynecology and Obstetrics in 2000. He is now the director of The Centers for Vulvovaginal Disorders, which has offices in New York City, Washington, DC, and Annapolis and is president of the International Society for the Study of Women's Sexual Health.

Here is more from Dr. Goldstein, a fit man of forty-six, who has lots of gray hair and a childlike enthusiasm when he discusses the intricacies and goal of his practice—to alleviate sexual pain for women.

DR. ANDREW GOLDSTEIN

When I started in this area of medicine, I would ask every woman who came in about basic things, such as: Do you have any problems with your libido during sex? Do you have difficulty having an orgasm? You know, frankly, on the libido subject, every other woman said, "I'd rather be gardening. What can you do about it?" And I didn't have an answer.

But then I started doing research into what literature was available and there was almost nothing out there at the time. There were lots of books about orgasms with titles like *The Key to Sexual Bliss,* but there were no books on what people were complaining about to me: low libido and pain during intercourse.

This was exactly at the same time that Viagra came out. And women's health expert Dr. Judith Reichman went on the *Today Show* and started talking about testosterone for women, and everyone started knocking down the doors for testosterone cream. And I started prescribing that and realized that people would get a boost in their libido for about two to three months. Then frequently they'd come back in and say, "My libido is not good anymore." It was a temporary thing. It wasn't working because there were a variety of other medical and relationship issues that weren't being addressed by the testosterone cream. I do recommend testosterone if the calculated free testosterone is low and I do not think the primary cause of a woman's lack of desire is a poor relationship or sexual boredom.

What I found out while looking into the source of low libido and difficulty orgasming was that a lot of these women had pain with sex, all the time. One cause of sexual pain that was frequently overlooked were dermatologic diseases of the vulva, such as lichen sclerosus and lichen planus. They're not

STDs. They are skin diseases. And when properly diagnosed, these diseases are very treatable with topical steroids. About 20 percent of my patients have a skin disease as the source of their pain.

There was a seventy-four-year-old woman I treated who came to me because she had tearing during sex. She was married to a fifty-nine-year-old guy and I discovered she had one of these skin diseases, which I was able to treat. She could be one of the happiest of any of my patients ever because she is able to keep having great sex with her husband, who is a lot younger than she.

At menopause, the number of people reporting vulva pain slightly increases. But while there is an increase in pain at that time, there are also women who are having pain from age sixteen through their senior years. There are some twenty different reasons why people have vulvodynia, which means vulvar pain of unknown reason. The most common cause of pain is actually because the patient has been on birth control pills for years and years, which causes dryness. Many young women don't know this when they start on pills in their teens, stop during childbearing years, then start up again until menopause. Often, women aren't told by their gynecologists when they are prescribed the pill that dryness is a major side effect.

I can help 90 percent of my patients with their vulvar pain. And all women of course feel a lot happier when the pain is lifted from performing the most basic of human pleasures and instincts. Clearly, at the level of our hypothalamus, there's nothing like sex to release the endorphins and oxytocin and dopamine that make us feel so good and that probably helps us live longer. Pain of the vulva is a fundamental block to what humans, the social primates, are hardwired to do, and that is to be intimate.

I leave Dr. Goldstein and rolling around in my mind is the fundamental issue that made me want to write this book in the first place, to discover the role of sex in our hardwired need for intimacy. I am wondering what will happen when women start popping pills that make them instantly aroused, like Viagra does for guys. Many women have told me they are no fans of Viagra because it means hard sex on demand when their mood may be for soft caresses. How will male partners feel if the tables are turned? A pill to bring on female desire is the predominant topic of discussion at our next Girls' Night Out with women ages fifty to seventy-five, a Cabernet-infused cluster in which opinions are as mixed as our libidos.

From the biggest supporter of the idea: "I would take it in a heartbeat. In my mind I want to have sex more often but I don't get that twang down there anymore."

And from the biggest opponent, who happens also to be the youngest: "Never would I take this. Why can't we just let our bodies age naturally and let our sex drive flow with them? It's just another designer drug that will make women feel like they need to be sexier, like some women already feel who are getting designer vaginas."

Designer vaginas is an umbrella term to describe an advancing area of plastic surgery in which vaginas are tightened and labia are shortened, not generally for vulvar pain or abnormality but because women want porno-perfect vulvas—even though much of that perfection is airbrushed and Photoshopped. There is a heated schism in the medical community about these procedures, as Dr. Goldstein and his dermatologist wife, Dr. Gail Goldstein, address in a comprehensive article they cowrote with other physicians on elective vulvar plastic surgery titled "Is Elective Vulvar Plastic Surgery Ever Warranted, and What Screening

Should Be Conducted Preoperatively?" that ran in a 2007 issue of *The Journal of Sexual Medicine*.

Dr. Gloria Bachmann's section in the article had some of the strongest language about what doctors and patients should consider before proceeding with what is called vaginal rejuvenation. As she wrote:

". . . I firmly believe that, preoperatively, the woman should be clearly told that excessive labial tissue or prominent labia minora are variations of normal genital anatomy and do not impair genital function. For example, it should not be inferred that labia minora are abnormal if they protrude through the labia majora, and that this condition will lead to sexual dysfunction, future problems, or pathology. Language should be avoided that implies that the labia minora, labia majora, clitoral hood, or the mons pubis are misshaped or ugly and, through surgery, can be 'restored' to be more appealing in size and shape. The woman should be clearly told that she is having cosmetic surgery, to make the area more pleasing to her and/or her partner, and that she is not having vulvar reconstruction, which denotes surgery for abnormal function."

I remember in the early 1970s when the iconic book on female sexual health, *Our Bodies, Ourselves*, came out and young women were using speculums to see how their vulvas looked, and how their friends' looked. Buoyed by feminism, women were beginning to embrace their imperfect bodies and to revere their hidden feminine parts as outwardly beautiful, like men have done with their penises for centuries. That the vulva deserves pride and not shame is celebrated through the enduring popularity of *The Vagina Monologues*, Eve Ensler's play that premiered in 1996 and sparked a global nonprofit movement that has raised more than $75 million for women's antiviolence groups through benefit productions.

I am composing this chapter on still another Southwest flight, and when we land, I begin a conversation with a woman named Deborah Nichols walking alongside me at Chicago's Midway Airport. I apologize for looking so bleary-eyed and explain I had been writing the whole flight, about sex. Turns out, serendipitously, Deborah is a board-certified women's health nurse practitioner, and had just returned from a Society for Sex Therapy and Research conference. Two weeks later, I resume a much longer conversation with Deborah, sixty, who doles out valuable insights on aging, vagina varieties, and natural ways to enhance desire from her experiences in her Berkeley, California, practice, one very cool town and a mecca for enlightened health care for women.

DEBORAH NICHOLS

My goal is to help women look at what libido really means to them, how it changes as we age, and to get strategies to help improve their quality of life. Many older women lose the familiar sensations of being aroused or having desire that tingles in the vulva or low abdomen, that tell her, "I want to make love." This is a big loss for many. There is hope, though; women can learn to rethink the whole nature of desire. A lot of it comes from the brain, rather than the vulva.

Desire runs the gamut. I see some women who say that they have no interest, no desire. They don't even think about sex—and in some cases, their partners are frustrated. I have seen older women who desire intimacy frequently. Some patients are unhappy because they have pain with penetration; some have had no penetration for twenty years and may be with a new partner and want to try again. The prescriptive path I take depends on what they are interested in achieving.

I will use hormone therapy when it is safe and indicated, but I steer away from hormones if a woman is past menopause more than ten years, following the Women's Health Initiative findings and the North American Menopause Society guidelines, which suggest that oral hormone therapy is most often contraindicated for women with breast and uterine cancers. Oncologists should always be consulted by women who have a history of breast cancer if estrogen is to be used, and their advice is usually on a case-by-case basis. There are other regimens to reduce vaginal dryness using natural lubricants internally and vulvar moisturizers for those who are not able to, or choose not to, use hormones.

Yesterday, I had a sixty-two-year-old woman come to see me. She was a lovely nurse married twenty-eight years who had been through menopause. She told me that intercourse was so painful she felt like shards of glass were shooting through her with deep penetration. I hear this complaint commonly. She went to her gynecologist, who gave her estrogen, and she kept saying to him, "I'm still having this horrible pain." He told her, "You are not having enough foreplay." She finally switched over to a female provider, who told her, "You need more estrogen cream, you are so dry"—then I saw her.

As it turned out, her vaginal tissue was perfectly healthy and the cause of the pain was from muscle spasms in her pelvic floor. I treated her with medication to correct the nerve dysfunction and sent her to physical therapy, an effective and relatively new treatment for this kind of response. The physical therapist will, among other treatment modalities, manually stretch the muscles of the pelvis and abdominal wall, which are accessed via the vaginal canal. These treatments help to release the internal spasm, like working out a charley horse you get in a leg muscle, thus reducing the pain.

I realize that I live in a very progressive part of the country, in Berkeley. Yet I also see that in general we are witnessing more progressive thinking across the board in the field of sexual health. Hopefully, some of the fears and stereotypes about not having the perfect female genitalia are disappearing, too.

Women often ask me what a normal vulva and vagina should look like. Some women express concern about the attractiveness of their vulvas when one labia is larger than the other, and have said, "I don't want to have oral sex because I don't think I look nice down there." I tell them, "I wish you could spend a day with me and you will see how different everybody is, and that there is no normal." I will recommend books such as *Petals* by Nick Karras or *Femalia* by Joani Blank, which illustrate with many photographs of vulvas from women of all ages and races how beautifully varied we are.

Variation is the theme. The clitoris comes in different sizes. Labia can be all shapes and sizes. Hair patterns are different, and as we age, pubic hair can become sparse. Some women have more profound vaginal atrophy after menopause. When we lose estrogen, the normal plump cells start to thin out and the vagina becomes less elastic and lubricated. The takeaway is that just as our noses are varied, so are our vulvas. Attitudes and experiences are different for everyone as we age.

I recently saw a very religious woman who was seventy-two and her husband had died several years earlier. She had connected with a man with whom she has been having amazing sex. She told me that she felt terribly guilty about it, that she was doing something wrong because it was out of wedlock. Then she lowered her voice and with great consternation stated that her boyfriend told her, when she has an orgasm, liquid squirted out of her—she was mortified. I said, "That's

fantastic! No need to be alarmed. That is known as female ejaculation." She was so relieved. Later I heard from her internist
that she said, "I am owning my sexuality now!"

You have just heard the voices of very different types of menopausal women who are all working toward owning their emerging sexuality as hormones shift, bodies change, and minds are
attempting to mold around all of it. I got a touching letter from a
fifty-five-year-old husband on the subject of his menopausal wife
who was both mystifying him and confusing him, alternating between tantrums and initiating great "makeup" sex. It seems only
fair to let a handpicked man speak out on the subject, so here is the
voice of Wayne, from Montreal:

WAYNE

During the lead-up to menopause and the height of it, my wife
was very much a different personality. In time, her turmoil
seemed to resemble what I saw in my daughters when they
passed through adolescence. It wasn't just bickering and making up that affected our sex life. Her sexual response became
stronger. We had always had similar appetites; when we got together, typically our lovemaking had a climax for each of us.

During menopause her appetite grew, and her capacity for
orgasms made me feel that my skills in pleasuring this woman
would become the stuff of legends. I used to tell her that she
was so wild that I hoped my wife wouldn't find out about her.
There is so much literature out there that says that, in general,
people as they age get happier. I love my wife; we're both in our
mid-fifties, and she is sexy as only a woman in her fifties can be.
I have this ongoing tension with men my age; a lot of these

friends make noises that younger women are more attractive than women our wives' ages.

My experience is that we have the opportunity to love every facet of a woman. I loved her as a twenty-two-year-old, I loved her when she was pregnant, then postpartum. I loved her in her mid-forties, and I will love her as a seventy-five-year-old.

Today I love her as a fifty-two-year-old.

PART FOUR

~

ADVENTURES IN OUTERCOURSE

CHAPTER 10
HIS AGING PARTS

There's no question about the fact that prostate cancer cuts to the heart of the masculine ego.

—DR. MARK SOLOWAY

I always find great source material in and around Miami, a hotbed (literally) for retired seniors who tend to live long and well, as they are religious about staying engaged with friends, exercising, and searching out the best doctors, habits that lead to longevity. And the wives are vigilant about not only advocating for their own health but also about looking out for their men.

I asked around to see who was the go-to urologist for the prostate problems that plague most men as they age. The name that kept recurring was Dr. Mark Soloway, who recently stepped down from his nineteen-year tenure as chairman of the Department of Urology at the University of Miami's Miller School of

Medicine, where he still has an active practice. Dr. Soloway has conducted extensive research in prostate cancer and the corresponding indication for surgery, and is recognized as one of the country's most influential urologic oncologists.

This is a cancer that forms in the tissues of the prostate, a gland the size of a plum in males that fronts the rectum and lies below the bladder. The gland secretes a milky fluid that makes up almost all of the volume of the sperm-packed semen. Based on 2014 statistics from the National Cancer Institute, there are 233,000 new cases of prostate cancer a year, and of that figure, 29,480 men will die of the disease. There is slightly more than 8 percent probability of a man developing cancer of the prostate between his fiftieth and seventieth birthday, and the average age of diagnosis is sixty-six.

Often when I speak to doctors, the interviews are muddled with jargon a lay person needs a medical dictionary to decipher. Dr. Soloway speaks in plain and straight language about the penis and prostate and cancer. And although performing surgery is a lucrative mainstay of his profession, he is out front in warning men with small tumors *not* to go under the knife as soon as they hear the words *prostate cancer*, for the procedure is overprescribed and frequently impairs erectile function.

I give Dr. Soloway a good chunk of space in this book geared toward women because, as we all know, the evolution of a couple's sex life is often in the female's hands. And if a spouse is diagnosed with prostate cancer, it is important that we are knowledgeable about his medical options and the corresponding side effects. Women are also more vocal about pushing for second opinions, something this doctor recommends.

DR. MARK SOLOWAY

The great majority of men with low-grade prostate cancer will never die of this cancer. But you hear the word *cancer* and the response is immediately "Get it out of me." So the men will go through with surgery when there was no threat of dying within the span of their lifetimes from this often slow-growing cancer. They might lose continence and erectile function, which is a real blow to the ego and causes a shift in intimate relationships.

There's no question about the fact that prostate cancer cuts to the heart of the masculine ego. This is a typical scene: The couple is in the room, they are about the same age, and as soon as you start talking about the sexual function after surgery, almost uniformly, the wife says: "Look, I just want this guy around. Take care of his cancer. I'm not worried about erections." Generally, his wife is probably postmenopausal and she is okay not to have the hard sexathons anymore.

But the man, when he's alone with me, will say, "Hey, you know what? I need to hear more about this, and let's explore other options." Maintaining the ability to have an erection is obviously something that many men think is important; it's what they associate with being a man. A big problem in our field is that there are often no open discussions in the office about sexuality; the doctor talks to prostate patients about the medical and surgical issues. I think that is one of our failings as urologists, and doctors in general, that we're not terribly comfortable talking about how medical procedures impact issues of intimacy. We are trained to discuss physical problems.

But I go there right away. As soon as they are diagnosed with prostate cancer, I say, "A lot of what we are going to talk about, treatment versus nontreatment, the biggest elephant in the room is sexual function." I tell them that once we start any consideration of treatment, erectile issues are definitely a potential problem.

When I get a patient who has prostate cancer, it's very important to see if that person is a candidate for what we call active surveillance—which means no treatment at all other than watching the tumor closely for changes. Because there is no doubt that there is a lot of overtreatment for prostate cancer. Many men, particularly as they get older, are candidates for this no-initial-treatment approach. This would avoid the side effects of surgery or radiation or other treatments such as focused ultrasound or freezing the prostate.

We actually did a study of prostate cancer patients through the Department of Urology at the University of Miami and we found that 30 percent of the doctors who made the diagnoses never mentioned active surveillance as one of the options, even though these men, because of their pathology, were candidates for this approach. They were told they could have either surgery or radiation. If a man gets this diagnosis and his doctor does not mention active surveillance as an option, he should get a second opinion, which is the correct route to go for any kind of cancer.

I would also advise this patient to get as accurate a determination as possible of how the treatments recommended are likely to affect his quality of life. We do see when radiation seeds are planted in the prostate that treatment is equally effective for most cancers and probably has much less impact specifically on erection problems.

When a man is tested for levels of prostate-specific antigen, or PSA, he is being tested for an enzyme that is made only in the prostate, and its purpose relates to fertility. Many factors can raise the blood level of PSA: prostate enlargement, which is normal for the aging man, inflammation of the prostate, and prostate cancer. There is no perfect normal level but in general, when the number is over 2.5, there is a 15 percent chance that a prostate biopsy will reveal prostate cancer. Yet if we removed the entire prostate from all men over fifty, a high percentage will have small foci of prostate cancer. This number increases with age and by eighty years old, more than one-half of prostates will have some cancer.

There is a big controversy now whether the PSA test should even be done, because even a slight elevation in PSA leads to prostate biopsies, then suddenly the man has a diagnosis of cancer. So even though it is a very tiny tumor, they wind up having a major intervention, be it surgery or radiation. Obviously, we aggressively treat high-grade cancers, which are potentially lethal.

Even without prostate surgery, the majority of men will start to have a decrease in their erectile function as they age. And as you get from age sixty to seventy-five, that percentage is going to go up. Basically, this is due to hardening of the arteries and the decrease of blood getting into the penis. For erections to work, blood has to rush into the penis, and stay there. So that's one whole category of erectile dysfunction, less blood getting into the penis. The other major cause is what we call venous leak, which is when the valves in the penile veins fail to shut down normally, causing the blood in the penis to escape. Then there is a whole category of medications that affect erections: diuretics, high blood pressure medications, beta-blockers.

Unrelated to cancer, a high percentage of men will show up in my office with an enlarged prostate and complaints about having trouble urinating. We may want to put them on a medication in a family of drugs that will shrink the prostate, a process that can take several months. Approximately between 5 to

10 percent of men taking these common drugs will experience a decrease in libido. And also because the gland is shrinking, it will cause a decrease in the amount of seminal fluid, which is made in the prostate. This lessening of semen and lower libido can be very disconcerting for some men, so they will discontinue the drug.

Then there is a whole other category of men affected by what we call andropause, which is really the male menopause and is now being much more openly discussed. Andropause is the time of life in males when testosterone may decrease. Testosterone replacement can be given by injection or more commonly in a topical salve that absorbs into the skin. I see this often. A man comes in and says, "You know, I feel tired. My sex drive is lousy." We measure his testosterone and if it's low, we try testosterone replacement. And we do see that when we get it to normal levels, many men are clearly seeing heightened libido and generally feel better.

When an enlarged prostate causes symptoms, a relatively common procedure is to trim out the obstructing prostate. To differentiate from surgery for cancer, this should not damage the nerves; this should not alter erections, but it will make it unlikely that fluid will come out with orgasm. It is very important that men be told prior to the procedure about this side effect so they won't be shocked after surgery once they have sex and no fluid comes out. The fluid instead goes back into the bladder, the neck of which has now been widened, which is what the operation was meant to do in the first place to improve the flow of urine. Some men are very upset with the thought of a dry ejaculation, and as was the case with pills that have the same effect, they may refuse to have the surgery because of it.

And of course, if that patient does end up with surgery and erectile dysfunction, he needs to be made aware by his doctor of all the potential options to help him along, from pills to pumps to prosthesis. The Viagra-type drugs are pretty safe. I rarely see someone having bad side effects from them. This family of drugs called PDE5 inhibitors, was developed by British scientists and became available in the United States in 1998. They work by closing off those valves that will then ward off the venous leak, and the blood stays in the penis. But the pills don't always work.

So then many patients use the vacuum pump, which is a plastic tube that fits over the penis and rests against the base. Air is pumped out and a vacuum is created; the blood is then sucked up and rushes into the penis—but then it has to stay there. With a normal erection, the venous valves keep the blood in the penis. But with ED, the man using a pump has to put a thick rubber band around the base of the penis to artificially keep the erection in place. The penis stays hard until you take the ring off.

There are also penile implants, or penile prostheses. In this procedure, a pump has been surgically implanted that contains a reservoir of saline solution. The man pumps up the implant by activating a small valve next to the scrotum, and this moves the fluid from the reservoir into the penis. Another procedure to produce erections is to inject a combination of medicines with a very thin, small needle directly into the side of the penis. These medications will open those arteries and close the veins, and the blood will enter the penis and stay there for up to an hour or so.

Overall, somewhere between 40 to 50 percent of men are going to have some alteration in their ability to have an erection after prostate surgery. Now, some urologists claim that it's only 5 percent of their patients that have these problems, but I don't believe it. I've been doing this for a long time, and that figure isn't accurate. We do find, though, if a young man has normal erections before surgery, and the nerves around the prostate are spared, 50 to 70 percent of such men will have a reasonable erection afterward. And I count in that group those we put on the PDE5 inhibitors.

My advice is to make a careful decision and discuss active surveillance with your doctor. Because the biggest side effect of surgery is a sexual side effect, there is no doubt about that. If someone has normal erectile function and a low-grade tiny cancer, I say, "You know what? We can watch you very carefully. I have three hundred patients with exactly what you have, with small low-grade cancers, who are not having surgery or radiation or any immediate treatment. I am watching them and I biopsy the prostate every year, and if there is no change, we just continue watching them."

There are about five or six institutions around the United States, including the University of Miami Miller School of Medicine, that are involved in a study showing that only about 30 to 40 percent of men are going to need treatment if they are being watched very carefully and have regular biopsies. These very small, slow-growing cancers are not going to kill a man, and we are sparing him from the potential side effects of surgery or radiation.

When we are not able to bring back erectile function, I have found that even my oldest men still want to continue to have sex, even if penetration is no longer possible. They want to continue being sexual beings until the day they die. I have many patients who are still having relatively active sex lives in their eighties—at least they tell me they are! How am I supposed to know if they are telling the truth? I hope it's true.

As you can imagine, in my line of work, I hear all sorts of personal things in my office. Size of the penis is an issue for some men. There are minor surgical procedures that divide the suspensory ligament of the penis to attempt to make it look longer, but it really does not do much. There is no way to make the penis longer. Some plastic surgeons place fat or other syn-thetic bulking agents in the penis to give it an increased girth. I think it looks ridiculous, actually, and fortunately I rarely see someone who has had this performed.

The issue of sexuality in men is related to so many aspects of their physical and mental status. It depends on factors such as whether they have been married for a long time, are single and looking, have other medical problems, as well as their part-ners' health and sexual desires. Nonetheless, many elderly men ask for a prescription for a PDE5 inhibitor even though we know the chance of its working may be low in that man. It gives them optimism. I guess it feels like buying a lottery ticket and knowing you have a chance to win.

I leave my conversation with Dr. Soloway and think about those guys who have insecurities that match the women who seek out "designer vagina" surgery, fooled by the vulvas air-brushed to perfection in porn. Any man who feels insecure about his own package when pitted against the cucumbers of male porn stars (many of them doctored by trick photography) should visit the Icelandic Phallological Museum in Reykjavik, Iceland, a palace of phalluses that houses dozens and dozens of penises representing every kind of mammal that inhabit Iceland.

But do not dwell upon the mammal organs beyond man, which will cause further insecurity. For example, the pickled whale penis wedged into a jar appears to be as large as a baby elephant's snout. Find the statue of the genitals of Iceland's entire men's handball team. I have no idea how replicas of their fifteen penises were made, yet there they are, alongside each other, necks craning, heads held high in slightly different directions, as if they were singing in a Christmas chorale.

Some have a curve, a few are lanky, others are stubby, each

is unique, and all are normal. Like the variety found in vulvas, penises come in an assortment of widths and lengths, and when erect average between five and six inches tall, according to Kinsey Institute research. Men who still think they fall short will be relieved to know that the human penis outguns all other primates—a male gorilla can weigh as much as four hundred pounds, but his erect penis is less than two inches.

Those men should also poll fifteen or two hundred women and they will find that a tape measure bears little measure of the breadth of their sexual fulfillment. What I hear most often is that thrilling sex is not mostly about what the penis can or cannot do, let alone how far it stretches out. It is the man who takes his time to discover what truly pleasures his partner all over her body—especially her brain—that gets the highest marks.

I am sharing information from Dr. Soloway with an eighty-one-year-old friend. She is shaking her head, and her mood shifts between grim and giggly as she relays that she is one of those women for whom sex has stopped cold, and not because of her lack of interest. Her husband is interested only in intercourse, and with his heart condition, he is afraid to take Viagra so they have a quick kiss goodnight and that is it.

"I would love to have sex, but my husband is afraid if he takes Viagra, he will die in bed," she says with a shrug. "I tell him, 'You should be so lucky.'"

I often get comments from women about Viagra, a subject that does seem to evoke loathing and loving. The loathing is from having to have sex when an erection takes hold but when the woman's desire may not be rising concurrently. The loving is frankly because a hard penis feels great. Then there is the opposite situation of my friend's above. The wives are worried about the side effects, and the guys would rather suffer those side effects than not get laid.

So who should take Viagra, and who should not? What fears are real?

Cardiologist Dr. Sam Green has to make this choice every day in his practice in Las Vegas, a city teeming with old men in second and third and fourth marriages, who are eager to perform with their partners, many of them who are substantially younger. Dr. Green said in his twenty-five years of practice, he has never had a patient die in bed from sex. He will not prescribe the Viagra family of drugs to patients who are taking nitroglycerin for angina—which causes a drop in blood pressure—or if the man has pain from heart blockages. In evaluating whether a man is a candidate for these medications, he also will take into consideration what other drugs the patient is taking that may be causing the erectile dysfunction, such as certain blood pressure pills and beta-blockers, which are commonly used to treat coronary heart disease.

Here is more from the Sin City doc.

DR. SAM GREEN

Let's say, though, that I have a patient who had a heart attack five years ago, and had a stent put in. He is now stable and on aspirin, a beta-blocker, his acid-reflux medicine, and his meds for high blood pressure. At some point, he may come to see me for erectile dysfunction. This is a patient who has been doing well, so I might wean him off the beta-blocker. It that doesn't work for the erection, then I'll try Viagra or Cialis.

I get many older men who are stable heart patients who want these drugs. Right now I am seeing an eighty-seven-year-old widowed man who just remarried a much younger woman. Because his prior heart dysfunction is not an active issue, I did put him on Viagra, and it works.

Then there are younger men who come in here and they'll say, "My penis isn't getting as hard anymore," but that's only in the eye of the beholder. We find that they are just very stressed and that is affecting sex. We tell them that if they still can get an erection in the middle of the night while they're sleeping, then it is likely not the plumbing or an organic problem. Here's a trick we learned in medical school to measure that: Lick a roll of stamps and put it around your penis, then go to bed. If the roll of stamps busts open while you are asleep, it means you are having nocturnal erections. If you don't break the stamps, then there is a real organic cause of the problem, which could be a lack of blood flow from diabetes or from medications. There are also more sophisticated tests for penile tumescence and erections, but they are a lot more expensive.

The drugs for erectile dysfunction work differently: Viagra has the shortest life. This is good if the patient suddenly gets chest pain or angina and then needs nitro because, with a shorter half-life, the Viagra will be out of the system quicker. Cialis has the longest half-life in your system—you can take it on a Friday and still get hard on Sunday. Levitra is in the middle range of time the effects last.

But it's not like the commercials, in which every man is eager to take these drugs so he can blissfully relax in a bathtub stuck in the woods next to his partner. I would say only 10 percent or so of my patients take them. They are expensive, for one, and many men are afraid of the side effects. Their wives are older and they have vaginal dryness, and both of them know that sexual intimacy between couples requires more than just an erection. As men and women age, they are more understanding of each other's sexual changes. But when the Viagra works, and each partner is into it, these drugs can be a very good thing.

In the 2009 movie *Play the Game*, Andy Griffith plays the part of Grandpa Joe, a widower who relocates to a senior community. Having slept with only one woman his entire life, Joe is hesitant to cave in to the admiring overtures of the many widows there. That is, until a sprightly octogenarian named Edna lures him out of his comfort zone and into bed—this after she has dropped that little blue pill into his drink.

Old Joe is ecstatic when he peers down to see the flagpole rising, and Edna gets so excited once they start their torrid romp she has a heart attack. When she learns of her mom's sex attack, Edna's daughter races to the hospital and insists on moving her hot mama out of the facility, away from revitalized Joe, and closer to her. Randy Andy is sad about Edna's exit, but he adores his ED pills and goes on to become the most popular bachelor on the premises.

The actors are flabby and wrinkly and real, which young people may find gross. But I thought this film really nailed the premise of this chapter, that we are never too old to want to be touched and held and, well, to shtup, if we so desire and can still do so. I also liked the twist of the woman having the heart attack in bed instead of the man. The usual shtick in films and the stereotype in real life is that it's the old guy having sex who is the one depicted gasping and grabbing his chest.

This was Andy Griffith's last film—he died July 3, 2012, at age eighty-six from a heart attack.

Play the Game is a movie with a happy ending, produced by Marc Fienberg, who loosely based the story line on his own grandfather, a widower who found a girlfriend in a senior community after the end of a long marriage. I talked to Marc, a father of four in his early forties, about what he learned about senior sexuality from his own production.

MARC FIENBERG

Preparing for this film, I reached out to a lot of widows and widowers in senior communities and learned about their dating worlds. I heard about getting back into having sex, this from people who grew up in a different age, when premarital sex was forbidden. The majority of these folks were feeling free; they said things like "Life is short; if it's good enough for the kids, it's good enough for us."

One funny story was from this ninety-year-old man who told me his doctor didn't want to prescribe Viagra because he thought it would endanger the man's health. So this older guy said, "Look, doctor. I'm ninety years old; I could have a heart attack on my own, five minutes from now. I'll take my chances. And if I do die, I'm going out with a bang."

I also heard from younger people that they don't want to envision older people having sex. Some of those young people were movie reviewers who said things like "I almost threw up when I saw Andy of Mayberry in bed." The response from the people in Florida in their seventies and eighties, though, was they thought the film was beautiful.

Andy's paramour was played by Liz Sheridan in a negligee, and, by the way, I didn't have to convince her to get into that thing. She was completely comfortable in her body and she wanted to show it off. My view is that if we show movies of younger people having sex, we should be showing older people doing it, too. Why not? This is what's going on with real life, even though their kids and grandkids don't want to see it.

The key thing I learned from observing and talking to my grandfather and other seniors is that, when we get older, happiness in relationships comes more from the companionship aspect than the sexual. The transformation I saw in my grandfather really drove this home: He lost his wife, his best friend, and he lost his will to live. He became sedentary and depressed. Then he meets a new friend in a senior community, who happened to be a woman. They had a spark, and it changed his whole life—overnight.

That flirty friendship gave him the will to exercise, the reason to get up in the morning. We truly are social creatures and we need to interact and we need to have friends or we will die. After talking to so many seniors, I also believe all those studies that say that touching one another makes us live longer, even holding hands. My grandfather's relationship with his lady friend, Ann, lasted six years; he died first, at the age of ninety-seven. I'm sure this relationship prolonged his life significantly.

CHAPTER 11
THE GIDDY GOLDEN GIRLS

Sex at every age can be gratifying if you have an
open and loving partner and you are open and
loving about yourself.

—DR. MARILYN CHARWAT

When I was ten, I wanted to be twenty. When I turned
fifty, I wanted to time travel back to forty. At fifty-eight,
I am savoring this moment, right here and right now, but hot
damn, things are looking bright for the next chapter. You, too,
will be hopeful about love after seventy and eighty when you
hear about the depths of intimacy and new sensations that
are rippling through older relationships—with, and without,
intercourse.

(Cuddling and kissing and oral sex decidedly rate higher
than Viagra-produced penetration.)

Are the seventies the new forties? I thought so when seventy-
eight-year-old Barbara Eden, star of the 1960s sitcom *I Dream of*

Jeannie, appeared on stage in her original genie costume, pink crop top, harem pants, and braided blond wig, at a May 2012 AIDS benefit in Austria.

Her abs were ripped.

Along with advice from sex educators, you will hear from a dynamic roster of senior women who are busting open any residual mythology that females of a certain age turn into fragile old ladies. I introduce you to Sylvia, Patricia, Shirley, and Dorothy, all hearty and horny and bravely facing change, which is necessary for successful aging.

"If you can adapt the mind to the changing body, anything is possible with a woman's sexuality," says Ellen Barnard, co-owner of A Woman's Touch Sexuality Resource Center in Madison, Wisconsin, which is like a candy store, only the items for sale are for sweetening the sexual experience.

Another incomparable voice and spirit I add to this mix is that of Dr. Ruth Westheimer, the legendary sex therapist who started the sexual self-help movement with her *Sexually Speaking* radio show in 1980. She now has her own YouTube channel that features videos on everything from anal sex to masturbation tutorials. Here is a tease from Dr. Ruth's interview: She tells older women, a demographic she notes is increasingly reaching out to her with queries, that if they are wary about giving oral sex, to practice first on an ice-cream cone or a banana—with eyes closed, so as not to hinder the fantasy effect.

I will introduce you to lots of true adventures in "outercourse," the all-encompassing term used in the field of sexual health that means the licking and snuggling and other really fun stuff that goes on when penetration is not wanted, or is impossible to achieve.

You may remember your own granny as someone who was knitting in her rocker; on the pages to come, you will be introduced to rocking grandmothers who attend Tantric sex workshops and are as lusty as teenagers. With females statistically outliving their male partners by several years, lots of wives who had sex with only one mate for forty and fifty-plus years are starting to date again, in their seventies and eighties, reaching unsurpassed levels of intimacy. Here is a snippet of one story to come, from Patricia, eighty, who lost her husband a year ago and has a new eighty-three-year-old boyfriend.

"The closeness, the love, the making love—this is sexual and intimate and exciting beyond exciting to discover another person after all these years."

I also heard stories of satisfied women going it alone, like the widow Sylvia, a master of masturbation who after six decades in a sexually charged marriage has no interest in becoming intimate with another man.

"I get about two women a month asking me, 'I've never used a vibrator; am I too old for one?'" relays sex therapist Ginger Manley, Associate in Psychiatry at Vanderbilt University and the author of *Assisted Loving: The Journey through Sexuality and Aging*, published by Westview in 2013.

"One woman in her early eighties came to me. Her husband had died and the issue with them was that she hadn't been able to have an orgasm. She said, 'I don't want to die without having an orgasm.' She got herself a good vibrator and that was that."

It is fitting that women who witnessed the starchy 1950s blooming into the tempestuous 1960s and early 1970s are feeling courageous and exploratory as they tackle their older years. Any adult female of that era, particularly the baby boomers, could not avoid getting ignited, and enlightened, by the sexual revolution and women's liberation. They are the hippies turned yuppies turned graying fitness addicts who are watching Mick Jagger still writhing at seventy and who believe that anything is possible in the final lap.

First up is Sylvia, eighty-eight, who has "marched to my own drummer" since her college days at Wellesley. She is wearing a skimpy black skirt and a royal blue blazer as she steps out of her silver Mercedes, having just come from teaching business classes at a senior center. The recently widowed Sylvia explains how she had such great sex in her sixty-year marriage that she has no interest in taking on any new lovers. Her solution is to golf when she can, have nightly dinners with younger friends, and pleasure herself with lessons she learned from "my horny husband":

SYLVIA

I have not gone on any dates since Roger died and I'm not the least bit interested. It was such a good and sexy marriage for fifty-six years, what's going to top that? I have gotten over the sadness and I just adore the independence. I don't have to cook and I can go out to eat every night—I never turn down invitations and I get many of them.

Let me tell you something: I do a lot of masturbation; that's my secret. I had sex for so long with my husband, I found I really do need that delightful feeling. So whammo, I give myself orgasms two to three times a week. It's one of those things I never talk about to my friends, but maybe I should just tell everyone that, at every age, as long as you are alive, you can psychologically and physically and magically have an orgasm— all by yourself!

An orgasm in your eighties feels like my orgasm of my sixties for sure. I don't really remember my twenties, but I'm sure it was good then, too. I really like the pleasure of taking my time and playing around for a while. I don't just slam-bam-thank-you-ma'am myself—I do it nice and slow, like my husband did. He was very good at foreplay and I guess I learned from him. I love the whole sexual act, the buildup, the orgasm, and the afterglow.

My husband was a very experienced lover and he was very good at pleasing women. We were horny for each other throughout our whole marriage. I'm still horny. I am so pleased that I am able to pleasure myself in this way. I have often thought to myself that maybe I should sit down with other older women and tell them, "Here are some of the tricks you can try. You don't have to dry up." I come from a family of women who live to be one hundred or more, and so it's good that I know this, I could be around for a while. My great-grandmother died at one hundred and five!

Sylvia can stick to teaching finance since there are hundreds of qualified experts that specialize in instructing seniors about sex. I met many of them in the fall of 2012 at the Sexuality and Aging Consortium at Widener University, outside of Philadelphia, an annual conference that attracts top experts on issues of intimacy relating to needs of older adults. One of my favorite finds was sex therapist Dr. Melanie Davis, copresident of the consortium at Widener, where she got her PhD in human sexuality. I sat next to Dr. Davis at the workshop on AIDS and seniors, then spoke to her afterward. Marilyn Burnett, a woman in her seventies with AIDS, was the workshop leader, and she tells her powerful story later in the chapter.

Dr. Davis operates a private sexual counseling center called Honest Exchange in Somerville, New Jersey, where a large segment of her clientele are curious older women.

Dr. Melanie Davis

The more we speak openly and listen to older adults, the more myths we see shattered. A pervasive myth is that older women stop wanting to be sexually active after menopause, when in fact, in heterosexual couples, the decision to stop is usually made by the male partner. Often the cause is a fear on the part of the man of being unable to perform sexually as he once did.

It's also a myth that the quality of sex declines with age. The truth is that, if you had great sex before you turned fifty, odds are you can still have great sex after the age of fifty. Studies have shown that many older adults thoroughly enjoy their sex lives, finding their experiences to be more sensual and satisfying than when they were younger.

It is true that sex after fifty may look very different from the sex people had when they were twenty. Couples aren't likely to have a hot and heavy quickie in the backseat of a car when they are seventy. But they may enjoy a lovemaking session that lasts long enough for them to enjoy exploring each other's bodies and giving each other pleasure, rather than racing to an imaginary finish line.

One of the best ways to improve sex when you're older is by taking the focus off orgasm—that imaginary finish line. When you focus on sensuality instead, you can have lots of fun being creative by yourself or with a partner.

Creativity is important because bodies change with age. People are generally less flexible, they may have gained weight or be dealing with health problems. Favorite sex positions may not be feasible anymore. Or you may lack the stamina you once enjoyed. Most men over the age of fifty have to deal with erections that ebb and flow during a lovemaking session, and older women may produce less lubrication than they need for comfortable sex play. It pays to maintain a sense of humor, to abandon self-consciousness, and to make adaptations as gracefully as possible.

A man with a soft penis can enjoy oral sex—even to orgasm— without ever getting hard. Partners can mutually masturbate, either touching themselves side by side or using their hands on each other. They can rub their bodies and genitals against each other for pleasure. You can introduce sex toys and try new lubricants. I have had older couples tell me that stripping for each other, then giving each other long body rubs is more enthralling than intercourse at this point in their lives. These pleasurable, non-intercourse activities are often called outercourse, because there is no penetration of the mouth, vagina, or anus.

In later life, many widowed and divorced older adults are dating and finding new partners, which can be intimidating. The rules of dating are very different from those of thirty years ago, let alone forty or fifty years ago. Straight women often complain that men expect sex on the first or second date, and if they don't get it, they move on to another woman. This can be disheartening for women who long for companionship and romance. Older men aren't immune to sexual disappointments, either. At one workshop I conducted, a man in his seventies asked, "I keep hearing about all these women looking for men, but where are they? How can I find someone to love?" A man at a sex and cancer program pulled me aside to ask how to deal with the embarrassment he felt about not being able to "ejaculate like a porn star" after surgery for prostate cancer.

I also meet many older adults who are simply done with sex. They have either lost interest or they find it too frustrating to try to have sex while dealing with relationship issues, physical challenges, and, in some cases, their own or a partner's cognitive changes. Some are also grieving the loss of a beloved spouse and cannot imagine intimacy with someone new.

On the other hand, older adulthood can be an exciting time for people who want to explore their sexuality. Whether by themselves, with a lifetime partner, or with a new partner, there are many ways for older adults to experiment with new techniques, positions, sex toys, erotica, and sensations. Anyone who wants a richer romantic or sexual life can benefit from asking, "What am I willing to do about it?" Some solutions are as simple as a penis ring to help maintain an erect penis, or a silicone lubricant for extra slickness. The bottom line is that older adult sexuality is as diverse as sexuality at other stages of life. There are times of great joy and passion as well as times of frustration and sadness.

Much of this sexual chutzpah among modern Golden Girls can be credited to Helen Gurley Brown. What Hugh Hefner did for the lucrative feeding of male fantasies when he founded *Playboy* magazine in 1953, Brown did for females when her book *Sex and the Single Girl* was released in 1962, a wildfire bestseller that was published in twenty-eight countries. Brown unleashed young boomer women to pursue their sexual curiosity and behaviors with as vehement a charge as their male counterparts. Under her extensive reign as editor in chief of *Cosmopolitan* magazine's sixty-four international editions, Brown became a global matriarch of the movement for women's sexual and financial freedom.

Long before the expression "having it all" became vogue for professional women balancing work and family, Brown was telling her devotees they deserved to have it all—"love, sex, and money." These orders fell on eager ears at a turning point in history when women were entering previously male-dominated professions, such as medicine and law, and the birth control pill was finally legal and becoming more accessible. We will remember

Brown, and forever be inspired by her tenacity, as the woman who wore stilettos and minis until her death at ninety in 2012.

Patricia spends her summers in Lake George, where we talked about what it means to be an ageless Cosmo girl, and other sexy topics. At the age of eighty, she has just begun dating an eighty-three-year-old man, the second person she has slept with in her life. Patricia's husband of fifty-five years died a year ago after being ill nearly all of their married life. He had his first heart attack at the age of thirty-eight. Next came throat cancer, then a chronic heart condition, and in his last years, he was stricken with leukemia.

As his health deteriorated, Patricia became more a loving caregiver than a lover. "Are you kidding? Sex? It would have killed him," she says with a husky laugh. I met Patricia while staying at the lakeside home of a childhood friend—and was dazzled, I mean knocked out, by her wry demeanor and high-styled exterior. My friend later told me this is how Patricia looks at any time of the day or night you might see her. She was wearing shiny red lipstick, red Chanel sunglasses, red bell-bottoms slit above the knee, black-and-white clunky jewelry. Her eyelashes are long and black and so is her hair, which is cinched tightly in a bun. She is a woman who has had "work done," and the work is good.

Patricia was a virgin when she married at the age of twenty-one and sixty years later is now that woman Dr. Melanie Davis speaks about, an older adult exploring her sexuality.

PATRICIA

I had such a wonderful love affair for almost fifty-five years, I never thought I would ever want to get involved with another man. When my husband developed leukemia, it made him very weak. They gave him three weeks to live, but he lasted sixteen months because of my encouragement and love.

We had known Steven for years because he lives in the same community. He had lost his wife, too, but had many paramours after. He was very patient with me. He would ask me out, but I would say, "I'm not ready." He was very persistent and romantic, though, and he would send me long-stemmed white roses every two weeks. When I finally went on a date with him, it was New Year's Eve, and he told me he had a temporary front tooth. I am thinking, "My luck if I kiss him at midnight, I'm going to choke on his tooth." Whether it was my fear or I was still afraid to touch another man, at midnight I wouldn't go near him.

He kept pursuing me, though, calling and saying, "Whenever you're ready." Then about a year after my husband died, Steven asked me to go to Paris with him. I said, "Okay, I guess it's time to try you out." My husband was the only man I've ever been with, so being intimate with another man was very scary, but he was very kind and respectful. Without giving you details, let me just say I feel wonderful, like a teenager.

He tells me "the only thing I want you to do is to look beautiful and sexy, and to have sex with me." It's not teenage sex, but it's very satisfying. We love to experiment. We love to dance. There is a lot of cuddling and snuggling. This man, my God, is a gem in every way, whether it's sexual or spiritual or cultural. It's so romantic it's almost electrifying.

The closeness, the love, the making love—this is sexual and intimate and exciting beyond exciting to discover another person after all these years. After he got that tooth fixed, a kiss led to more things, and our life just keeps getting better and better and better. After taking care of someone so ill for so many years, this is so fantastic.

We are writing our final chapter together, and we are loving every minute of it. Finding love in my eighties is like opening another world I never knew could exist. I would never think at this stage of my life I could have this. Not only do I have a golf partner and a life partner, but the sex part is very, very good. It is not *Fifty Shades of Grey* but it is definitely erotic and warm and beautiful.

Patricia did not want to give me physical details, but she tells plenty with her blush and giddy laughs. A younger Golden Girl in a senior community on the other coast does give me details, tantalizing tidbits that will make you blush like Patricia, and perhaps a tad envious.

Radiant in an orange pantsuit and lipstick to match, Shirley sparkled from the crowd of one hundred senior women I addressed in the clubhouse of a West Coast oceanfront community. After my talk on female generational angst, she bought a copy of *Surrendering to Yourself,* my book about the bracing self-discovery that arises at every stage in a woman's life. After I signed her book with this inscription: *May you never be afraid to be wild and free, and to follow the passion in your soul,* Shirley leaned over, in a whoosh of Shalimar, and whispered: "I've got stories of passion that will make your hair stand up."

She handed me her card, then winked. "Call me. I'm seventy-two and I am having the best sex I've ever had in my life. At every age, I've always made sure that I am having the best sex of my life. In fact, I have always made sure I am having the best life every day of my life."

Who could resist this offer? I met Shirley in her home, and curled up in high-backed rattan chairs on her patio, we talked for an entire day and well into the night about Tantric sex, Erica Jong, Shirley's penchant for pot, and how hard she works at keeping her marriage hot. Here she goes, uncensored.

Shirley

I married for the first time in 1959 at the age of eighteen. In those days, you could not have sex until you got married, and I was very sexually oriented. Remember, there was no birth control pill yet, and I was petrified of my father. I used to have nightmares that if I got pregnant, I would have to kill myself because I would be so ashamed. Back then, there was so much shame with unmarried pregnancy. You had to hide; people did not get abortions.

My father used to wait up for me every night. He would click our house light on if he saw I was in the car parked outside. It didn't stop me from experimenting with everything. Like Bill Clinton says, "I did not have sexual relations." Ha! But we did everything else. I thought I was a bad girl, giving blow jobs in cars, because people just didn't talk about it. I basically got married so I could go all the way without feeling guilty.

I quit college after one year, and I got married in a big dress at a big wedding. Going down the aisle, I felt like Cinderella, like I hit the jackpot, like I was the luckiest girl in the world. I couldn't have been happier that night. Ah, that magic didn't last long.

You would think after all this steamy foreplay in parked cars, we would have been hot to finally make love. Well, my new husband instead fell asleep on our wedding night. He obviously was scared to death. We were both virgins. I had gone into the bathroom to get into my drop-dead pure white nightgown. When I came out, he was snoring on the bed. We didn't have sex until the next morning and it was over in, like, ten seconds. Just like that. My first intercourse experience was terrible.

I didn't know then that there was such a thing as a premature ejaculator. Again, no one openly talked about sex, especially to eighteen-year-old girls. It was very confusing; before I got married, I had many orgasms during foreplay. But as the months went on in our new marriage, I never had an orgasm from the actual act of lovemaking. I thought there was something horribly wrong with me.

The young wives in the neighborhood started to gather in each other's kitchens for morning coffee and conversation. One day, we started talking about sex, and one woman was boasting about how great her sex life was. And I'm thinking to myself, *I love sex, and I know that I should love making love. But we have quick intercourse and my husband just rolls over and goes to sleep. It's over in a minute, and that's the way it has been for our entire five-year marriage.* I was too embarrassed to bring it up.

Lonely and horny, I masturbated every single day. No one talked about masturbation then, or advised each other on types of vibrators, like women do today. For a long time, I suffered in silence, thinking there was something wrong with me and that I was the only woman alive not having an orgasm from intercourse.

After my third child was born, when I was still only thirty-two, I had an awakening. We were putting an addition on to our house, and I would take my baby and go outside and watch the construction crew. One day, I found myself growing tingly as I watched one of the workmen. I was having sexual feelings for this carpenter. He was balding, and there was nothing classically handsome about him. But he told me I was beautiful and sexy. He had his shirt off and he was sweating, and he had these great muscles. I don't know how this happened, but one day, we met in the basement of my house, and I let him kiss me, I let him touch me, and I felt so guilty.

I think of these moments long ago, when I had three kids

under the age of four, as the first real sensual awakening of my adult life. Remembering the passion of those embraces in my basement, I still get unbelievable sexual feelings.

If husbands could have affairs, which they did openly through history, why couldn't wives? I wasn't hurting anyone, and I felt like I was definitely saving myself. And I thought I was saving my marriage.

From the minute I got married, I was always looking for ways to keep our passion alive. By the early 1970s, feminism was exploding and along with that came the sexual revolution. I attended a meeting on open marriage called "Designing Your Perfect Relationship," put on by a group of humanistic psychologists. It was amazing for me to hear that you could make your own rules in your marriage, rules that you could change when you both agree.

I asked my husband to accompany me to the next seminar. I knew that we were changing and that we needed a new way to relate to each other. So we ended up together at this seminar and it was mind-boggling that there was this secret world going on with marriages we had never heard of in our little town. It was not spouse swapping; it was having actual loving relationships with other people yet still staying committed to your marriage.

My husband and I decided we would open our marriage. We were both scared and excited. These are the rules we made for ourselves: One night a week, we could go out with whomever. We would tell each other everything. We would sleep at home and not out. There would be no secrets. And if we found ourselves getting too attached to anyone, and the other person felt threatened, we would immediately end that relationship. We both agreed our marriage would remain more important than anyone else.

Surprisingly, our marriage bed started to heat up. My husband came home after a few affairs and he no longer ejaculated prematurely. He became a much better lover. He could actually now stay inside a woman for a very long time. Who knows? This freedom to be with random partners must have freed his inhibitions. Our sex life got way more romantic because the new tricks we learned, we brought home to each other.

During the first months of our open marriage, I read Erica Jong's book *Fear of Flying*, and its tales of zipless sex really opened up my life. I went after the zipless experience, too, having sex with no real attachment, what this young generation today calls hooking up. In those days, we weren't worried about sexually transmitted diseases; there was no AIDS. Because of Erica Jong, I started to do some crazy, crazy things. I wanted to make up for the teenage years I missed, because the rules of virginity had changed.

These were the wild 1970s when I would occasionally hang out at a place called Plato's Retreat in New York. You got a big all-you-could-eat buffet, all you could drink, and all you could screw for forty dollars a person. There was loud music and naked people dancing, and a room with nothing but mattresses. But I did not have sex with anyone but my date. Meanwhile, I am telling my husband everything that I am doing, We actually became much closer during this time because we talked about everything. We always felt like the luckiest people alive because we could have our cake and eat it, too.

During this astounding period of growth, this one date was becoming my primary lover and I realized very quickly that our relationship was not just an affair. I broke the rules of our open marriage agreement by falling in love. He was my Omar Sharif! I loved how he looked. I loved how he spent hours making love. I loved how he talked to me. This extramarital relationship went on for seven years, and during this time I saw only him and my husband.

We arranged to have a weekend trip to Baja, and here we were in a magnificent room overlooking the ocean. I can picture everything as it happened that day. We had the balcony doors open, and the setting sun was streaming across the bed. We were gazing out at the shimmering Pacific and we had just made love. There was this moment when we looked at each other and we both just knew; we knew that we were really in love and that we were going to be together for the rest of our lives. Telling my husband was the hardest conversation I have ever had with anyone in my life, this person I really loved.

We have been married now for twenty-four years: Thomas was my true awakening to who I really am, and what I am capable of becoming. In the right relationship, we are able to unlock parts of ourselves that are underdeveloped and grow in ways we never dreamed possible.

Every week we make a date, and we put it on the calendar, for a time to make love. We both look forward to that day; there is a palpable sense of anticipation. On that day, I put on a gorgeous, sexy anything and we feel like it is still that forbidden, exciting act of long ago, and that keeps it exciting today. We also find that a little bit of marijuana is a nice addition to our sex lives.

I am having some of the hottest sex now, better than I had in my twenties or thirties or forties. There are times after lovemaking that Thomas and I look at each other and become hysterical with laughter because we can't believe how great sex still is. One of my secrets is that I still will try anything to keep things hot. About twenty years ago, we went to a Tantric sex training seminar. This was a big turnaround for us: Tantric training takes the focus off of intercourse. Although Thomas is not on Viagra, he has no trouble getting an erection.

But now we are more into loving each other, eye contact, touching each other. We are really making love and not just having sex and orgasm. We've also incorporated some very inventive sex toys into our sessions, and that combination of feeling wild abandon has been just amazing. We learned about conscious loving and intimacy. A lot of the men who take Viagra just want a blow job or a long intercourse, and the women just want to be fondled and touched and to hear whispered sweet nothings, like "I love you sooooo." I don't want a long intercourse at this stage.

After seventy, there comes a sweetness about making love, touching sexually becomes more important, and intercourse becomes less important. With a vibrator, I can have multiple orgasms in a row, and Thomas loves watching and assisting—we play together. We go slowly, there is no rush anymore. When you're younger, it's all about the orgasm, then it's over. I love the suspended feeling.

We actually start our lovemaking with him giving me a massage as a warm-up, which definitely puts me in the mood. I recommend the Celebrator—I went out and bought a dozen of those vibrators and gave them to my friends for their birthdays. They all love it! It looks like a toothbrush that has a little bulb on the top. It's so strong, it's better to let the batteries run down a little. Honestly, I've never felt anything like this in my life. I'm seventy-two and we still make love three times a week.

Ice bath, anyone? How many of your younger friends are this breathless about their sex lives? Empowered since youth by their sixties revolution, which trumpeted free love and birthed the Me Decade, boomers and the bodacious septuagenarians like Shirley are the target market for products designed to enhance and prolong sexuality. In North America alone, vibrators and other sex toys account for a $500-million-per-year industry.

Even the crunchy Vermont Country Store catalog features state-of-the-art vibrators, devices that women used to be able to purchase only in sleazy R-rated venues and now come in the size of a lipstick, easy to pop in a purse or briefcase. I would never promise that vibrating gadgets coupled with partners who will try anything will result in streaming orgasms like Shirley's. But I do know from talking to a lot of older women and sex educators that sexual fulfillment can be mighty fine in old age. I am often reminded of this by Dr. Marilyn Charwat, seventy-nine, a sex therapist in Boca Raton, home to many women in her age range hankering for wisdom about dating after widowhood. I quote Dr. Charwat often in my writings because she does not mince words, as you will see. Her titillating portion below boils down to this: Use it or lose it.

DR. MARILYN CHARWAT

I always encourage the use of vibrators and masturbation, which still comes with some guilt for women. Throughout history, men have been masturbating regularly without bad conscience while women often feel guilty about it. I am a big believer in women having orgasms once a day, or at least three times a week. Why? Because an orgasm, like a Kegel, lifts and tightens the pelvis. An orgasm provides tremendous relaxation and it helps keep the vagina in operation and healthy and lubricated. If you get used to having regular orgasms that whole part of your body is being revitalized, your whole life is revitalized.

Also, if you learn to bring yourself to orgasm, you can have more fulfilling sex with a partner because you know what you need. Interestingly, I do a lot of work with overweight people and I find that it is a real help for women who are dieting to learn how to masturbate, and not be ashamed of it. Many women are emotional eaters; they eat when they are bored or depressed. I say instead of digging into the refrigerator, have a quick orgasm with a vibrator—it creates a whole shift in thinking. The clitoris is there for your pleasure; that's what it was designed for. So reach down there and have a good time.

And for older women who still have a partner, I turn them on to the joy of oral sex as a completely reliable, completely natural way to have sex. When women describe the experience who have never had it before, they are berserk with joy! Sex at every age can be gratifying if you have an open and loving partner and you are open and loving about yourself. Sex is all about attitude, particularly as we age. These older men who are dancing in the streets because of Viagra often miss out on the most important part of a woman's sexual pleasure, and that is being touched in the right way, and being held.

Happily, I can report there is a lot of sex going on with people my age, because most people in their seventies and eighties feel internally like they did when they were thirty-five and forty-five. Orgasms are just as deep or deeper and just as possible. Although the man might not be able to get it up, and the woman may need some help lubricating, there are many different paths to take that are even more enjoyable.

I am at an event near Newark, New Jersey, speaking to a group of raucous senior women about the different paths—and secret lives—wives have created to sustain intimate relationships.

One woman with curly silver hair, wearing stretch pants tucked into knee-high boots, lingers as I am putting my notes in my canvas bag and preparing to leave. Dorothy introduces herself, then starts by saying, "You're going to think I'm terrible." I reply that in my decades of writing about love and romance, I have heard every type of story imaginable, including one that involved a wife who discovered her husband had slept with sheep. Her face softened, she laughed, and then she said: "My husband has early Alzheimer's and other diseases and we put him into a home a few months ago." She paused, sighed deeply, and added: "And I just started an affair."

I had heard other stories from older women, still dynamic and healthy, whose husbands have become incapacitated. They react to this passage in various ways. Some would never think of taking on another love prospect while their mates are still alive. Others say they compensate for the lack of intimacy and communication by spending more time with their girlfriends. Then there are cases like Dorothy's, married to someone with whom she feels deeply committed yet who is flattened by various illnesses, including early Alzheimer's. While her husband is losing his memory, Dorothy has fallen "madly in love." Therapy practices and clergy offices are filled with spouses wrestling with the same kind of angst and guilt over how to go forward in life when a life partner is going backward.

Here is how therapist Marge Coffey handles this increasingly common issue in her Washington-area practice, which caters mostly to midlife to older women who generally hold on to good health longer than their husbands.

"We are all sexual human beings until we die," says Coffey. "If the ill spouse is being well cared for, I think it's reasonable for the well spouse to be discreetly involved with a new partner, should she choose. Some couples discuss this issue before illness strikes and come to an agreement about how they would like the issue to be addressed if the time comes. It's a loving and respectful way to acknowledge that we're sexual beings until we stop breathing."

Seventy-three-year-old Dorothy tells me she is "feeling

terrible and wonderful at the same time" about a lover who is seventy-five and who, as you will see below, brings on some heavy breathing. They are from the same hometown where, when growing up, they were acquaintances, not friends, and they had not spoken to each other for fifty years. In 2012 they ran into each other at a funeral. He gave her a hug, and that was that.

DOROTHY

My two closest girlfriends know about this and they are jealous. They are horny as hell and having sex at the most about every six months with their husbands, some every six years. This kind of sexual fulfillment I'm having I've never had before. Never. There is warmth. There is love. There is passion. In order to have an erection, he has to take Viagra. But even when the Viagra doesn't work, this is just sensational.

Maybe it's my age, but I just feel so free now. My kids have their own kids. I live alone. And since I've known this man for so long, we share so many memories from childhood, I have never been this comfortable with a man. I have never been this comfortable with sex.

Even in my long marriage, I was self-conscious about sex. I couldn't ever really relax. I liked it but always I felt deep down it was wrong. I'm from the old school. Now I'm like you see in the movies—I get out of bed after we have sex, and I walk into the bathroom naked. I can't believe it's me!

There was a big celebration-of-life party after the funeral of this woman we both knew, and he walked over to me and put his hand on my shoulder. I knew he looked familiar. I smiled at him and then he told me who he was and I reminded him about something we did in seventh grade. Then we gave each other a hug and it was electric; a shock went through my entire body.

We held each other longer than a quick hug. We just stood there. It was amazing. It was like magic.

Funny I was never attracted to him when we were young, hadn't thought about him for fifty years. I didn't see him at all. Not after I graduated from college or after I got married. He had been married for twenty or so years, got a divorce after and did not remarry.

I married someone who is very nice and a good man, but it was never like that electric shock kind of romance. I have grown used to our relationship, but I always felt that he loved me more than I love him. We had a friendship marriage more than a sexy marriage, and we had three great children together, who are now in their forties. I have been a loyal wife always. I would never have had an affair; this just wasn't me! I'm a good Christian and brought up with Puritanical thoughts—you just don't do these things.

My husband's health has gone from bad to worse over the last fifteen years, affecting not only his mind but his ability to be mobile. Finally, we had to put him in a nursing home because there are so many things going wrong. I visit him all the time, and sometimes he will talk to me and he knows me, other times, nothing. Believe me, having an affair was not something I could ever dream would happen.

Then I go to this funeral—I was wearing a black suit with a very pretty black-and-red blouse with ruffles around the neck. After we hugged, we sat down and talked for a while. Before I left, I wrote down my phone number, then went home and couldn't stop thinking about him. That night, I called one of my girl-friends and I said, "I just fell in love." And she told me, "I am not shocked, after all you've been through."

He called me the next day and we set up a lunch date. We went out to a really discreet place because everyone knows us in this town. We rehashed our childhood and everybody we knew in common as children. We both knew there was a connection. When he took me home, all of a sudden, he said, "You want to go into the bedroom?" This was our first date!

Then he just took my hand and there we went, and I'm thinking, *What is going on? This isn't me! I have never gotten involved with anyone else.* Well, we stayed in bed for five hours. We had sex, then we took a little nap, then we had sex again. And we talked and we talked, and he said, "We're not done yet." I said, "Listen, we've got to stop. I'm not used to this."

And this has been going on for six months now. I love my husband; he's the nicest guy you'd ever want to meet. But I have never felt this passion in my life. I never made mad passionate love like they do in the movies and we do every time we see each other, which is about twice a week. It's more than sex—we sit and gab and have a drink together; our history, remember, goes way back.

It surprises me how amazing our sex life is because he definitely has a problem in the erection area. All I can tell you is I never had sex like this in my life—he just makes up for it in other ways. He's a fabulous lover, adventurous; there's so much else you can do. Oh God, the way he kisses me, the way he holds me, he is always sucking my neck, he loves my feet. I'm like a teenager in love who is having this explosive intimacy.

And I feel wonderful about him but terrible when I juggle this with reality—I still have a husband. My way of coping is that I don't think about the future. I just try to think of him as someone who is doing good for me right now, and I'm not hurting anyone. I feel more sad about my husband than guilty. I went to a weekend seminar for well spouses of people who are ill. And during one session, this man shared, "I do have a friend I sleep with from time to time." Now so do I. It's a good feeling to be touched when it comes to a time that your partner can't do it.

I just heard on the radio that if you have sex twice a week, you can live five years longer. I told my two best girlfriends, and one of them said, "I'm lucky if I have sex twice a year." The other said, "I'm lucky if I have sex every five years." I tell them, "Get off your ass, get on his lap, start snuggling. If you want it, maybe you can get it."

Former Supreme Court Justice Sandra Day O'Connor also found herself dealing with the pull of infidelity with an Alzheimer's spouse, only this time it was his pull, not hers. She married John Jay O'Connor III in 1952 and had three sons with him. He suffered from Alzheimer's disease for twenty years, until his death in 2009. Justice O'Connor never commented on this experience, though her son did speak about the fact that when his dad was seventy-seven years old and living at a Phoenix facility for Alzheimer's patients, he found a new romance with a woman who is referred to only as Kay in news reports.

The son, Scott O'Connor, said in an interview with KPNX, an Arizona TV station, that "Mom was thrilled that Dad was relaxed and happy and comfortable living there and wasn't complaining." He also described his father as "a teenager in love."

"For Mom to visit when he's happy . . . visiting with his girlfriend, sitting on his porch holding hands," was a relief after a painful period, Scott said, particularly since John O'Connor no longer recognized his wife, even after fifty-four years of marriage.

Dr. Ruth addresses this shift in marital expectations and affairs in older years when a spouse has this disease, in her new book, *Dr. Ruth's Guide for the Alzheimer's Caregiver*, cowritten with her longtime communications director, Pierre A. Lehu, and published in 2012 by Quill Driver Books. She says that when you live with someone with Alzheimer's, the choice to have sex with your partner—if it works—or not is your individual choice. And for people like Dorothy, who choose to have sex with someone else, here is the dictum of Dr. Ruth:

"If you need the love, the companionship and, yes, the sexual gratification of a relationship, then by all means seek one out."

The big voice from the tiny (four feet seven) Dr. Ruth is unmistakable, bossy and frank. At eighty-five, the thrice-married Dr. Ruth Westheimer is still doling out advice, with her own YouTube channel and a namesake website on which she answers readers' questions. The psychosexual therapist was introduced to a broad audience when her radio show, *Sexually Speaking*, was launched in 1980, and she later became a worldwide icon with cable television programs, and hysterically funny appearances on David Letterman's *Late Show*. Many of us, as we were becoming sexual, would sneak a listen to Dr. Ruth on our transistor radios to hear her plain-spoken, unabashed explanations about sex.

Born Karola Ruth Siegel in Germany, at the age of ten she was sent to a children's home in Switzerland, which became an orphanage for many German Jewish students escaping the Holocaust. At the age of seventeen, she immigrated to Israel and joined the Haganah, a Jewish paramilitary organization, and during a 1948 bombing she was struck in both legs with shrapnel. It was in Israel where she really discovered sex. As Dr. Ruth recalls in her 1987 autobiography, *All in a Lifetime*—one of the thirty-five books she has written—she "first had sexual intercourse on a starry night, in a haystack, without contraception."

"I am not happy about that," she said about unprotected sex in a *New York Times* article written by Georgia Dullea that appeared October 26, 1987. "But I know much better now and so does everyone who listens to my radio program."

I spoke to Dr. Ruth about the awakening and changes she has seen in our culture's sexual curiosity and activity as her earliest listeners are now entering their senior citizen years.

DR. RUTH WESTHEIMER

Older people who might not have had sex in a long time, a widow or a widower, I don't want to put any pressure on them. What is important for them to know is how their ability to be aroused may have changed. For example, they need to know to take their time with sex, and the better it will be. I want to say to older people not to put into their minds the experiences they had when they were younger; that the orgasmic response is not going to be as intense, the erection is not going to be as hard. Older people have to know that in order to not be disappointed.

The best data on sexual functioning in the United States shows that in our culture, no question, most adults want to have a significant other in their lives. I'm not saying that someone necessarily has to be for a whole lifetime, but they do want to have a significant other. Wherever I go, I do find older and younger people who are lonely, either because they are separated, or divorced, or widowed. So it proves what I have been saying all along because I'm very old-fashioned about this—people basically do want to have a loving partner. Life has changed over the many years I've been doing this, but that hasn't changed.

When I started in this business, I was already fifty. It became very clear right away that my values were old-fashioned about relationships, and my opinions were respected. I really was fortunate. From the time I started the radio show, I had no hate mail. I had no demonstration against me for talking about progressive subjects. Now I hear from people who remember me from those early days and they tell me they are thankful that I talked openly about the subject of sex. From the time I was in an orphanage as a young girl, I knew that I wanted to make a dent in this world. Because I was spared as a child during the Holocaust and millions of children did not make it.

My old-fashioned values haven't changed, but I have seen that the attitude toward sexuality and older people in this country has drastically changed. There's no question that people have realized that older people have to be sexually literate. This means knowing not to engage in sex when they are tired. Older people definitely need to be touched, and they do need to be sexually active only if they desire.

I'm not on a bandwagon to say that every older person has to find a sexual outlet, or that every woman has to have a vibrator. I'm saying only if they so desire. If a widow says to me, "I'm not interested in another sexual relationship," I say, "Leave it alone." I am also saying that those who do feel sexual arousal, who do feel loneliness, "go out and do something about it."

If you are missing having intimacy, you can have that without sex. You can have intimate relationships with a member of your own sex or the opposite sex and not have it become sexual, yet you still feel there is a person who cares about you. Maybe that's enough for some people—just to have a person in your life who is interested in you, in what you think, in spending time with you. This could also be a person with whom there is some snuggling without other sexual activities.

Snuggling is so nice because it feels good and doesn't have to involve intercourse. Snuggling is not necessarily even having an erection or an indication of being aroused. It would be ideal if every older person had somebody with whom they could just snuggle, someone who was a true friend. They could satisfy each other, and it doesn't have to be intercourse.

For people who do want more, I think Viagra is a wonderful

drug, if prescribed by a physician. No man should ever take Viagra because a friend gives it to him. More important, with Viagra the relationship between the two people has to be a good one. What happened across the United States when Viagra first came out: Men went to their doctors. They got Viagra. They came home. They told their wives, "Hop into bed," because they now had an erection from the floor to the ceiling. They think it's the last erection of their life, so they want to act quickly. Meanwhile, they forgot her birthday. They forgot Valentine's Day. And in our culture, if there was a sports event on television at night, maybe the man hadn't talked to the wife in three days. And now he wants sex.

You know what all of these women want to tell their partners to do with that erection, when after all this, he just says, "Hop into bed!" So my point is, for the Viagra part to be good and productive for both people, the relationship has to be a good one, with communication.

It was really thought that, at a certain time in life, women particularly weren't that interested in sex. But in the Jewish tradition and in the Talmud, which I use a lot because the sages were very smart, there is a rule that even after menopause, a man is still obligated to provide sexual satisfaction to his wife so he can prove that sex is not only for procreation, but also for recreation.

Men need to know this: Speak to her softly so that she will want to engage in sex. It takes a woman a longer time to be aroused. That's particularly important for older woman. They must use a lubricant, or otherwise sex will be painful. I also tell older people not to compare lovers, not to say "my late husband was better than this one"—that's a destructive thought. Don't compare. Enjoy what you have when you have it, and keep your mouth shut about past experiences.

Other changes I have seen are in the vocabulary about sex. Now people talk in more explicit terms, even older people. I get more questions about anal intercourse than I ever got when I was on the radio. I get questions from older women that I never did before on how to perform oral sex. I tell them, "Close your eyes and practice on a banana or an ice-cream cone. Then it will be easier to engage in oral sex with your partner." What hasn't changed are the questions of wanting to find the right person, of wanting to be in a relationship. That holds true for young and older people, too.

Some people are happy just finding someone with whom to go to the opera. I'm not on a bandwagon of saying everybody has to have sex. However, I do say if you feel sexual arousal and you don't have a partner, then learn how to masturbate. And learn how to masturbate without feeling sadness that you are alone. Masturbate, and then go out, satisfied, with a smile on your face. Then you will find a partner.

Sex is a very important life force, and the more sexually literate people of all ages become, the better off they will be. Read something arousing—from *Lady Chatterley's Lover* to *Fear of Flying* to *Fifty Shades of Grey*, women do get aroused from sexually explicit material. In Israel, *Fifty Shades* sold out in one day.

I hear from people who tell me that they used to go to bed listening to me on the radio, under their covers if parents were around, as I talked about sex. I want to be remembered as somebody who made sure that people know how important relationships are in order to have a good spirit and a good outlook on life. I want to be remembered as a person who taught them how important it was to be sexually literate, and to have good sex.

A crucial part of sexual literacy and aging is the urgent push for seniors to use protection to safeguard against rampant STDs, which used to be thought of as solely a plague of young people. Not anymore: The rise in retirement romps that exude youthful pleasure are bringing on youthful problems. Widows and older divorcées, eager for a renewal of sexual activity, are increasingly being exposed to diseases. This is what happens in the age of elongated life spans and the advent of potions and pharmaceuticals that make it possible for men and women to have sex until death do us part. Another reason for the spread of sexual diseases in grandparents is the trend toward older women-younger men equations and vice versa. It may feel great to be in bed with a hot, young body—not so great if he or she leaves a dreaded and permanent token of affection.

I refer back to the advice of therapist Marge Coffey in the chapter "Sex after Divorce." Her stern warning to all: When you are ready to sleep with a new partner, have him or her get tested for everything.

In the five years from 2005 through 2009, the number of reported cases of syphilis and chlamydia among those fifty-five and older increased 43 percent, according to an *Orlando Sentinel* analysis of data provided by the Centers for Disease Control and Prevention. (In Florida, where the newspaper is based, nearly 18 percent of the population is age sixty-five or older.) The CDC data states that in communities where retirees flock, such as Maricopa and Pima counties in Arizona, cases of syphilis and chlamydia increased twice as fast as the national average. In Riverside County, California, home to lots of robust older folks in Palm Springs, reported cases were up 50 percent over the five-year span, according to data from that county's health department.

Many seniors who are dating for the first time after losing a spouse to death or divorce were not privy to the detailed sex education their grandchildren received as a part of their curricula in middle school.

HIV/AIDS is also striking older populations at higher than average rates. According to statistics compiled by the CDC, people at age fifty and older represent almost one-fourth of all people with HIV/AIDS in the United States. Because older people do not get tested for HIV/AIDS on a regular basis, there are probably more cases than currently reported and people are spreading the virus unknowingly.

Marilyn Burnett was diagnosed with the HIV virus in 1991, acquired through unprotected heterosexual sex. Five years later, the virus progressed to AIDS, yet she kept her illness a secret for the next decade, even from her mom, suffering silently with what she believed to be a "sure death sentence." More than a quarter century later, I met Marilyn at Widener University's Sexuality, Intimacy and Aging Conference, where she was the speaker at a workshop called "HIV with Joy and Wrinkles." Marilyn is tall and black and elegant, in a flowing silk tunic and billowy pants.

She smiles often and speaks openly about love and sex with HIV, and how she has made it her mission to help other women afflicted with the disease. Burnett is the cofounder of a Baltimore-based organization called OWEL, that stands for Older Women Embracing Life and offers advocacy services for seniors living with HIV/AIDS.

Seventy and single now, after a lengthy and disappointing relationship, Burnett puts a face on that little-known segment of the aging population who are infected with the most deadly of STDs, many of whom do not even know they carry the virus.

Marilyn Burnett

It was my own painful secret for so long. I was very afraid to disclose the truth because of the stigma of the disease. And I had a lot of shame and guilt on my part, too. What would people think if they knew I had AIDS? So that's kind of how I dealt with it in the beginning, but so much has happened since then that has led me to this healthy emotional place where I am today.

A couple of years after I was diagnosed, I had to tell the truth when I met a gentleman I was interested in. After a whole lot of anxiety, I was able to disclose to him that I was infected. I needed to give him the opportunity to back out of the relationship if he couldn't handle this. And also I needed to protect myself—you know, this is something I tell other women now, too: It's better to disclose sooner than later in relationships because you protect yourself emotionally, before you get involved, in case the person decides he's going to run. This man was comfortable with what I told him and we ended up in a sexual relationship very quickly that lasted nearly seven years. We practiced safe sex and it felt good to be close to somebody, though the relationship was far from perfect.

Finally, it just became such a burden keeping AIDS a secret. I decided I was going to tell my mother, and eventually I told my son. I also told a few of my best friends. Around this time, I met Dorcas Baker, a registered nurse who implements HIV/AIDS education programs at Johns Hopkins University. She grabbed ahold of me and guided me into becoming a real activist and advocate for women living with the disease.

I came to the point where I was ready to share my story to help other women, and I told my boyfriend right away. He decided this was something he could not deal with, and he left me as quickly as the relationship began. He didn't want people to think he was HIV-infected, too. You know, again we come back to the stigma. As long as AIDS was a secret, he was okay with it. But when I said I was going to talk about it, he was out of there.

This was an *aha* moment for me. I realized that over the years there had been red flags that the relationship was unhealthy. Out of the bedroom, he was consistently aloof and condescending. I was so relieved to have a man in my life who seemed to accept me with AIDS that I looked the other way to avoid the fact that he was emotionally abusive. Then when he bailed, the red flags were jumping up and down in my face. So it wasn't much of a surprise that he left, but it didn't make it any less painful.

Sexually, we had a good relationship, protected by condoms, so the physical part really wasn't an issue. Sex doesn't make the relationship, intimacy does, and that's where he was lacking. Intimacy is all about revealing who we really are to each other. It's the cuddling and the touching that happens before you get into the bed and after sex that makes for intimacy, and that didn't happen with us. I hung on to something that was unhealthy because I felt like I needed a man in my life.

I haven't been in a relationship since then. Initially, it was because I shut down after he left. I wasn't going to put myself at risk of feeling that kind of pain again. I am finally open to love again, but I haven't met anybody. I'm not lonely by any stretch of the imagination, but I do miss the physical touch and pleasure of sex. I am not looking forward, though, to going through the whole process again with a new partner, disclosing, practicing safe sex, the stress. Because even when you do practice safe sex, there's a risk. And it would really, really destroy me if I infected somebody. So yeah, I keep that in the back of my head as I think about starting up again.

Practicing safe sex when one of you has HIV is something that takes a lot of attention. You need a partnership with someone who would be willing to work with you, with condoms, and female condoms if you choose, and making sure you're doing it each and every time. Women have to really insist on this because the first thing many men will say when they want to sleep with you is they don't want to use a condom because "it doesn't feel good." Just remember, it doesn't feel so good to have any STDs, especially AIDS.

I'm seventy years old, so I don't know if that time for me to have a lover in my life has come and gone. But then I talk to women who just got married again and they're sixty-four and seventy-two, and older, and that gives me hope.

I do miss being touched. The importance of physical touch as you get older becomes even more important. It adds to your self-esteem and it allows you to feel supported; it makes you feel loved. Even when I hug a girlfriend, it's such a good feeling from that warmth and that affection. We have found with our work with HIV/AIDS in the senior community that human interaction has so much to do with the healing process. Women who are isolated don't do as well healthwise. I can speak from experience: When I made the choice to share my story, I turned my life around.

When you are happy in your soul, it heals the body; it all works together, mind, body, and soul. When I was stuck in that mode of unhappiness, thinking, *I'm going to die* and telling nobody, my health examinations started to go downhill. My emotional state is very strong right now, but my physical health is just fair. Research is showing that people like me who have been living with the virus for a long time, in addition to the side effects of all the medications I take, the aging process itself is accelerated. I have a lot of aches and pains; my cholesterol is high. My blood pressure fluctuates, and then there are all of these side effects from taking the AIDS drugs for so many years.

I am meeting more and more people like me who have been carrying the virus for more than twenty years. The drugs are working. There is a growing number of long-term survivors who are seniors and who became infected at the early stages of the epidemic, when scientists and doctors had no idea what was going to happen. They didn't expect people to live, and now here we are pushing seventy and beyond, and there is a lot of research being done now with seniors living with HIV. They are finding that a lot of these seniors are having to get hip and knee replacements because the virus robs calcium from your bones.

Everyone should get tested in their routine medical exams. I will never forget one of our OWEL women who came to us at the age of ninety-two. Such a vibrant and sophisticated lady, you could tell she lived a good life, by her manner and her dress. Her husband had died a few years earlier of AIDS. She chose to believe that she was infected through a blood transfusion, but we had a suspicion it was the husband. By the time she was diagnosed, she had full-blown AIDS; doctors had not thought to test her earlier when she came in with various other ailments. Too often, if you have gray hair and wrinkles, the doctors won't push you to get tested. You need to push them. The woman died of pneumonia.

AIDS is a chronic disease that is treatable, so the earlier you know your status, the sooner you can start these medications that absolutely work. It's not a death sentence.

I tell my newly diagnosed women not to jump into bed with someone right away. Allow yourself that period of time when you actually date; the true personality of the man is going to show up. Then you will find out if you really want that person in your life. This also allows you time to process the news of your diagnosis.

When the character of a man comes out, you know how he is going to treat you. Then when you feel there is sexual chemistry between you, honesty is the way to go. Tell him the truth, the sooner the better, because it does two things: You protect yourself emotionally when you put it out there before you get caught up in your feelings and are crushed; and it gives the man a chance to really think over whether he can deal with the situation.

You can find love again. When you hear the news, you may be in a state of shock, so you have to deal with your diagnosis first, and the depression. But you will come to a place when you hold your head up and know that you are worthy. When you know you are worthy, you are in a mind-set where the next man in your life will be someone who treats you the way you deserve to be treated.

In Madison, Wisconsin, a town teeming with ageless renegades, there is an illustrious store with pale pink walls for women who want guidance on how to explore healthy sex, in new directions or to expand old routes. Founded in 1996, A Woman's Touch offers one-stop sex shopping—sexual health counseling and adult toys and other erotica. The 2,000-square-foot enterprise is an adult fantasy store with a huge online market, featuring a classy smorgasbord of products to entice even the prudes who have never ventured beyond the mission position.

Just browsing through the array of merchandise is arousing, a selection that spans G-spot stimulators, nipple toys, and shocking-pink dildos, a store bestseller, and food-grade flavored lubricants. The most popular flavor is Frutopia: "I've been told it's so tasty you could eat Frutopia over ice cream," says Ellen

Barnard, a sex educator and social worker, and co-owner of A Woman's Touch with Dr. Myrtle Wilhite, who is trained in internal medicine and epidemiology.

Along with frivolous offerings, there are also serious gadgets such as vibrating massage wands that relax tight pelvic floor muscles, as well as guides for women recovering from cancer. This is a drug-free operation, emphasizing natural approaches over pharmacology, all geared to educate women on ways to address changes in their sexual function. Like nurse practitioner Deborah Nichols in Berkeley, Ellen knows a whole lot about sex, as she, too, is based in a college town that is a holistic hotbed of health and wellness activism. Ellen talks about the importance of "being adaptable" as the secret to achieving deep intimacy as we age.

ELLEN BARNARD

If you can adapt the mind to the changing body, which you have to do as you age, anything is possible with a woman's sexuality. We provide that opportunity for midlife and older women to reaffirm that they can be sexual their whole lives, even as they deal with health-related issues such as cancer and diabetes.

Type 2 diabetes has a big effect on sexual function; it damages the nerves of the genitals and blocks genital blood vessels the same way it affects hands and feet. You need a healthy and flexible mental attitude, adequate blood flow, and responsive nerves to enjoy good sexual function and arousal. Often, people aren't necessarily aware of what is possible in their sexual potential until things really start changing or falling apart. And when things aren't working, in most cases, you can fix it.

Before they take hormones, there are many lifestyle changes that women can make as a first course of action to facilitate

blood flow and reduce inflammation of the vessels, thus increasing the ability to become aroused. The women I talk to
who do really well after cancer and who glide through menopause into their older years are the ones who eat well: nuts,
fruits, vegetables with only a little bit of healthy meats, lots of
healthy oils. They exercise every day no matter what, at least
thirty minutes to an hour. They take time to keep their stress
levels down; stress releases the hormone cortisol, which causes
more stress and raises inflammation levels in the body.

These women keep their weight down; obesity invites high
blood pressure and Type 2 diabetes, and damages blood vessels. They are light drinkers and they don't smoke. There is
nothing like exercise to get the blood flowing everywhere, including into the genitals.

The women who are doing everything they are supposed
to do as they age are the ones that tell me, "I'm wet and still
very interested in sex." And most of these women aren't taking
hormones. While each woman comes to A Woman's Touch with
her own story, I find that it is the woman who is overweight or
who has a very stressful and demanding life—that she is not
trying to or is unable to balance—who struggles the most with
sexual function after menopause. Cortisol is surging through
her body; she may already have damaged blood vessels from
undiagnosed diabetes. And she may be too stressed and tired
to make the lifestyle changes that are not only affecting her sex
life but also endangering her life.

We do not prescribe drugs here, but there aren't any drugs
in the world that are going to fix this woman. She needs to
make healthier lifestyle choices. I know there is a lot of talk now
about a female Viagra hitting the market, but all Viagra does is
help with blood flow. This woman may already have damaged
blood vessels, and diabetes may be starting to damage her

nerves. Viagra helps support the function of sex organs, but it doesn't fix the cause of arousal dysfunction or help women have orgasms more easily. We guide this woman toward more exercise, healthy eating, sleeping enough, and de-stressing her life, and we see hopeful results.

I'm not saying that everybody is going to leave our shop on the path to great sex, but they will leave with a realistic view of what's possible. We direct them to the right kind of lubricants and teach them how to do massage on the vulva and inside the vagina that will help with blood flow and maintain healthy func- tion. We see many women in their sixties and seventies who are super-healthy, busy women and their only complaint is that the vulva is dry. We can help them with this very easily with products.

But older women also need to hear this important message as they age: You aren't going to be able to go backward. You are probably not going to get that strong twang in the vulva that lets your body lead the way like you did when you were young. But if you want to have sex, there is nothing stopping you as long as you know it requires healthy choices. We en- courage women as they age to be consciously sexual, and not turn their sexuality over to a physician who will immediately say, "Honey, all you need is to take hormones."

Hormones will not fix desire or arousal issues, though they may be useful topically when the skin is getting too fragile to allow for pleasurable sex play. This is my problem with the idea of a female Viagra or other desire drugs; the two new medica- tions currently being explored are Lybrido and Lybridos. I don't believe we want to be thinking of sex as something you can turn on and off like a lightbulb.

We have a brain that is so able to get us to that point; I would prefer that women make intentional choices that move them toward arousal and pleasurable play with themselves or with a partner, not take a pill and wait for it to propel them toward sex.

You should hear my eighty-year-olds and ninety-year-olds talk about how much sex still means to them, and it surprises them. They come to us because they have made the conscious choice to keep at it; they say, "I'm dry and it's a little painful, so I need some help there. But I want to keep this part of my life going." I had a ninety-eight-year-old come in recently to buy her first vibrator. It may take some tools and some instruction, but a woman can have an orgasm at any age.

We also find older women discovering the joys of oral sex for the first time as a way to transition with partners who aren't getting those strong erections anymore. I love to talk to them about nonintercourse-based play, and steer them toward delicious techniques and products to help them in this new phase of life. Too many people stop sex cold because they can't have intercourse. Our job is to remind them that the capacity for intimacy never has to stop cold.

I am flooded with so many visuals and so much empathy about so many lives as I write these final words in this chapter on our final years. We can all be inspired by these stories of forging onward with fortitude and adventurous spirits amidst loss, illness and heartbreak. I think of my own quarter of a century of marriage, and how staying on the roller coaster has paid off. I am rolling into a mature "sweetness" in the relationship, as Shirley describes hers, and rolling out of youthful restlessness. Expectations for love and sex are individual for all of us, but for anyone to achieve intimacy in its purest sense, I believe it takes both love and sex—and time. I will leave you with a scene that is neither high nor low but rather a steady and soothing hum of what may be ours if we make conscious and consistent loving, body and soul, a priority as time goes by.

My friend Susan, who just turned fifty, was leaving Washington to spend a month in Florida with her parents, Helen, eighty-five, and Gus, eighty-nine. Helen has arthritis, but "nothing slows her down," says Susan. Gus has just been diagnosed with early Alzheimer's. I asked her to pay close attention to how they interact. Susan had often shared with me how romantic her parents still were, and I was hoping I could extract some of her observations for the book. She sent me this note during week three of her visit.

SUSAN

My mother got up early and joined me for coffee. We had watched a movie the night before, and Dad slept during the movie. He sleeps a lot. My mother had been experiencing a bit of caregiver distress, although she would hardly admit it, she is just so happy to still have him. Her rock-solid husband of fifty-five years is losing his short-term memory and he has become more childlike.

Helen and Gus are starting to sing a lot together, old show tunes. When they were younger, Dad played guitar and my mother played piano, so singing is a fun tradition for them that has always bound them together.

The sun was pouring into the condo, reflecting on the man-made lake. Mother was checking the outdoor thermometer to see if it was warm enough for them to take their water aerobics class. She went into the bedroom to talk to Dad, then she came out abruptly and said to me, with a deep sigh that was a happy sigh:

"I need to go back to bed. Your father wants to cuddle."

EPILOGUE

That Vicki Kowaleski is the woman you will read about on these final pages does not make her an afterthought. Vicki stands on her own as the epilogue, because the beautiful forty-nine-year-old with long brown hair and the purple heart tattoo behind her left ear does not fit into any one category. In many ways she is the core message of this book, summed up eloquently in these words of Ellen Barnard, the co-owner of the store A Woman's Touch:

"If you can adapt the mind to a changing body anything is possible in a woman's sexuality."

Vicki swam competitively for many years for elite YMCA teams and for Naperville North High School, located thirty-two miles from downtown Chicago. Her high school team was undefeated in dual meets and Vicki placed third in the 100-yard breaststroke, earning All State recognition. She went on to swim her freshman year at Southern Illinois University.

A night out drinking with high school friends during the summer of 1986 altered her physical capacity, yet her emotional and mental stamina has never been stronger. Nor has her marriage of twenty years.

On that fateful night a lifetime ago, following rounds of mixed drinks and shots, Vicki and some friends hopped a fence and crashed a private pool. At the sight of an approaching flashlight, Vicki ran toward the pool and dove. She hit her head against the wall on the other side of the pool, compressing the bones in her neck, and has never walked again.

Today, she sits in a Quantum 600 power wheelchair in her home nestled into three acres of Connecticut woods. Her able-bodied husband, Billy, is at work at the grocery store they own. Their daughter, Kylie, whom she carried to term, gave birth to naturally, and breast-fed, recently graduated from high school.

Vicki is talking to me on her day off from her job as a vocational rehabilitation supervisor of counselors who help persons with all types of disabilities get back into the work force. She drives herself to the office in a "fancy" Honda Odyssey, complete with leather seats, moonroof, voice controls for everything she needs, a back-up camera, DVD player, and navigation system. It is modified for her to be able to drive with a lowered floor, wheelchair-lockdown system, hand controls, and rain-sensing windshield wipers.

Inspired by their experiences with Vicki's accident and recovery, her father, Bob Hill, and his wife, Thea Flaum, developed an organization called the Hill Foundation for Families Living with Disabilities. A website was created called facing disability.com, which is an informational and support website for families facing spinal cord injuries. This is an online resource to share stories and information to educate and empower other individuals with spinal cord injuries, as well as to offer guidance to their family members.

I spoke at length with Vicki, who acquired a master's degree in rehabilitation counseling following her accident, on how far she has come since those scary first ten days following her accident when she was immobilized on a board called a Stryker frame, with bolts drilled into each side of her shaven head, fearing: "No man will ever want me like this":

VICKI

Swimming was at the core of my identity; it was what I liked to do the most. In the water you are just in there by yourself; it is peaceful and relaxing; you are free. Swimming taught me to set goals, and it boosted my self-esteem. You feel really good about yourself if you excel at something you love. At first I was only really good at breaststroke, but eventually I became better in butterfly and backstroke. My favorite was the 400-yard individual medley, where I had to swim 100 yards each of butterfly, backstroke, breaststroke, and freestyle.

Normally girls peak at swimming in high school, but I just kept getting better as I got older. I didn't learn how to swim until I was ten years old, so maybe it was because I started later than most competitive swimmers that I improved as I got older. My coaches really challenged me at Southern Illinois University, which is a Division I swimming program. I was in excellent shape as a result of weight training, running, and biking.

But then I started thinking, *Why am I doing this to myself? It's not like I'm going to be a professional swimmer, and here I am doing the same kind of conditioning as football and basketball players who could go on to become professional athletes.* So I retired from swimming after my freshman year and instead of swim practice I started partying and running around, and I got a little chubby. But I do credit the fact that I had a strong body when I had my accident, and that I was used to the discipline and tenacity it takes to be a competitive swimmer, for my ability and drive to recover.

Typically, when accidents happen to people there is someone else to blame. In those cases, I think it is harder to rationalize and to move forward emotionally, like if you were hit by a drunk driver. But for me, it was 100 percent my fault; I had nobody to blame but myself.

Thursday, July 24, 1986, I was home from college for the summer and my mom said, "Are you sure you should go out?" It was a weeknight and I had work the next morning. Of course, I did go out. I went to the mall and I bought two cassettes; ironically one was the Ramones's *Too Tough to Die*. After seeing the movie *About Last Night* with a friend, we ended up at a bar, Millie and Maxwell's in Aurora, Illinois, and we ran into so many people from our high school class. After the bar closed around 1:00 A.M. or so, a couple of the guys said to us, "Let's go pool hopping," which was a common occurrence in our town during the summer. I did think, *Hmm, this is a pretty stupid thing to do. I've had way too much to drink.* The three people who were with me were in no condition to drive either.

I don't know how we all made it to the pool at Cress Creek Commons in Naperville, which was on the other side of town, on July 25 at around 2:00 A.M. When I parked my car I said to myself again, *Vicki, what are you doing? Maybe you should just go home.* I don't know how many times that voice inside of my head tried to tell me to stop. But I wasn't listening. I got out of my car, saw the NO TRESPASSING sign, and we jumped the fence.

Before we started swimming that voice in my head came

back, and I even said to everyone, "Don't anyone dive. It's really dark out." But I wasn't listening to myself. This is where things got fuzzy; you know when you are drinking, the alcohol continues to get stronger in your body.

I saw a light of some sort, like a flashlight, so I said to my friend, "I don't know what's going on, let's get the heck out of here." But instead of running away from the pool, idiot me, I dived into the pool that was not really very wide. Taking a running start, I did what breaststrokers do: they dive in the water, take an underwater pull, arms down at their sides, then they pop up and swim along. Instead, I smashed into the wall.

I do remember hitting my head, right where you would part your hair down the middle, and I felt a sickening crunch. Underwater everything is kind of muffled, but immediately I heard buzzing in my head. I had hit it so hard, and I thought, *Oh my God, that really hurt*. I went to try and move my arms and they didn't move.

I did immediate damage right in that instant. My spinal cord had been compressed in between the fifth and seventh vertebrae; the sixth vertebrae in my neck just burst. I knew right away when I hit that I was in really bad shape, and the last thought that I remember was: *My parents are going to kill me. I just broke my neck.* I knew right away that I had done this. I couldn't even roll over in the water, and that's all I remember before I passed out.

That light I had seen was the cops, it turned out. I was unconscious so I don't know exactly what happened, but one of my friends had pulled me out of the water as the police got to us. I was lying there, basically in my glory for all to see, as we had been mostly unclothed. But when I did wake up I was in the ambulance and the paramedic said to me, "You were in an accident. We're going to the hospital. You're going to be okay."

At Northwestern Memorial Hospital I was put on the

Stryker frame. The doctors shaved the sides of my head, then drilled into each side of my skull just above my ears to place metal tongs, which were attached to wires and weights. The reason for this was to stabilize my cervical spine before surgery. Then for ten days they flipped me over every two hours, to relieve the pressure and try to decrease the swelling of the spinal cord so they could do surgery.

It was terrible. They don't do that anymore with spinal cord injuries. Nowadays they shoot you with steroids quickly and they do surgery as fast as they can, to reduce the swelling immediately. Because the more swelling there is the more damage there is to the nerves. I did terrible damage to my nerves and really messed up my lung capacity. To this day, I still don't have full use of my lungs.

As I talk to you today, I am more than okay. The universe works in strange and powerful ways. Flash forward to July 25, 1995, and my baby girl was born, nine years to the day after I had my accident. Kylie's birth turned that awful day into a day of celebration, instead of a day of reflection when I would constantly be asking myself, "What if, what if, what if?"

The fact that I did get pregnant was somewhat of a surprise, even though I wasn't using birth control. I had blood clots shortly after my accident, so I couldn't be on the pill. We had talked about having a baby but hadn't decided for sure what the timing should be.

I had an interesting pregnancy, with morning sickness and gestational diabetes. At my seven-month mark, the doctors decided I should stop working. I had a normal delivery despite being considered a high-risk pregnancy. At around 2:00 A.M. on Tuesday July 25, 1995, my water broke. My husband, Bill, and I drove to the hospital, the doctors hooked me up with an epidural to avoid complications of what is called autonomic dysreflexia (sudden onset of high blood pressure that occurs in persons with spinal cord injuries and can be life-threatening).

At 12:07 P.M., Kylie came into our world, six and a half pounds and nineteen inches, after two involuntary pushes on my part, a quick episiotomy, and the help of a thing that looked like a suction cup. My doctors had insisted that they weren't going to do a mandatory C-section, that I could do a natural birth. When my milk came in, it was the greatest thing ever. I did it! I was so happy. My husband, Bill, was the one who did the diaper changes, basically my only job was the breast-feeding. And I was petrified to hold her because I was so afraid she was going to roll and drop. So it took a little while to get the baby thing down. As she got older, she would sit on my lap in my wheelchair and I would double as her stroller, and Bill could push us both.

I do have some sensation below my level of injury (around my upper chest area) but not like before my accident. But with sex, it's more of a mind connection, and it's hard to explain, but I will try. I did have sexual relationships before the accident. So I can remember what it feels like. My husband understood from the beginning that it would be different with us. He lets me know where and how he is touching me and it helps to have the lights on so I can see what is going on. For me during intimacy, the visuals are very important. It's strange, but the places where I still do have sensation are so much more sensitive, like my neck and shoulders.

I think of everything I have today and remember those terrible days when I thought, *Who is going to want me this way?* When I was twenty-two and coming out of this terrible accident, having children was the farthest thing from my mind. But almost the first thing my dad asked the doctors was "Can she ever have kids?" I said, "Dad, why the heck would you ever ask that? I'm just trying to survive." But a few years later, I met Bill and my mind shifted about everything.

I was finishing up my graduate degree, and I had been dating someone else. I had messed up my elbow, so I had to be in the hospital again, and I was supposed to go on a date with this other guy. I called my sister and asked her if she could please tell him I'm in the hospital and can't make our date. I figured he might come to the hospital with balloons or flowers to cheer me up. Instead, he told my sister when she called: "Thanks for letting me know. I don't do hospitals. Tell her to call me when she's out." I thought, *Screw you, buddy.*

A few months before that, I had met Bill when he was visiting Chicago from Connecticut. We met through a friend of mine who also happened to be Bill's best friend. And when I was in the hospital, Bill started calling me, and then he kept calling me after I was released. We really opened up to each other on the phone and got to be good friends. Before, I'd be scared to tell somebody I was dating that I have an internal catheter. Basically it's like having a Porta Potty on my leg. I didn't want anyone to think that it was gross.

But I was honest with Bill. I'd say things like, "You know, sometimes my body doesn't work the way I would like it to. And I have these issues with doing Number Two." He was so cool and funny about it, he'd say, "I get it, like sometimes you are sitting two inches higher in your chair." I felt very comfortable talking to him about anything, and there was no end to what I would tell him.

Eventually, he started flying out to visit me, and from that beginning of our relationship, it felt so natural. He knew exactly how to pop me up and down curbs in my wheelchair. I asked him, "How do you know how to do that?" He told me that his father had worked with Easter Seals, and he had grown up around people with disabilities. And this is a guy who did bring me flowers.

I felt drawn to Bill right away. He is six foot, 225 pounds, and beyond his body he is just a solid guy. I could tell him anything. I didn't feel awkward talking to him about sex; instead he was awkward about the whole sex thing. After a couple of months of dating, he was so shy I had to finally attack him! I said, "It's time. Come on let's do this!"

What I say to other women in my situation is not to be afraid of intimacy. You have to first feel comfortable with yourself. And you need to trust in the other person that he is not going to take advantage of you. Because there are a lot of men out there who are into kinky stuff; they would like to mess around with a woman in a wheelchair, just to try it. From the age of twenty-two to twenty-eight, when I met Bill, I did date other men. And in my experience they were either put off: "No way, she's a gimp," or they were very intrigued. I didn't sleep with any of them because, before Bill, I never felt safe enough to tell anybody about what was going on with my body after the accident.

I would also tell other people in my position to believe you can do anything. I credit my father for this belief in me. After this happened to me he said, "Vicki, whatever it is you want to do you can do. People in your situation can work, and you've got to think about how you are going to support yourself and be independent." This is how I came to define myself as a person first and not as someone who is disabled in a wheelchair.

I've been married for twenty years and we are not only best friends but we also have true intimacy. Intimacy is being completely honest with each other, being connected by soul and by mind. I had an accident a couple of years ago where I broke both of my legs. So when it comes to sexual intimacy, it didn't happen a lot for a while because it was frightening for both of us; we were afraid that I was going to "break." But sex ebbs and flows in every married relationship, and in that regard, we are like everyone else.

When we first got together, Bill was going through a divorce. I asked him what was most important to him in a relationship. And he said, "Companionship." He didn't have that in his first marriage, and we do have that in this marriage: We are sounding boards for each other; we are best friends; we trust each other. He also told me from the beginning, "I don't have to have sex all the time." Some men have to; my husband is more of a connector of the mind.

Over time that quality of true intimacy has strengthened because we have been through many hard times over the years. Right after I had Kylie I had severe postpartum depression. I was constantly crying and we thought we weren't going to make it, as we were heading into our fifth year of marriage. We each went into therapy and with medication, my depression lifted and we pushed through the challenges of those first five years.

Around the ten-year mark, we almost called it quits—but again we made the decision to stay together and work through our issues out of respect for ourselves and our family. It wasn't just Bill, Kylie, and me but also Bill's three children from his previous marriage, BJ, Sarah, and Kris, who made up our family. As a stepparent, challenges existed that strained our relationship significantly. But every struggle was worth it because as adults, ages thirty-four, twenty-eight, and twenty-five respectively, his kids and I have developed strong relationships. They are wonderful adults and I appreciate that I had a hand in helping them grow. They love their little sister Kylie, who looks up to them and I look to my stepkids to guide and support Kylie as she endures her teenage years with Bill and me!

Each time we experienced serious issues in our marriage, we talked about what we had promised each other before we got married. And that was "I'm getting married for life. So if you feel I'm not there for you, or you are feeling attracted to someone else, you need to tell me so we can work on that."

I know that I couldn't have come this far without him. When I think back to when I was in the Rehabilitation Institute of Chicago it is as if I'm thinking about a totally different person. Oh my God, it was so awful. But I do sometimes like to talk about this, because I never want to forget how far I have come. I've got scars from my surgeries to remind me.

Though I have gotten a lot of sensation back, it's mostly slight pain sensation. I have what's called sacral sparing, so if I feel tingly I know I have to move in my chair to avoid getting a pressure sore. I can't voluntarily move my legs. I can move my hands but I can't pinch or grasp. I can feel both of my thumbs, both of my index fingers, and the inside half of one of my middle fingers. I have no sensation below my armpits and my balance isn't great.

As a former athlete, my upper body was very strong, so as a result I can dress myself, though most of my clothes and my shoes have Velcro closures. I just wanted to have a normal life, and I have accomplished that, for the most part. I learned at the Rehabilitation Institute how to transfer from my wheelchair to my bed using a board, how to dress myself, put on makeup and nail polish—totally essential skills—as well as how to direct others to care for me for the things I cannot do.

My husband helps me with a lot of things that probably a lot of other men would not do. He changes catheters. He administers IV meds when I have needed them. He is there for me for anything I need, like a nurse on call. Once in a while he will be helping me with something, then we will start messing around a bit. We laugh, and I say, "Oh, Nurse Bill, you better stop that or I'm going to have to file a complaint."

We know that what we have is not going to be this lovey-dovey, butterflies, stomach flutters the entire time. No couple has that. For us the unbreakable bond of intimacy comes from constantly being there for each other, for the long haul. Our routine with each other, we don't even have to talk. It's amazing. It's like a dance.

Vicki is obviously an exceptional woman, who has braved the unthinkable with courage and spunk and perseverance and an admirable sense of humor. Curious to know how rare it is to come back from a spinal cord injury with the force of a Vicki, I contacted Diane Rowles, a nurse practitioner specializing in sexuality and fertility for spinal cord injury [SCI] patients. Rowles worked with Vicki when she was a patient at the Rehabilitation Institute of Chicago after her accident. She moderates videos on the facingdisability.com site in clear and frank lay language that addresses the psychological and physical transitions, and obstacles, an SCI patient can expect, on issues that span everything from erectile dysfunction to oral sex to inventing new positions. The Rowles's videos get more hits than anything else on the site.

"Sexuality is very much a part of these patients' lives, but some parts of sex may be different due to their injuries," Diane explained, adding that the definition of orgasm is different with SCI patients, in that many do experience a peak sensation during sexual activity yet the arousal is not genital-focused. Here is more from Diane, who is now a nurse practitioner with University Neurosurgery at Rush University Medical Center in Chicago.

DIANE ROWLES

Sexual function is often one of the first things that people are concerned about, sometimes even before whether or not they will regain function of the bladder or their bowels. Sex is simply a crucial part of everyone's life. Some people have little or no sensation after a spinal cord injury, so it is key to recognize all forms of enjoyment and arousal.

I spend a lot of time talking to patients about ways to enjoy the act without normal sensation, and other ways to enjoy sensations that are not totally focused on the genitals. I suggest to patients and their significant others experimenting in finding areas of their bodies that are erogenous. In my years of experience I do see that people find very sensitive areas of their bodies beyond their genitals, from which they can get a sense of reaching peak sensory enjoyment. Some people also enjoy watching their partners getting pleasure, and find that arousing.

Women with spinal cord injuries have healthy pregnancies and healthy babies. There is a slightly higher incidence of forceps and suction-device deliveries in this group as compared to the general population, and a slightly higher incidence of C-sections.

It is important to realize that a spinal cord injury does not generally interfere with a woman's ability to have children. Men are also frequently able to father children despite their sexual response cycle being interrupted by their spinal cord injury. Many men are able to get some kind of erection on their own after a spinal cord injury, and for those who do not have adequate erections there are medications and devices available that are successful in treating the erectile dysfunction.

One of the greatest joys in my work has been to see families, like Vicki's, grow after a spinal cord injury. They will often bring me a first sonogram and it is just wonderful to witness. Not every person with a spinal cord injury can go on to do what Vicki has been able to do, but it is not rare either. There are many people who go on and have full lives like Vicki.

Beyond surmounting physical challenges, Vicki has worked through the emotional challenges that many women face in sustaining long-term relationships. Like the tenacious Vicki, they have made love last through hard work, commitment, and determination.

You have heard the voices of these women resound in this book, young moms and old grandmothers, women with different bodies and varying stories and unique areas of angst. Yet they understand, nonetheless, the secret that Vicki does: that true intimacy comes not from hot and fleeting physical highs. The intimate connection that endures is fueled by a flame within that, if stoked properly, can burn for a lifetime.

Sex? It is a very good thing. Yet the sensations that women crave most in an intimate relationship are some really warm, perpetually rocking brain waves.

ACKNOWLEDGMENTS

First off, I would like to thank Bill Shinker and Lauren Marino, publisher and editorial director of Gotham Books, respectively, for letting me loose once again to further untangle my favorite subject, the complexity of intimate relationships. They are the best of the best in the literary field, astute, bold, and original. Lauren is a writer's dream editor, that great combination of flexible and disciplined. She pushed me to the edge while keeping me reined in to focus on the issues that matter most, to most women.

I am also deeply appreciative of Lisa Johnson, associate publisher, and Lindsay Gordon Bezalel, assistant publicity director, who unfailingly *get* my writing, and relentlessly communicate that message. An enormous thank-you to Gail Ross, my irrepressible agent who connected me to my beloved Gotham gang. I am so lucky to have had Gail's abiding friendship and brilliant advice for so many years. May our journey together continue to be fun and fruitful—and long.

Freelance journalist Nicole Glass did an impeccable and exhaustive job as my research assistant. I could not have built a book without her. Nicole is unflappable and a night owl, two great qualities in a lieutenant whose job required digging up lots of gritty information about sex and aging, at all hours. A recent college graduate, Nicole also consistently fed me topics of interest to younger readers, resulting in the construction of a project with multigenerational reach.

Another savvy woman in her twenties was indispensable in composing *Sex After . . . .* Thank you to newlywed and new mama Anna Sproul-Latimer, an agent at the Ross Yoon Agency. Anna gave my chapters a read-through for style and timeliness. While Nicole kept me abreast of post-college relationship trends, Anna's feeds were enlightening as I researched the next step—new marriage and new motherhood. Another big nod of appreciation goes to Howard Yoon, Gail's partner in the literary agency. As in my other books, Howard was instrumental in reminding me to counter some of the girl-talk with perspectives from men.

To John Turco, thank you for letting me occupy your beachside cottage for a writer's retreat. I did some of my best work at your dining room table and some of my best thinking on the nearby bluff overlooking the Pacific Ocean. I'd also like to thank my circle of girlfriends who always say "I'm in" whenever I feel the urge to go out for wine and a few whines. In our community of rivers and hills near the Chesapeake Bay, this sisterhood sustains me in work and in play. And what would we do without Les Folies Brasserie? Alain Matrat, and Eric Frazier—you are the cherished Other Men in my life!

Emily Wunderlich, an assistant editor at Gotham, and Jennifer Manguera, literary manager at the Ross Yoon Agency, have also been essential allies in the grueling process of assembling hundreds of pages. Emily, thank you for kindly taking my dozens and dozens of phone calls and for working behind the scenes to artfully piece the elements together. Jennifer, you are my trusty rapid responder on every front and I am so grateful to you, and for you.

And to the adult students in my Voices of Women classes at American University, your voices of raw truth have enhanced my own voice and spirit in so many ways. You are a blessing.

I would also like to give deep thanks to the physicians and assorted mental and physical health practitioners who squeezed me in between patients, or made yourselves available for late-night visits and phone conversations. This stellar group served as a sounding board and as an astounding source of pioneering experiences and research: Anthony Atala, Ellen Barnard, Carmen Calvo, Marilyn Charwat, Marge Coffey, Melanie Davis, Justin Garcia, Andrew Goldstein, Sam Green, Christine Hall, Debby Herbenick, Ginger Manley, Angela Moses, Deborah Nichols, Diane Rowles, Janet Schaffel, Mark Soloway, Lorraine Tafra, and Ruth Westheimer.

My own astounding source of strength comes from my steadfast husband, Chuck, and our four sons, Theodore, Isaac, Zane, and Jackson. The unwavering support of my tribe makes it possible for me to be a woman and mother and wife who feels like she has it all, an engaging career and a solid family. I am also fortunate to have as lifelong cheerleaders, my sister, Fran, and brother, Greg. I love you for sticking by me faithfully during our very long journey together.

Finally, thank you, thank you, to all you brave and generous women who allowed me to root around the most private areas of your lives, to which you answered openly and powerfully. Your startling honesty forms the spine of this book, which should give every reader a sense of resiliency and hope, as they pass through the evolving stages of intimacy and love.

Also by Iris Krasnow

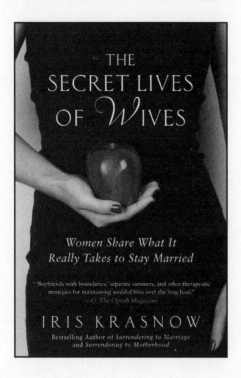

In raw, candid, and sometimes titillating stories, Krasnow offers a groundbreaking exploration of wives who thrive, sharing their uncensored strategies for staying married.

GOTHAM BOOKS